Machine Learning in Java
Second Edition

Helpful techniques to design, build, and deploy powerful machine learning applications in Java

AshishSingh Bhatia
Bostjan Kaluza

BIRMINGHAM - MUMBAI

Machine Learning in Java
Second Edition

Commissioning Editor: Amey Varangaonkar
Acquisition Editor: Divya Poojari
Content Development Editor: Athikho Sapuni Rishana
Technical Editor: Joseph Sunil
Copy Editor: Safis Editing
Project Coordinator: Kirti Pisat
Proofreader: Safis Editing
Indexer: Mariammal Chettiyar
Graphics: Jisha Chirayil
Production Coordinator: Tom Scaria

First published: April 2016
Second edition: November 2018

Production reference: 1231118

Published by Packt Publishing Ltd.
Livery Place
35 Livery Street
Birmingham
B3 2PB, UK.

ISBN 978-1-78847-439-9

www.packtpub.com

Contributors

About the authors

AshishSingh Bhatia is a reader and learner at his core. He has more than 11 years of rich experience in different IT sectors, encompassing training, development, and management. He has worked in many domains, such as software development, ERP, banking, and training. He is passionate about Python and Java, and has recently been exploring R. He is mostly involved in web and mobile development in various capacities. He likes to explore new technologies and share his views and thoughts through various online media and magazines. He believes in sharing his experience with the new generation and also takes part in training and teaching.

Bostjan Kaluza is a researcher in artificial intelligence and machine learning with extensive experience in Java and Python. Bostjan is the chief data scientist at Evolven, a leading IT operations analytics company. He works with machine learning, predictive analytics, pattern mining, and anomaly detection to turn data into relevant information. Prior to Evolven, Bostjan served as a senior researcher in the department of intelligent systems at the Jozef Stefan Institute and led research projects involving pattern and anomaly detection, ubiquitous computing, and multi-agent systems. In 2013, Bostjan published his first book, *Instant Weka How-To*, published by Packt Publishing, exploring how to leverage machine learning using Weka.

About the reviewer

Yogendra Sharma is a developer with experience in architecture, design, and the development of scalable and distributed applications, with a core interest in microservices and Spring. He is currently working as an IoT and cloud architect at Intelizign Engineering Services, Pune. He also has hands-on experience with technologies such as AWS Cloud, IoT, Python, J2SE, J2EE, Node.js, Angular, MongoDB, and Docker. He is constantly exploring technical novelties, and is open-minded and eager to learn more about new technologies and frameworks.

Packt is searching for authors like you

If you're interested in becoming an author for Packt, please visit `authors.packtpub.com` and apply today. We have worked with thousands of developers and tech professionals, just like you, to help them share their insight with the global tech community. You can make a general application, apply for a specific hot topic that we are recruiting an author for, or submit your own idea.

`mapt.io`

Mapt is an online digital library that gives you full access to over 5,000 books and videos, as well as industry leading tools to help you plan your personal development and advance your career. For more information, please visit our website.

Why subscribe?

- Spend less time learning and more time coding with practical eBooks and Videos from over 4,000 industry professionals

- Improve your learning with Skill Plans built especially for you

- Get a free eBook or video every month

- Mapt is fully searchable

- Copy and paste, print, and bookmark content

Packt.com

Did you know that Packt offers eBook versions of every book published, with PDF and ePub files available? You can upgrade to the eBook version at `www.packt.com` and as a print book customer, you are entitled to a discount on the eBook copy. Get in touch with us at `customercare@packtpub.com` for more details.

At `www.packt.com`, you can also read a collection of free technical articles, sign up for a range of free newsletters, and receive exclusive discounts and offers on Packt books and eBooks.

Table of Contents

Preface

Machine Learning in Java, Second Edition, will provide you with the techniques and tools you need to quickly gain insights from complex data. You will start by learning how to apply machine learning methods to a variety of common tasks, including classification, prediction, forecasting, market basket analysis, and clustering.

This is a practical tutorial that uses hands-on examples to step through some real-world applications of machine learning. Without shying away from the technical details, you will explore machine learning with Java libraries using clear and practical examples. You will explore how to prepare data for analysis, choose a machine learning method, and measure the success of the process.

Who this book is for

If you want to learn how to use Java's machine learning libraries to gain insights from your data, this book is for you. It will get you up and running quickly and provide you with the skills you need to successfully create, customize, and deploy machine learning applications with ease. You should be familiar with Java programming and some basic data mining concepts in order to make the most of this book, but no prior experience with machine learning is required.

What this book covers

Chapter 1, *Applied Machine Learning Quick Start*, introduces the field of **natural language processing** (**NLP**). The tools and basic techniques that support NLP are discussed. The use of models, their validation, and their use from a conceptual perspective are presented.

Chapter 2, *Java Libraries and Platforms for Machine Learning*, covers the purpose and uses of tokenizers. Different tokenization processes will be explored, followed by how they can be used to solve specific problems.

`Chapter 3`, *Basic Algorithms – Classification, Regression, and Clustering*, covers the problems associated with sentence detection. Correct detection of the end of sentences is important for many reasons. We will examine different approaches to this problem using a variety of examples.

`Chapter 4`, *Customer Relationship Prediction with Ensembles*, covers the process and problems associated with name recognition. Finding names, locations, and various things in a document is an important step in NLP. The techniques available are identified and demonstrated.

`Chapter 5`, *Affinity Analysis*, covers the process of determining the part of speech that is useful in determining the importance of words and their relationships in a document. It is a process that can enhance the effectiveness of other NLP tasks.

`Chapter 6`, *Recommendation Engine with Apache Mahout*, covers traditional features that do not apply to text documents. In this chapter, we'll learn how text documents can be presented.

`Chapter 7`, *Fraud and Anomaly Detection*, covers information retrieval, which entails finding documents in an unstructured format, such as text that satisfies a query.

`Chapter 8`, *Image Recognition with Deeplearning4J*, covers the issues surrounding how documents and text can be classified. Once we have isolated the parts of text, we can begin the process of analyzing it for information. One of these processes involves classifying and clustering information.

`Chapter 9`, *Activity Recognition with Mobile Phone Sensors*, demonstrates how to discover topics in a set of documents.

`Chapter 10`, *Text Mining with Mallet – Topic Modeling and Spam Detection*, covers the use of parsers and chunkers to solve text problems that are then examined. This important process, which normally results in a parse tree, provides insights into the structure and meaning of documents.

`Chapter 11`, *What is Next?*, brings together many of the topics in previous chapters to address other more sophisticated problems. The use and construction of a pipeline is discussed. The use of open source tools to support these operations is presented.

To get the most out of this book

This book assumes that the user has a working knowledge of the Java language and a basic idea about machine learning. This book heavily uses external libraries that are available in JAR format. It is assumed that the user is aware of using JAR files in Terminal or Command Prompt, although the book does also explain how to do this. The user may easily use this book with any generic Windows or Linux system.

Download the example code files

You can download the example code files for this book from your account at `www.packt.com`. If you purchased this book elsewhere, you can visit `www.packt.com/support` and register to have the files emailed directly to you.

You can download the code files by following these steps:

1. Log in or register at `www.packt.com`.
2. Select the **SUPPORT** tab.
3. Click on **Code Downloads and Errata**.
4. Enter the name of the book in the **Search** box and follow the onscreen instructions.

Once the file is downloaded, please make sure that you unzip or extract the folder using the latest version of:

- WinRAR/7-Zip for Windows
- Zipeg/iZip/UnRarX for Mac
- 7-Zip/PeaZip for Linux

The code bundle for the book is also hosted on GitHub at `https://github.com/PacktPublishing/Machine-Learning-in-Java-Second-Edition`. In case there's an update to the code, it will be updated on the existing GitHub repository.

We also have other code bundles from our rich catalog of books and videos available at `https://github.com/PacktPublishing/`. Check them out!

Download the color images

We also provide a PDF file that has color images of the screenshots/diagrams used in this book. You can download it here: `http://www.packtpub.com/sites/default/files/downloads/9781788474399_ColorImages.pdf`.

Conventions used

There are a number of text conventions used throughout this book.

`CodeInText`: Indicates code words in text, database table names, folder names, filenames, file extensions, pathnames, dummy URLs, user input, and Twitter handles. Here is an example: "Unzip the archive and locate `weka.jar` within the extracted archive."

A block of code is set as follows:

```
data.defineSingleOutputOthersInput(outputColumn);

EncogModel model = new EncogModel(data);
model.selectMethod(data, MLMethodFactory.TYPE_FEEDFORWARD);
model.setReport(new ConsoleStatusReportable());
data.normalize();
```

Any command-line input or output is written as follows:

```
$ java -cp moa.jar -javaagent:sizeofag.jar moa.gui.GUI
```

Bold: Indicates a new term, an important word, or words that you see on screen. For example, words in menus or dialog boxes appear in the text as bold. Here is an example: "We can convert it to a **Comma Separated Value** (**CSV**) format by clicking **File** | **Save As** and picking CSV in the saving dialog."

Warnings or important notes appear like this.

Tips and tricks appear like this.

Get in touch

Feedback from our readers is always welcome.

General feedback: If you have questions about any aspect of this book, mention the book title in the subject of your message and email us at customercare@packtpub.com.

Errata: Although we have taken every care to ensure the accuracy of our content, mistakes do happen. If you have found a mistake in this book, we would be grateful if you would report this to us. Please visit www.packt.com/submit-errata, selecting your book, clicking on the Errata Submission Form link, and entering the details.

Piracy: If you come across any illegal copies of our works in any form on the internet, we would be grateful if you would provide us with the location address or website name. Please contact us at copyright@packt.com with a link to the material.

If you are interested in becoming an author: If there is a topic that you have expertise in, and you are interested in either writing or contributing to a book, please visit authors.packtpub.com.

Reviews

Please leave a review. Once you have read and used this book, why not leave a review on the site that you purchased it from? Potential readers can then see and use your unbiased opinion to make purchase decisions, we at Packt can understand what you think about our products, and our authors can see your feedback on their book. Thank you!

For more information about Packt, please visit packt.com.

1
Applied Machine Learning Quick Start

This chapter introduces the basics of machine learning, laying down common themes and concepts and making it easy to follow the logic and familiarize yourself with the topic. The goal is to quickly learn the step-by-step process of applied machine learning and grasp the main machine learning principles. In this chapter, we will cover the following topics:

- Machine learning and data science
- Data and problem definition
- Data collection
- Data preprocessing
- Unsupervised learning
- Supervised learning
- Generalization and evaluation

If you are already familiar with machine learning and are eager to start coding, then quickly jump to the chapters that follow this one. However, if you need to refresh your memory or clarify some concepts, then it is strongly recommend revisiting the topics presented in this chapter.

Machine learning and data science

Nowadays, everyone talks about machine learning and data science. So, what exactly is machine learning, anyway? How does it relate to data science? These two terms are commonly confused, as they often employ the same methods and overlap significantly. Therefore, let's first clarify what they are. Josh Wills tweeted this:

> *"A data scientist is a person who is better at statistics than any software engineer and better at software engineering than any statistician."*
>
> *– Josh Wills*

More specifically, data science encompasses the entire process of obtaining knowledge by integrating methods from statistics, computer science, and other fields to gain insight from data. In practice, data science encompasses an iterative process of data harvesting, cleaning, analysis, visualization, and deployment.

Machine learning, on the other hand, is mainly concerned with generic algorithms and techniques that are used in analysis and modelling phases of the data science process.

Solving problems with machine learning

Among the different machine learning approaches, there are three main ways of learning, as shown in the following list:

- Supervised learning
- Unsupervised learning
- Reinforcement learning

Given a set of example inputs X, and their outcomes Y, supervised learning aims to learn a general mapping function f, which transforms inputs into outputs, as f: (X,Y).

An example of supervised learning is credit card fraud detection, where the learning algorithm is presented with credit card transactions (matrix X) marked as normal or suspicious (vector Y). The learning algorithm produces a decision model that marks unseen transactions as normal or suspicious (this is the f function).

In contrast, unsupervised learning algorithms do not assume given outcome labels, as they focus on learning the structure of the data, such as grouping similar inputs into clusters. Unsupervised learning can, therefore, discover hidden patterns in the data. An example of unsupervised learning is an item-based recommendation system, where the learning algorithm discovers similar items bought together; for example, people who bought book A also bought book B.

Reinforcement learning addresses the learning process from a completely different angle. It assumes that an agent, which can be a robot, bot, or computer program, interacts with a dynamic environment to achieve a specific goal. The environment is described with a set of states and the agent can take different actions to move from one state to another. Some states are marked as goal states, and if the agent achieves this state, it receives a large reward. In other states, the reward is smaller, non-existent, or even negative. The goal of reinforcement learning is to find an optimal policy or a mapping function that specifies the action to take in each of the states, without a teacher explicitly telling whether this leads to the goal state or not. An example of reinforcement learning would be a program for driving a vehicle, where the states correspond to the driving conditions, for example, current speed, road segment information, surrounding traffic, speed limits, and obstacles on the road; and the actions could be driving maneuvers, such as turn left or right, stop, accelerate, and continue. The learning algorithm produces a policy that specifies the action that is to be taken in specific configurations of driving conditions.

In this book, we will focus on supervised and unsupervised learning only, as they share many concepts. If reinforcement learning sparked your interest, a good book to start with is *Reinforcement Learning: An Introduction* by Richard S. Sutton and Andrew Barto, MIT Press (2018).

Applied machine learning workflow

This book's emphasis is on applied machine learning. We want to provide you with the practical skills needed to get learning algorithms to work in different settings. Instead of math and theory in machine learning, we will spend more time on the practical, hands-on skills (and dirty tricks) to get this stuff to work well on an application. We will focus on supervised and unsupervised machine learning and learn the essential steps in data science to build the applied machine learning workflow.

A typical workflow in applied machine learning applications consists of answering a series of questions that can be summarized in the following steps:

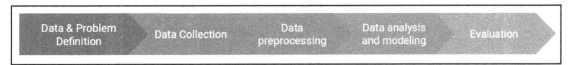

1. **Data and problem definition**: The first step is to ask interesting questions, such as: *What is the problem you are trying solve? Why is it important? Which format of result answers your question? Is this a simple yes/no answer? Do you need to pick one of the available questions?*

2. **Data collection**: Once you have a problem to tackle, you will need the data. Ask yourself what kind of data will help you answer the question. *Can you get the data from the available sources? Will you have to combine multiple sources? Do you have to generate the data? Are there any sampling biases? How much data will be required?*

3. **Data preprocessing**: The first data preprocessing task is **data cleaning**. Some of the examples include filling missing values, smoothing noisy data, removing outliers, and resolving consistencies. This is usually followed by integration of multiple data sources and data transformation to a specific range (normalization), to value bins (discretized intervals), and to reduce the number of dimensions.

4. **Data analysis and modelling**: Data analysis and modelling includes unsupervised and supervised machine learning, statistical inference, and prediction. A wide variety of machine learning algorithms are available, including k-nearest neighbors, Naive Bayes classifier, decision trees, **Support Vector Machines** (**SVMs**), logistic regression, k-means, and so on. The method to be deployed depends on the problem definition, as discussed in the first step, and the type of collected data. The final product of this step is a model inferred from the data.

5. **Evaluation**: The last step is devoted to model assessment. The main issue that the models built with machine learning face is how well they model the underlying data; for example, if a model is too specific or it overfits to the data used for training, it is quite possible that it will not perform well on new data. The model can be too generic, meaning that it underfits the training data. For example, when asked how the weather is in California, it always answers sunny, which is indeed correct most of the time. However, such a model is not really useful for making valid predictions. The goal of this step is to correctly evaluate the model and make sure it will work on new data as well. Evaluation methods include separate test and train sets, cross-validation, and leave-one-out cross-validation.

We will take a closer look at each of the steps in the following sections. We will try to understand the type of questions we must answer during the applied machine learning workflow, and look at the accompanying concepts of data analysis and evaluation.

Data and problem definition

When presented with a problem definition, we need to ask questions that will help in understanding the objective and target information from the data. We could ask very common questions, such as: *what is the expected finding once the data is explored? What kind of information can be extracted after data exploration? Or, what kind of format is required so the question can be answered?* Asking the right question will give a clearer understanding of how to proceed further. Data is simply a collection of measurements in the form of numbers, words, observations, descriptions of things, images, and more.

Measurement scales

The most common way to represent data is using a set of attribute-value pairs. Consider the following example:

```
Bob = {
height: 185cm,
eye color: blue,
hobbies: climbing, sky diving
}
```

For example, `Bob` has attributes named `height`, `eye color`, and `hobbies` with the values `185cm`, `blue`, `climbing`, and `sky diving` respectively.

A set of data can be presented simply as a table, where columns correspond to attributes or features and rows correspond to particular data examples or instances. In supervised machine learning, the attribute whose value we want to predict the outcome, Y, from the values of the other attributes, X, is denoted as the class or target variable, as shown in the following table:

Name	Height [cm]	Eye color	Hobbies
Bob	185.0	Blue	Climbing, sky diving
Anna	163.0	Brown	Reading
...	...	...	...

The first thing we notice is how much the attribute values vary. For instance, height is a number, eye color is text, and hobbies are a list. To gain a better understanding of the value types, let's take a closer look at the different types of data or measurement scales. Stanley Smith Stevens (1946) defined the following four scales of measurement with increasingly expressive properties:

- **Nominal data** consists of data that is mutually exclusive, but not ordered. Examples include eye color, marital status, type of car owned, and so on.
- **Ordinal data** correspond to categories where order matters, but not the difference between the values, such as pain level, student letter grades, service quality ratings, IMDb movie ratings, and so on.
- **Interval data** consists of data where the difference between two values is meaningful, but there is no concept of zero, for instance, standardized exam scores, temperature in Fahrenheit, and so on.
- **Ratio data** has all of the properties of an interval variable and also a clear definition of zero; when the variable is equal to zero, this variable would be missing. Variables such as height, age, stock prices, and weekly food spending are ratio variables.

Why should we care about measurement scales? Well, machine learning depends heavily on the statistical properties of the data; hence, we should be aware of the limitations that each data type possesses. Some machine learning algorithms can only be applied to a subset of measurement scales.

The following table summarizes the main operations and statistics properties for each of the measurement types:

	Property	Nominal	Ordinal	Interval	Ratio
1	Frequency of distribution	True	True	True	True
2	Mode and median		True	True	True
3	Order of values is known		True	True	True
4	Can quantify difference between each value			True	True
5	Can add or subtract values			True	True
6	Can multiply and divide values				True
7	Has true zero				True

Furthermore, nominal and ordinal data correspond to discrete values, while interval and ratio data can correspond to continuous values as well. In supervised learning, the measurement scale of the attribute values that we want to predict dictates the kind of machine algorithm that can be used. For instance, predicting discrete values from a limited list is called classification and can be achieved using decision trees, while predicting continuous values is called regression, which can be achieved using model trees.

Data collection

Once questions are asked in the right direction, the target of data exploration is clear. So, the next step is to see where the data comes from. Data collected can be much unorganized and in very diverse formats, which may involve reading from a database, internet, file system, or other documents. Most of the tools for machine learning require data to be presented in a specific format in order to generate the proper result. We have two choices: observe the data from existing sources or generate the data via surveys, simulations, and experiments. Let's take a closer look at both approaches.

Finding or observing data

Data can be found or observed in many places. An obvious data source is the internet. With an increase in social media usage, and with mobile phones penetrating deeper as mobile data plans become cheaper or even offer unlimited data, there has been an exponential rise in data consumed by users.

Now, online streaming platforms have emerged—the following diagram shows that the hours spent on consuming video data is also growing rapidly:

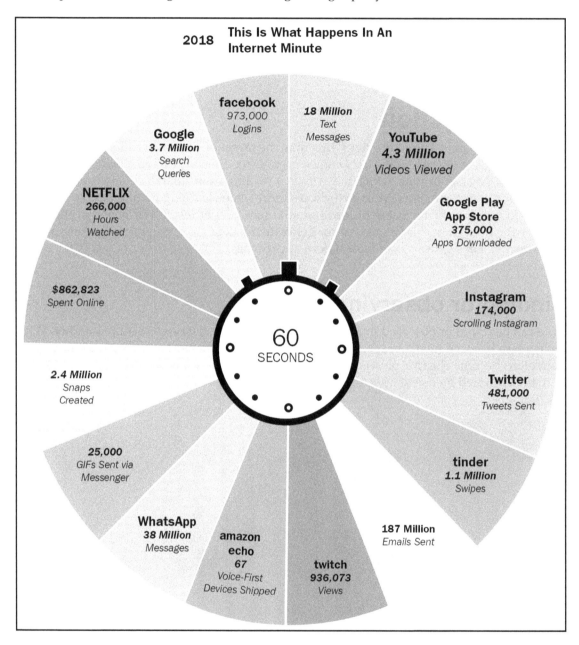

To get data from the internet, there are multiple options, as shown in the following list:

- Bulk downloads from websites such as Wikipedia, IMDb, and the *Million Song Dataset* (which can be found here: `https://labrosa.ee.columbia.edu/millionsong/`).
- Accessing the data through APIs (such as Google, Twitter, Facebook, and YouTube).
- It is okay to scrape public, non-sensitive, and anonymized data. Be sure to check the terms and conditions and to fully reference the information.

The main drawbacks of the data collected is that it takes time and space to accumulate the data, and it covers only what happened; for instance, intentions and internal and external motivations are not collected. Finally, such data might be noisy, incomplete, inconsistent, and may even change over time.

Another option is to collect measurements from sensors such as inertial and location sensors in mobile devices, environmental sensors, and software agents monitoring key performance indicators.

Generating data

An alternative approach is to generate the data by you, for example, with a survey. In survey design, we have to pay attention to data sampling; that is, who the respondents are that are answering the survey. We only get data from the respondents who are accessible and willing to respond. Also, respondents can provide answers that are in line with their self-image and researcher's expectations.

Alternatively, the data can be collected with simulations, where a domain expert specifies the behavior model of users at a micro level. For instance, crowd simulation requires specifying how different types of users will behave in a crowd. Some of the examples could be following the crowd, looking for an escape, and so on. The simulation can then be run under different conditions to see what happens (Tsai et al., 2011). Simulations are appropriate for studying macro phenomena and emergent behavior; however, they are typically hard to validate empirically.

Furthermore, you can design experiments to thoroughly cover all of the possible outcomes, where you keep all of the variables constant and only manipulate one variable at a time. This is the most costly approach, but usually provides the best quality.

Sampling traps

Data collection may involve many traps. To demonstrate one, let me share a story. There is supposed to be a global, unwritten rule for sending regular mail between students for free. If you write student to student in the place where the stamp should be, the mail is delivered to the recipient for free. Now, suppose Jacob sends a set of postcards to Emma, and given that Emma indeed receives some of the postcards, she concludes that all of the postcards are delivered and that the rule indeed holds true. Emma reasons that, as she received the postcards, all of the postcards are delivered. However, she does not know of the postcards that were sent by Jacob, but were undelivered; hence, she is unable to account for this in her inference. What Emma experienced is survivorship bias; that is, she drew the conclusion based on the data that survived. For your information, postcards that are sent with a student to student stamp get a circled black letter T stamp on them, which mean postage is due and the receiver should pay it, including a small fine. However, mail services often have higher costs on applying such fees and hence do not do it. (Magalhães, 2010).

Another example is a study that found that the profession with the lowest average age of death was student. Being a student does not cause you to die at an early age; rather, being a student means you are young. This is why the average is so low. (Gelman and Nolan, 2002).

Furthermore, a study that found that only 1.5% of drivers in accidents reported they were using a cell phone, whereas 10.9% reported another occupant in the car distracted them. Can we conclude that using a cell phone is safer than speaking with another occupant? (Uts, 2003) To answer this question, we need to know the prevalence of the cell phone use. It is likely that a higher number of people talked to another occupant in the car while driving than talked on a cell phone during the period when the data was collected.

Data preprocessing

The goal of data preprocessing tasks is to prepare the data for a machine learning algorithm in the best possible way, as not all algorithms are capable of addressing issues with missing data, extra attributes, or denormalized values.

Data cleaning

Data cleaning, also known as data cleansing or data scrubbing, is a process consisting of the following steps:

1. Identifying inaccurate, incomplete, irrelevant, or corrupted data to remove it from further processing
2. Parsing data, extracting information of interest, or validating whether a string of data is in an acceptable format
3. Transforming data into a common encoding format, for example, UTF-8 or int32, time scale, or a normalized range
4. Transforming data into a common data schema; for instance, if we collect temperature measurements from different types of sensors, we might want them to have the same structure

Filling missing values

Machine learning algorithms generally do not work well with missing values. Rare exceptions include decision trees, Naive Bayes classifier, and some rule-based learners. It is very important to understand why a value is missing. It can be missing due to many reasons, such as random error, systematic error, and sensor noise. Once we identify the reason, there are multiple ways to deal with the missing values, as shown in the following list:

- **Remove the instance**: If there is enough data, and only a couple of non-relevant instances have some missing values, then it is safe to remove these instances.
- **Remove the attribute**: Removing an attribute makes sense when most of the values are missing, values are constant, or an attribute is strongly correlated with another attribute.
- **Assign a special value (N/A)**: Sometimes a value is missing due to valid reasons, such as the value is out of scope, the discrete attribute value is not defined, or it is not possible to obtain or measure the value. For example, if a person never rates a movie, their rating on this movie is nonexistent.
- **Take the average attribute value**: If we have a limited number of instances, we might not be able to afford removing instances or attributes. In that case, we can estimate the missing values by assigning the average attribute value.
- **Predict the value from other attributes**: Predict the value from previous entries if the attribute possesses time dependencies.

As we have seen, the value can be missing for many reasons, and hence, it is important to understand why the value is missing, absent, or corrupted.

Remove outliers

Outliers in data are values that are unlike any other values in the series and affect all learning methods to various degrees. These can be extreme values, which could be detected with confidence intervals and removed by using a threshold. The best approach is to visualize the data and inspect the visualization to detect irregularities. An example is shown in the following diagram. Visualization applies to low-dimensional data only:

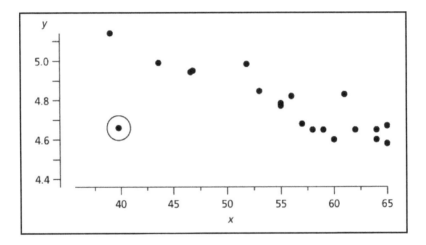

Data transformation

Data transformation techniques tame the dataset to a format that a machine learning algorithm expects as input and may even help the algorithm to learn faster and achieve better performance. It is also known as data munging or data wrangling. Standardization, for instance, assumes that data follows Gaussian distribution and transforms the values in such a way that the mean value is 0 and the deviation is 1, as follows:

$$X = \frac{X - mean(X)}{st.\, dev}$$

Normalization, on the other hand, scales the values of attributes to a small, specified range, usually between 0 and 1:

$$X = \frac{X - min}{max - min}$$

Many machine learning toolboxes automatically normalize and standardize the data for you.

The last transformation technique is discretization, which divides the range of a continuous attribute into intervals. Why should we care? Some algorithms, such as decision trees and Naive Bayes prefer discrete attributes. The most common ways to select the intervals are as follows:

- **Equal width**: The interval of continuous variables is divided into k equal width intervals
- **Equal frequency**: Supposing there are N instances, each of the k intervals contains approximately N or k instances
- **Min entropy**: This approach recursively splits the intervals until the entropy, which measures disorder, decreases more than the entropy increase, introduced by the interval split (Fayyad and Irani, 1993)

The first two methods require us to specify the number of intervals, while the last method sets the number of intervals automatically; however, it requires the class variable, which means it won't work for unsupervised machine learning tasks.

Data reduction

Data reduction deals with abundant attributes and instances. The number of attributes corresponds to the number of dimensions in our dataset. Dimensions with low prediction power contribute very little to the overall model, and cause a lot of harm. For instance, an attribute with random values can introduce some random patterns that will be picked up by a machine learning algorithm. It may happen that data contains a large number of missing values, wherein we have to find the reason for missing values in large numbers, and on that basis, it may fill it with some alternate value or impute or remove the attribute altogether. If 40% or more values are missing, then it may be advisable to remove such attributes, as this will impact the model performance.

The other factor is variance, where the constant variable may have low variance, which means the data is very close to each other or there is not very much variation in the data.

To deal with this problem, the first set of techniques removes such attributes and selects the most promising ones. This process is known as feature selection, or attributes selection, and includes methods such as ReliefF, information gain, and the Gini index. These methods are mainly focused on discrete attributes.

Another set of tools, focused on continuous attributes, transforms the dataset from the original dimensions into a lower-dimensional space. For example, if we have a set of points in three-dimensional space, we can make a projection into a two-dimensional space. Some information is lost, but in a situation where the third dimension is irrelevant, we don't lose much, as the data structure and relationships are almost perfectly preserved. This can be performed by the following methods:

- **Singular value decomposition (SVD)**
- **Principal component analysis (PCA)**
- Backward/forward feature elimination
- Factor analysis
- **Linear discriminant analysis (LDA)**
- Neural network autoencoders

The second problem in data reduction is related to too many instances; for example, they can be duplicates or come from a very frequent data stream. The main idea is to select a subset of instances in such a way that distribution of the selected data still resembles the original data distribution, and more importantly, the observed process. Techniques to reduce the number of instances involve random data sampling, stratification, and others. Once the data is prepared, we can start with the data analysis and modeling.

Unsupervised learning

Unsupervised learning is about analyzing the data and discovering hidden structures in unlabeled data. As no notion of the right labels is given, there is also no error measure to evaluate a learned model; however, unsupervised learning is an extremely powerful tool. Have you ever wondered how Amazon can predict what books you'll like? Or how Netflix knows what you want to watch before you do? The answer can be found in unsupervised learning. We will look at a similar example of unsupervised learning in the following section.

Finding similar items

Many problems can be formulated as finding similar sets of elements, for example, customers who purchased similar products, web pages with similar content, images with similar objects, users who visited similar websites, and so on.

Two items are considered similar if they are a small distance apart. The main questions are how each item is represented and how the distance between the items is defined. There are two main classes of distance measures:

- Euclidean distances
- Non-Euclidean distances

Euclidean distances

In Euclidean space, with the n dimension, the distance between two elements is based on the locations of the elements in such a space, which is expressed as **p-norm distance**. Two commonly used distance measures are L2- and L1-norm distances.

L2-norm, also known as Euclidean distance, is the most frequently applied distance measure that measures how far apart two items in a two-dimensional space are. It is calculated as follows:

$$L_2\,norm\;d(a,b) = \sqrt{\sum_{i=1}^{n}(a_i - b_i)^2}$$

L1-norm, also known as Manhattan distance, city block distance, and taxicab norm, simply sums the absolute differences in each dimension, as follows:

$$L_1\,norm\;d(a,b) = \sum_{i=1}^{n}|a_i - b_i|$$

Non-Euclidean distances

A non-Euclidean distance is based on the properties of the elements, but not on their location in space. Some well known distances are Jaccard distance, cosine distance, edit distance, and Hamming distance.

Jaccard distance is used to compute the distance between two sets. First, we compute the Jaccard similarity of two sets as the size of their intersection divided by the size of their union, as follows:

$$sim(A, B) = \frac{A \bigcap B}{A \bigcup B}$$

The Jaccard distance is then defined as per the following formula:

$$d(A, B) = 1 - sim(A, B) = 1 - \frac{A \bigcap B}{A \bigcup B}$$

Cosine distance between two vectors focuses on the orientation and not magnitude, therefore, two vectors with the same orientation have a cosine similarity of 1, while two perpendicular vectors have a cosine similarity of 0. Supposing that we have two multidimensional points, think of a point as a vector from origin *(0, 0, ..., 0)* to its location. Two vectors make an angle, whose cosine distance is a normalized dot-product of the vectors, as follows:

$$d(A, B) = arcos \frac{A \times B}{\|A\| \, \|B\|}$$

Cosine distance is commonly used in a high-dimensional feature space; for instance, in text mining, where a text document represents an instance, features that correspond to different words, and their values correspond to the number of times the word appears in the document. By computing cosine similarity, we can measure how likely two documents match in describing similar content.

Edit distance makes sense when we compare two strings. The distance between the a=a1,a2,a3,...an and b=b1,b2,b3,...bn strings is the smallest number of the insert/delete operation of single characters required to convert the string from a to b, for example, a = abcd and b = abbd. To convert a into b, we have to delete the second b and insert c in its place. No smallest number of operations would convert a into b, hence the distance is d(a, b) =2.

Hamming distance compares two vectors of the same size and counts the number of dimensions in which they differ. In other words, it measures the number of substitutions required to convert one vector into another.

There are many distance measures focusing on various properties, for instance, correlation measures the linear relationship between two elements; **Mahalanobis distance** measures the distance between a point and distribution of other points and **SimRank**, which is based on graph theory, measures similarity of the structure in which elements occur, and so on. As you can already imagine, selecting and designing the right similarity measure for your problem is more than half of the battle. An impressive overview and evaluation of similarity measures is collected in Chapter 2, *Similarity and Dissimilarity Measures,* in the book *Image Registration: Principles, Tools and Methods* by A. A. Goshtasby, Springer Science and Business Media (2012).

The curse of dimensionality

The curse of dimensionality refers to a situation where we have a large number of features, often hundreds or thousands, which lead to an extremely large space with sparse data and, consequently, to distance anomalies. For instance, in high dimensions, almost all pairs of points are equally distant from each other; in fact, almost all of the pairs have distance close to the average distance. Another manifestation of the curse is that any two vectors are almost orthogonal, which means all of the angles are close to 90 degrees. This practically makes any distance measurement useless.

A cure for the curse of dimensionality might be found in one of the data reduction techniques, where we want to reduce the number of features; for instance, we can run a feature selection algorithm, such as ReliefF, or a feature extraction or reduction algorithm, such as PCA.

Clustering

Clustering is a technique for grouping similar instances into clusters according to some distance measures. The main idea is to put instances that are similar (that is, close to each other) into the same cluster, while keeping the dissimilar points (that is, the ones further apart from each other) in different clusters. An example of how clusters might look like is shown in the following diagram:

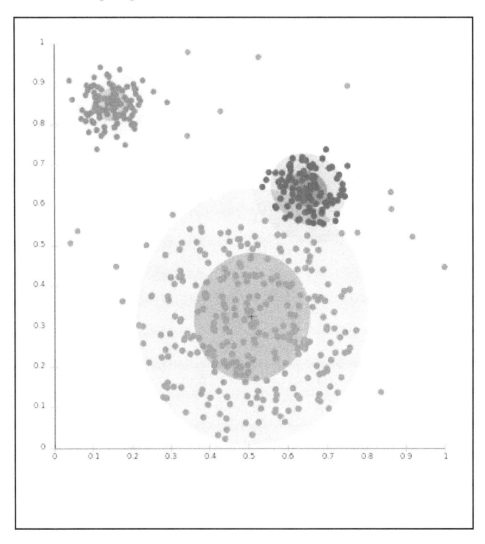

The clustering algorithms follow two fundamentally different approaches. The first is a hierarchical or agglomerative approach that first considers each point as its own cluster, and then iteratively merges the most similar clusters together. It stops when further merging reaches a predefined number of clusters, or if the clusters to be merged are spread over a large region.

The other approach is based on point assignment. First, initial cluster centers (that is, centroids) are estimated, for instance, randomly, and then, each point is assigned to the closest cluster, until all of the points are assigned. The most well known algorithm in this group is k-means clustering.

The k-means clustering either picks initial cluster centers as points that are as far as possible from one another, or (hierarchically) clusters a sample of data and picks a point that is the closest to the center of each of the k-clusters.

Supervised learning

Supervised learning is the key concept behind such amazing things as voice recognition, email spam filtering, and face recognition in photos, and detecting credit card frauds. More formally, given a set, D, of learning examples described with features, X, the goal of supervised learning is to find a function that predicts a target variable, Y. The function, f ,that describes the relation between features X and class Y is called a model:

$$f(X) \rightarrow Y$$

The general structure of supervised learning algorithms is defined by the following decisions (Hand et al., 2001):

1. Define the task
2. Decide on the machine learning algorithm, which introduces specific inductive bias; that is, and a priori assumptions that it makes regarding the target concept
3. Decide on the score or cost function, for instance, information gain, root mean square error, and so on
4. Decide on the optimization/search method to optimize the score function
5. Find a function that describes the relation between X and Y

Many decisions are already made for us by the type of the task and dataset that we have. In the following sections, we will take a closer look at the classification and regression methods and the corresponding score functions.

Classification

Classification can be applied when we deal with a discrete class, where the goal is to predict one of the mutually exclusive values in the target variable. An example would be credit scoring, where the final prediction is whether the person is credit liable or not. The most popular algorithms include decision trees, Naive Bayes classifiers, SVMs, neural networks, and ensemble methods.

Decision tree learning

Decision tree learning builds a classification tree, where each node corresponds to one of the attributes; edges correspond to a possible value (or intervals) of the attribute from which the node originates; and each leaf corresponds to a class label. A decision tree can be used to visually and explicitly represent the prediction model, which makes it a very transparent (white box) classifier. Notable algorithms are ID3 and C4.5, although many alternative implementations and improvements exist (for example, J48 in Weka).

Probabilistic classifiers

Given a set of attribute values, a probabilistic classifier is able to predict a distribution over a set of classes, rather than an exact class. This can be used as a degree of certainty; that is, how sure the classifier is about its prediction. The most basic classifier is Naive Bayes, which happens to be the optimal classifier if, and only if, the attributes are conditionally independent. Unfortunately, this is extremely rare in practice.

There is an enormous subfield denoted as probabilistic graphical models, comprising hundreds of algorithms for example, Bayesian networks, dynamic Bayesian networks, hidden Markov models, and conditional random fields that can handle not only specific relationships between attributes, but also temporal dependencies. Kiran R Karkera wrote an excellent introductory book on this topic, *Building Probabilistic Graphical Models with Python*, Packt Publishing (2014), while Koller and Friedman published a comprehensive theory bible, *Probabilistic Graphical Models*, MIT Press (2009).

Kernel methods

Any linear model can be turned into a non-linear model by applying the kernel trick to the model—replacing its features (predictors) by a kernel function. In other words, the kernel implicitly transforms our dataset into higher dimensions. The kernel trick leverages the fact that it is often easier to separate the instances in more dimensions. Algorithms capable of operating with kernels include the kernel perceptron, SVMs, Gaussian processes, PCA, canonical correlation analysis, ridge regression, spectral clustering, linear adaptive filters, and many others.

Artificial neural networks

Artificial neural networks are inspired by the structure of biological neural networks and are capable of machine learning, as well as pattern recognition. They are commonly used for both regression and classification problems, comprising a wide variety of algorithms and variations for all manner of problem types. Some popular classification methods are **perceptron**, **restricted Boltzmann machine (RBM)**, and **deep belief networks**.

Ensemble learning

Ensemble methods compose of a set of diverse weaker models to obtain better predictive performance. The individual models are trained separately and their predictions are then combined in some way to make the overall prediction. Ensembles, hence, contain multiple ways of modeling the data, which hopefully leads to better results. This is a very powerful class of techniques, and as such, it is very popular. This class includes boosting, bagging, AdaBoost, and random forest. The main differences among them are the type of weak learners that are to be combined and the ways in which to combine them.

Evaluating classification

Is our classifier doing well? Is this better than the other one? In classification, we count how many times we classify something right and wrong. Suppose there are two possible classification labels of yes and no, then there are four possible outcomes, as shown in the following table:

		Predicted as positive?	
		Yes	No
Really positive?	**Yes**	TP-True Positive	FN- False Negative
	No	FP- False Positive	TN-True Negative

The four variables:

- **True positive** (**hit**): This indicates a yes instance correctly predicted as yes
- **True negative** (**correct rejection**): This indicates a no instance correctly predicted as no
- **False positive** (**false alarm**): This indicates a no instance predicted as yes
- **False negative** (**miss**): This indicates a yes instance predicted as no

The basic two performance measures of a classifier are, firstly, classification error:

$$Classification\ error = \frac{errors}{totals} = \frac{FP + FN}{FP + FN + TP + FN}$$

And, secondly, classification accuracy is another performance measure, as shown here:

$$Classification\ accuracy = 1 - error = \frac{correct}{totals} = \frac{TP + TN}{FP + FN + TP + FN}$$

The main problem with these two measures is that they cannot handle unbalanced classes. Classifying whether a credit card transaction is an abuse or not is an example of a problem with unbalanced classes: there are 99.99% normal transactions and just a tiny percentage of abuses. The classifier that says that every transaction is a normal one is 99.99% accurate, but we are mainly interested in those few classifications that occur very rarely.

Precision and recall

The solution is to use measures that don't involve true negatives. Two such measures are as follows:

- **Precision**: This is the proportion of positive examples correctly predicted as positive (*TP*) out of all examples predicted as positive (*TP* + *FP*):

$$Precision = \frac{TP}{TP + FP}$$

- **Recall**: This is the proportion of positives examples correctly predicted as positive (*TP*) out of all positive examples (*TP* + *FN*):

$$Recall = \frac{TP}{TP + FN}$$

It is common to combine the two and report the *F-measure*, which considers both precision and recall to calculate the score as a weighted average, where the score reaches its best value at 1 and worst at 0, as follows:

$$F - measure = \frac{2 \times Precision \times Recall}{Precision + Recall}$$

Roc curves

Most classification algorithms return a classification confidence denoted as *f(X)*, which is, in turn, used to calculate the prediction. Following the credit card abuse example, a rule might look similar to the following:

$$F(X) = \begin{cases} abuse, if\ f(X) > threshold \\ not\ abuse, else \end{cases}$$

The threshold determines the error rate and the true positive rate. The outcomes of all the possible threshold values can be plotted as **receiver operating characteristics** (**ROC**) as shown in the following diagram:

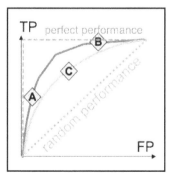

A random predictor is plotted with a red dashed line and a perfect predictor is plotted with a green dashed line. To compare whether the **A** classifier is better than **C**, we compare the area under the curve.

Most of the toolboxes provide all of the previous measures out of the box.

Regression

Regression deals with a continuous target variable, unlike classification, which works with a discrete target variable. For example, in order to forecast the outside temperature of the following few days, we would use regression, while classification will be used to predict whether it will rain or not. Generally speaking, regression is a process that estimates the relationship among features, that is, how varying a feature changes the target variable.

Linear regression

The most basic regression model assumes linear dependency between features and target variable. The model is often fitted using least squares approach, that is, the best model minimizes the squares of the errors. In many cases, linear regression is not able to model complex relations; for example, the following diagram shows four different sets of points having the same linear regression line. The upper-left model captures the general trend and can be considered as a proper model, whereas the bottom-left model fits points much better (except for one outlier, which should be carefully checked), and the upper and lower-right side linear models completely miss the underlying structure of the data and cannot be considered proper models:

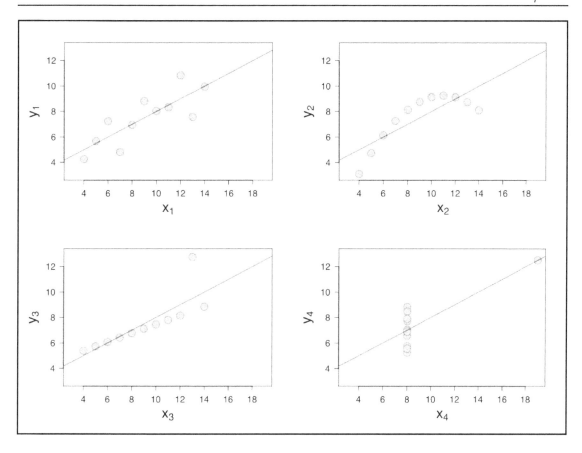

Logistic regression

Linear regression works when the dependent variable is continuous. If, however, the dependent variable is binary in nature, that is, 0 or 1, success or failure, yes or no, true or false, survived or died, and so on, then logistic regression is used instead. One such example is a clinical trial of drugs where the subject under study either responds to the drugs or does not respond. It is also used in fraud detection where the transaction is either a fraud or not fraud. Normally, a logistic function is used to measure the relationship between dependent and independent variables. It is seen as a Bernoulli distribution and, when plotted, looks similar to a curve in the shape of characters.

Evaluating regression

In regression, we predict numbers, Y, from input, X, and the predictions are usually wrong or not exact. The main question that we have to ask is: by how much? In other words, we want to measure the distance between the predicted and true values.

Mean squared error

Mean squared error (**MSE**) is an average of the squared difference between the predicted and true values, as follows:

$$MSE(X,Y) = \sqrt{\frac{1}{n} \sum_{i=1}^{n} (f(X_i) - Y_i)^2}$$

The measure is very sensitive to the outliers, for example, 99 exact predictions and 1 prediction off by 10 is scored the same as all predictions wrong by 1. Moreover, the measure is sensitive to the mean. Therefore, a relative squared error that compares the MSE of our predictor to the MSE of the mean predictor (which always predicts the mean value) is often used instead.

Mean absolute error

Mean absolute error (**MAS**) is an average of the absolute difference between the predicted and the true values, as follows:

$$MAS(X,Y) = \frac{1}{n} \sum_{i=1}^{n} |f(X_i) - Y_i|$$

The MAS is less sensitive to the outliers, but it is also sensitive to the mean and scale.

Correlation coefficient

Correlation coefficient (**CC**) compares the average of prediction relative to the mean, multiplied by training values relative to the mean. If the number is negative, it means weak correlation; a positive number means strong correlation; and zero means no correlation. The correlation between true values X and predictions Y is defined as follows:

$$CC_{XY} = \frac{\sum_{i=1}^{n}(X_i - \overline{X})(Y_i - \overline{Y})}{\sqrt{\sum_{i=1}^{n}(X_i - \overline{X})^2}\sqrt{\sum_{i=1}^{n}(Y_i - \overline{Y})^2}}$$

The CC measure is completely insensitive to the mean and scale and less sensitive to the outliers. It is able to capture the relative ordering, which makes it useful for ranking tasks, such as document relevance and gene expression.

Generalization and evaluation

Once the model is built, how do we know it will perform on new data? Is this model any good? To answer these questions, we'll first look into the model generalization, and then see how to get an estimate of the model performance on new data.

Underfitting and overfitting

Predictor training can lead to models that are too complex or too simple. The model with low complexity (the leftmost models in the following diagram) can be as simple as predicting the most frequent or mean class value, while the model with high complexity (the rightmost models) can represent the training instances. Modes that are too rigid, shown on the left-hand side, cannot capture complex patterns; while models that are too flexible, shown on the right-hand side, fit to the noise in the training data. The main challenge is to select the appropriate learning algorithm and its parameters, so that the learned model will perform well on the new data (for example, the middle column):

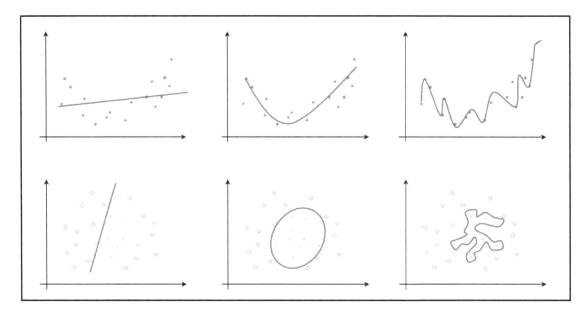

The following diagram shows how errors in the training set decreases with model complexity. Simple rigid models underfit the data and have large errors. As model complexity increases, it describes the underlying structure of the training data better and, consequentially, the error decreases. If the model is too complex, it overfits the training data and its prediction error increases again:

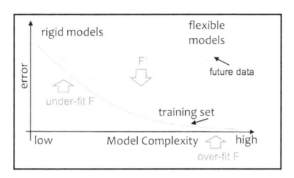

Depending on the task complexity and data availability, we want to tune our classifiers toward more or less complex structures. Most learning algorithms allow such tuning, as follows:

- **Regression**: This is the order of the polynomial
- **Naive Bayes**: This is the number of the attributes
- **Decision trees**: This is the number of nodes in the tree—pruning confidence
- **K-nearest neighbors**: This is the number of neighbors—distance-based neighbor weights
- **SVM**: This is the kernel type; cost parameter
- **Neural network**: This is the number of neurons and hidden layers

With tuning, we want to minimize the generalization error; that is, how well the classifier performs on future data. Unfortunately, we can never compute the true generalization error; however, we can estimate it. Nevertheless, if the model performs well on the training data but performance is much worse on the test data, then the model most likely overfits.

Train and test sets

To estimate the generalization error, we split our data into two parts: training data and testing data. A general rule of thumb is to split them by the training: testing ratio, that is, 70:30. We first train the predictor on the training data, then predict the values for the test data, and finally, compute the error, that is, the difference between the predicted and the true values. This gives us an estimate of the true generalization error.

The estimation is based on the two following assumptions: first, we assume that the test set is an unbiased sample from our dataset; and second, we assume that the actual new data will reassemble the distribution as our training and testing examples. The first assumption can be mitigated by cross-validation and stratification. Also, if it is scarce, one can't afford to leave out a considerable amount of data for a separate test set, as learning algorithms do not perform well if they don't receive enough data. In such cases, cross-validation is used instead.

Cross-validation

Cross-validation splits the dataset into k sets of approximately the same size—for example, in the following diagram, into five sets. First, we use sets 2 to 5 for learning and set 1 for training. We then repeat the procedure five times, leaving out one set at a time for testing, and average the error over the five repetitions:

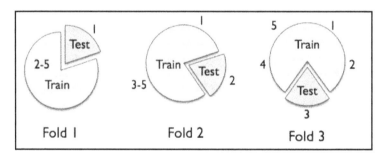

This way, we use all of the data for learning and testing as well, while avoiding using the same data to train and test a model.

Leave-one-out validation

An extreme example of cross-validation is the leave-one-out validation. In this case, the number of folds is equal to the number of instances; we learn on all but one instance, and then test the model on the omitted instance. We repeat this for all instances, so that each instance is used exactly once for the validation. This approach is recommended when we have a limited set of learning examples, for example, less than 50.

Stratification

Stratification is a procedure to select a subset of instances in such a way that each fold roughly contains the same proportion of class values. When a class is continuous, the folds are selected so that the mean response value is approximately equal in all of the folds. Stratification can be applied along with cross-validation or separate training and test sets.

Summary

In this chapter, we refreshed our knowledge of machine learning basics. We revisited the workflow of applied machine learning and clarified the main tasks, methods, and algorithms. We learned about different types for regression and how to evaluate them. We also explored cross-validation and where it is applied.

In the next chapter, we will learn about Java libraries, the tasks that they can perform, and different platforms for machine learning.

Java Libraries and Platforms for Machine Learning

2

Implementing machine learning algorithms by yourself is probably the best way to learn machine learning, but you can progress much faster if you step on the shoulders of the giants and leverage one of the existing open source libraries.

This chapter reviews various libraries and platforms for machine learning in Java. The goal is to understand what each library brings to the table and what kind of problems it is able to solve.

In this chapter, we will cover the following topics:

- The requirement of Java for implementing a machine learning application
- Weka, a general purpose machine learning platform
- The Java machine learning library, a collection of machine learning algorithms
- Apache Mahout, a scalable machine learning platform
- Apache Spark, a distributed machine learning library
- Deeplearning4j, a deep learning library
- MALLET, a text mining library

We'll also discuss how to design the complete machine learning application stack for both single-machine and big data apps by using these libraries with other components.

The need for Java

New machine learning algorithms are often first scripted at university labs, gluing together several languages such as shell scripting, Python, R, MATLAB, Scala, or C++ to provide a new concept and theoretically analyze its properties. An algorithm might take a long path of refactoring before it lands in a library with standardized input or output and interfaces. While Python, R, and MATLAB are quite popular, they are mainly used for scripting, research, and experimenting. Java, on the other hand, is the de facto enterprise language, which could be attributed to static typing, robust IDE support, good maintainability, as well as decent threading model and high performance concurrent data structure libraries. Moreover, there are already many Java libraries available for machine learning, which makes it really convenient to apply them in existing Java applications and leverage powerful machine learning capabilities.

Machine learning libraries

There are over 70 Java-based open source machine learning projects listed on the `MLOSS.org` website, and probably many more unlisted projects live at university servers, GitHub, or Bitbucket. In this section, we will review the major libraries and platforms, the kind of problems they can solve, the algorithms they support, and the kind of data they can work with.

Weka

Waikato Environment for Knowledge Analysis (**WEKA**) is a machine learning library that was developed at the University of Waikato, New Zealand, and is probably the most well-known Java library. It is a general purpose library that is able to solve a wide variety of machine learning tasks, such as classification, regression, and clustering. It features a rich graphical user interface, command-line interface, and Java API. You can check out Weka at `http://www.cs.waikato.ac.nz/ml/weka/`.

At the time of writing this book, Weka contains 267 algorithms in total: data preprocessing (82), attribute selection (33), classification and regression (133), clustering (12), and association rules mining (7). Graphical interfaces are well suited for exploring your data, while the Java API allows you to develop new machine learning schemes and use the algorithms in your applications.

Weka is distributed under the **GNU General Public License** (**GNU GPL**), which means that you can copy, distribute, and modify it as long as you track changes in source files and keep it under GNU GPL. You can even distribute it commercially, but you must disclose the source code or obtain a commercial license.

In addition to several supported file formats, Weka features its own default data format, ARFF, to describe data by attribute-data pairs. It consists of two parts. The first part contains a header, which specifies all of the attributes and their types, for instance, nominal, numeric, date, and string. The second part contains the data, where each line corresponds to an instance. The last attribute in the header is implicitly considered the target variable and missing data is marked with a question mark. For example, returning to the example from Chapter 1, *Applied Machine Learning Quick Start*, the Bob instance written in an ARFF file format would be as follows:

```
@RELATION person_dataset @ATTRIBUTE `Name` STRING @ATTRIBUTE `Height`
NUMERIC @ATTRIBUTE `Eye color`{blue, brown, green} @ATTRIBUTE `Hobbies`
STRING @DATA 'Bob', 185.0, blue, 'climbing, sky diving' 'Anna', 163.0,
brown, 'reading' 'Jane', 168.0, ?, ?
```

The file consists of three sections. The first section starts with the @RELATION <String> keyword, specifying the dataset name. The next section starts with the @ATTRIBUTE keyword, followed by the attribute name and type. The available types are STRING, NUMERIC, DATE, and a set of categorical values. The last attribute is implicitly assumed to be the target variable that we want to predict. The last section starts with the @DATA keyword, followed by one instance per line. Instance values are separated by commas and must follow the same order as attributes in the second section.

More Weka examples will be demonstrated in Chapter 3, *Basic Algorithms – Classification, Regression, and Clustering*, and Chapter 4, *Customer Relationship Prediction with Ensembles*.

To learn more about Weka, pick up a quick-start book—*Weka Howto,* by *Kaluza, Packt Publishing* to start coding, or look into *Data Mining: Practical Machine Learning Tools and Techniques with Java Implementations* by *Witten and Frank, Morgan Kaufmann Publishers* for theoretical background and in-depth explanations.

Weka's Java API is organized into the following top-level packages:

- `weka.associations`: These are data structures and algorithms for association rules learning, including **Apriori**, **predictive Apriori**, **FilteredAssociator**, **FP-Growth**, **Generalized Sequential Patterns (GSP)**, **hotSpot**, and **Tertius**.
- `weka.classifiers`: These are supervised learning algorithms, evaluators, and data structures. The package is further split into the following components:
    - `weka.classifiers.bayes`: This implements Bayesian methods, including Naive Bayes, Bayes net, Bayesian logistic regression, and so on.
    - `weka.classifiers.evaluation`: These are supervised evaluation algorithms for nominal and numerical prediction, such as evaluation statistics, confusion matrix, ROC curve, and so on.
    - `weka.classifiers.functions`: These are regression algorithms, including linear regression, isotonic regression, Gaussian processes, **Support Vector Machines (SVMs)**, multilayer perceptron, voted perceptron, and others.
    - `weka.classifiers.lazy`: These are instance-based algorithms such as k-nearest neighbors, K*, and lazy Bayesian rules.
    - `weka.classifiers.meta`: These are supervised learning meta-algorithms, including AdaBoost, bagging, additive regression, random committee, and so on.
    - `weka.classifiers.mi`: These are multiple-instance learning algorithms, such as citation k-nearest neighbors, diverse density, AdaBoost, and others.
    - `weka.classifiers.rules`: These are decision tables and decision rules based on the separate-and-conquer approach, RIPPER, PART, PRISM, and so on.
    - `weka.classifiers.trees`: These are various decision trees algorithms, including ID3, C4.5, M5, functional tree, logistic tree, random forest, and so on.
    - `weka.clusterers`: These are clustering algorithms, including k-means, CLOPE, Cobweb, DBSCAN hierarchical clustering, and FarthestFirst.
    - `weka.core`: These are various utility classes such as the attribute class, statistics class, and instance class.
    - `weka.datagenerators`: These are data generators for classification, regression, and clustering algorithms.

- weka.estimators: These are various data distribution estimators for discrete/nominal domains, conditional probability estimations, and so on.
- weka.experiment: These are a set of classes supporting necessary configuration, datasets, model setups, and statistics to run experiments.
- weka.filters: These are attribute-based and instance-based selection algorithms for both supervised and unsupervised data preprocessing.
- weka.gui: These are graphical interface implementing explorer, experimenter, and knowledge flow applications. The Weka Explorer allows you to investigate datasets, algorithms, as well as their parameters, and visualize datasets with scatter plots and other visualizations. The Weka Experimenter is used to design batches of experiments, but it can only be used for classification and regression problems.The Weka KnowledgeFlow implements a visual drag-and-drop user interface to build data flows and, for example, load data, apply filter, build classifier, and evaluate it.

Java machine learning

The **Java Machine Learning Library** (**Java-ML**) is a collection of machine learning algorithms with a common interface for algorithms of the same type. It only features the Java API, and so it is primarily aimed at software engineers and programmers. Java-ML contains algorithms for data preprocessing, feature selection, classification, and clustering. In addition, it features several Weka bridges to access Weka's algorithms directly through the Java-ML API. It can be downloaded from http://java-ml.sourceforge.net.

Java-ML is also a general-purpose machine learning library. Compared to Weka, it offers more consistent interfaces and implementations of recent algorithms that are not present in other packages, such as an extensive set of state-of-the-art similarity measures and feature-selection techniques, for example, **dynamic time warping** (**DTW**), random forest attribute evaluation, and so on. Java-ML is also available under the GNU GPL license.

Java-ML supports all types of files as long as they contain one data sample per line and the features are separated by a symbol such as a comma, semicolon, or tab.

The library is organized around the following top-level packages:

- `net.sf.javaml.classification`: These are classification algorithms, including Naive Bayes, random forests, bagging, self-organizing maps, k-nearest neighbors, and so on
- `net.sf.javaml.clustering`: These are clustering algorithms such as k-means, self-organizing maps, spatial clustering, Cobweb, ABC, and others
- `net.sf.javaml.core`: These are classes representing instances and datasets
- `net.sf.javaml.distance`: These are algorithms that measure instance distance and similarity, for example, Chebyshev distance, cosine distance/similarity, Euclidean distance, Jaccard distance/similarity, Mahalanobis distance, Manhattan distance, Minkowski distance, Pearson correlation coefficient, Spearman's footrule distance, DTW, and so on
- `net.sf.javaml.featureselection`: These are algorithms for feature evaluation, scoring, selection, and ranking, for instance, gain ratio, ReliefF, Kullback-Leibler divergence, symmetrical uncertainty, and so on
- `net.sf.javaml.filter`: These are methods for manipulating instances by filtering, removing attributes, setting classes or attribute values, and so on
- `net.sf.javaml.matrix`: This implements in-memory or file-based arrays
- `net.sf.javaml.sampling`: This implements sampling algorithms to select a subset of datasets
- `net.sf.javaml.tools`: These are utility methods on dataset, instance manipulation, serialization, Weka API interface, and so on
- `net.sf.javaml.utils`: These are utility methods for algorithms, for example, statistics, math methods, contingency tables, and others

Apache Mahout

The Apache Mahout project aims to build a scalable machine learning library. It is built atop scalable, distributed architectures, such as Hadoop, using the MapReduce paradigm, which is an approach for processing and generating large datasets with a parallel, distributed algorithm using a cluster of servers.

Mahout features a console interface and the Java API as scalable algorithms for clustering, classification, and collaborative filtering. It is able to solve three business problems:

- **Item recommendation**: Recommending items such as *People who liked this movie also liked*

- **Clustering**: Sorting of text documents into groups of topically-related documents
- **Classification**: Learning which topic to assign to an unlabelled document

Mahout is distributed under a commercially friendly Apache license, which means that you can use it as long as you keep the Apache license included and display it in your program's copyright notice.

Mahout features the following libraries:

- `org.apache.mahout.cf.taste`: These are collaborative filtering algorithms based on user-based and item-based collaborative filtering and matrix factorization with ALS
- `org.apache.mahout.classifier`: These are in-memory and distributed implementations, including logistic regression, Naive Bayes, random forest, **hidden Markov models** (**HMM**), and multilayer perceptron
- `org.apache.mahout.clustering`: These are clustering algorithms such as canopy clustering, k-means, fuzzy k-means, streaming k-means, and spectral clustering
- `org.apache.mahout.common`: These are utility methods for algorithms, including distances, MapReduce operations, iterators, and so on
- `org.apache.mahout.driver`: This implements a general-purpose driver to run main methods of other classes
- `org.apache.mahout.ep`: This is the evolutionary optimization using the recorded-step mutation
- `org.apache.mahout.math`: These are various math utility methods and implementations in Hadoop
- `org.apache.mahout.vectorizer`: These are classes for data presentation, manipulation, and MapReduce jobs

Apache Spark

Apache Spark, or simply Spark, is a platform for large-scale data processing builds atop Hadoop, but, in contrast to Mahout, it is not tied to the MapReduce paradigm. Instead, it uses in-memory caches to extract a working set of data, process it, and repeat the query. This is reported to be up to ten times as fast as a Mahout implementation that works directly with data stored in the disk. It can be grabbed from `https://spark.apache.org`.

There are many modules built atop Spark, for instance, GraphX for graph processing, Spark Streaming for processing real-time data streams, and MLlib for machine learning library featuring classification, regression, collaborative filtering, clustering, dimensionality reduction, and optimization.

Spark's MLlib can use a Hadoop-based data source, for example, **Hadoop Distributed File System** (**HDFS**) or HBase, as well as local files. The supported data types include the following:

- **Local vectors** are stored on a single machine. Dense vectors are presented as an array of double-typed values, for example, (2.0, 0.0, 1.0, 0.0), while sparse vector is presented by the size of the vector, an array of indices, and an array of values, for example, [4, (0, 2), (2.0, 1.0)].
- **Labelled point** is used for supervised learning algorithms and consists of a local vector labelled with double-typed class values. The label can be a class index, binary outcome, or a list of multiple class indices (multiclass classification). For example, a labelled dense vector is presented as [1.0, (2.0, 0.0, 1.0, 0.0)].
- **Local matrices** store a dense matrix on a single machine. It is defined by matrix dimensions and a single double-array arranged in a column-major order.
- **Distributed matrices** operate on data stored in Spark's **Resilient Distributed Dataset** (**RDD**), which represents a collection of elements that can be operated on in parallel. There are three presentations: row matrix, where each row is a local vector that can be stored on a single machine, row indices are meaningless; indexed row matrix, which is similar to row matrix, but the row indices are meaningful, that is, rows can be identified and joins can be executed; and coordinate matrix, which is used when a row cannot be stored on a single machine and the matrix is very sparse.

Spark's MLlib API library provides interfaces for various learning algorithms and utilities, as outlined in the following list:

- `org.apache.spark.mllib.classification`: These are binary and multiclass classification algorithms, including linear SVMs, logistic regression, decision trees, and Naive Bayes
- `org.apache.spark.mllib.clustering`: These are k-means clustering algorithms
- `org.apache.spark.mllib.linalg`: These are data presentations, including dense vectors, sparse vectors, and matrices

- `org.apache.spark.mllib.optimization`: These are the various optimization algorithms that are used as low-level primitives in MLlib, including gradient descent, **stochastic gradient descent** (**SGD**), update schemes for distributed SGD, and the limited-memory **Broyden–Fletcher–Goldfarb–Shanno** (**BFGS**) algorithm

- `org.apache.spark.mllib.recommendation`: These are model-based collaborative filtering techniques implemented with alternating least squares matrix factorization

- `org.apache.spark.mllib.regression`: These are regression learning algorithms, such as linear least squares, decision trees, Lasso, and Ridge regression

- `org.apache.spark.mllib.stat`: These are statistical functions for samples in sparse or dense vector format to compute the mean, variance, minimum, maximum, counts, and nonzero counts

- `org.apache.spark.mllib.tree`: This implements classification and regression decision tree-learning algorithms

- `org.apache.spark.mllib.util`: These are a collection of methods used for loading, saving, preprocessing, generating, and validating the data

Deeplearning4j

Deeplearning4j, or DL4J, is a deep learning library written in Java. It features a distributed as well as a single-machine deep learning framework that includes and supports various neural network structures such as feedforward neural networks, RBM, convolutional neural nets, deep belief networks, autoencoders, and others. DL4J can solve distinct problems, such as identifying faces, voices, spam, or e-commerce fraud.

Deeplearning4j is also distributed under the Apache 2.0 license and can be downloaded from `http://deeplearning4j.org`. The library is organized as follows:

- `org.deeplearning4j.base`: These are loading classes
- `org.deeplearning4j.berkeley`: These are math utility methods
- `org.deeplearning4j.clustering`: This is the implementation of k-means clustering
- `org.deeplearning4j.datasets`: This is dataset manipulation, including import, creation, iterating, and so on
- `org.deeplearning4j.distributions`: These are utility methods for distributions

- `org.deeplearning4j.eval`: These are evaluation classes, including the confusion matrix
- `org.deeplearning4j.exceptions`: This implements the exception handlers
- `org.deeplearning4j.models`: These are supervised learning algorithms, including deep belief networks, stacked autoencoders, stacked denoising autoencoders, and RBM
- `org.deeplearning4j.nn`: These are the implementations of components and algorithms based on neural networks, such as neural networks, multi-layer networks, convolutional multi-layer networks, and so on
- `org.deeplearning4j.optimize`: These are neural net optimization algorithms, including back propagation, multi-layer optimization, output layer optimization, and so on
- `org.deeplearning4j.plot`: These are various methods for rendering data
- `org.deeplearning4j.rng`: This is a random data generator
- `org.deeplearning4j.util`: These are helper and utility methods

MALLET

The **Machine Learning for Language Toolkit** (**MALLET**) is a large library of natural language processing algorithms and utilities. It can be used in a variety of tasks such as document classification, document clustering, information extraction, and topic modelling. It features a command-line interface as well as a Java API for several algorithms such as Naive Bayes, HMM, Latent Dirichlet topic models, logistic regression, and conditional random fields.

MALLET is available under the Common Public License 1.0, which means that you can even use it in commercial applications. It can be downloaded from `http://mallet.cs.umass.edu`. A MALLET instance is represented by name, label, data, and source. However, there are two methods to import data into the MALLET format, as shown in the following list:

- **Instance per file**: Each file or document corresponds to an instance and MALLET accepts the directory name for the input.
- **Instance per line**: Each line corresponds to an instance, where the following format is assumed—the `instance_name` label token. Data will be a feature vector, consisting of distinct words that appear as tokens and their occurrence count.

The library is comprised of the following packages:

- `cc.mallet.classify`: These are algorithms for training and classifying instances, including AdaBoost, bagging, C4.5, as well as other decision tree models, multivariate logistic regression, Naive Bayes, and Winnow2.
- `cc.mallet.cluster`: These are unsupervised clustering algorithms, including greedy agglomerative, hill climbing, k-best, and k-means clustering.
- `cc.mallet.extract`: This implements tokenizers, document extractors, document viewers, cleaners, and so on.
- `cc.mallet.fst`: This implements sequence models, including conditional random fields, HMM, maximum entropy Markov models, and corresponding algorithms and evaluators.
- `cc.mallet.grmm`: This implements graphical models and factor graphs such as inference algorithms, learning, and testing, for example, loopy belief propagation, Gibbs sampling, and so on.
- `cc.mallet.optimize`: These are optimization algorithms for finding the maximum of a function, such as gradient ascent, limited-memory BFGS, stochastic meta ascent, and so on.
- `cc.mallet.pipe`: These are methods as pipelines to process data into MALLET instances.
- `cc.mallet.topics`: These are topics modelling algorithms, such as Latent Dirichlet allocation, four-level pachinko allocation, hierarchical PAM, DMRT, and so on.
- `cc.mallet.types`: This implements fundamental data types such as dataset, feature vector, instance, and label.
- `cc.mallet.util`: These are miscellaneous utility functions such as command-line processing, search, math, test, and so on.

The Encog Machine Learning Framework

Encog is a machine learning framework in Java/C# that was developed by Jeff Heaton, a data scientist. It supports normalizing and processing data and a variety of advanced algorithm such as SVM, Neural Networks, Bayesian Networks, Hidden Markov Models, Genetic Programming, and Genetic Algorithms. It has been actively developed since 2008. It supports multi-threading, which boosts performance on multi-core systems.

It can be found at `https://www.heatonresearch.com/encog/`. MLMethod is the base interface, which includes all of the methods for the models. The following are some of the interfaces and classes that it includes:

- `MLRegression`: This interface defines regression algorithms
- `MLClassification`: This interface defines classification algorithms
- `MLClustering`: This interface defines clustering algorithms
- `MLData`: This class represents a vector used in a model, either for input or output
- `MLDataPair`: The functionality of this class is similar to that of `MLData`, but can be used for both input and output
- `MLDataSet`: This represents the list of `MLDataPair` instances for trainers
- `FreeformNeuron`: This class is used as a neuron
- `FreeformConnection`: This shows the weighted connection between neurons
- `FreeformContextNeuron`: This represents a context neuron
- `InputSummation`: This value specifies how the inputs are summed to form a single neuron
- `BasicActiveSummation`: This is the simple sum of all input neurons
- `BasicFreeConnection`: This is the basic weighted connection between neurons
- `BasicFreeformLayer`: This interface provides a layer

ELKI

ELKI creates an environment for developing KDD applications supported by index structures, with an emphasis on unsupervised learning. It provides various implementations for cluster analysis and outlier detection. It provides index structures such as R*-tree for performance boosting and scalability. It is widely used in research areas by students and faculties up until now and has been gaining attention from other parties recently.

ELKI uses the AGPLv3 license, and can be found at `https://elki-project.github.io/`. It is comprised of the following packages:

- `de.lmu.ifi.dbs.elki.algorithm`: Contains various algorithms such as clustering, classification, itemset mining, and so on
- `de.lmu.ifi.dbs.elki.outlier`: Defines an outlier-based algorithm
- `de.lmu.ifi.dbs.elki.statistics`: Defines a statistical analysis algorithm

- `de.lmu.ifi.dbs.elki.database`: This is the ELKI database layer
- `de.lmu.ifi.dbs.elki.index`: This is for index structure implementation
- `de.lmu.ifi.dbs.elki.data`: Defines various data types and database object types

MOA

Massive Online Analysis (**MOA**) contains a vast collection of various machine learning algorithms that includes algorithms for classification, regression, clustering, outlier detection, concept drift detection and recommender system, and tools for evaluation. All algorithms are designed for large-scale machine learning, with the concept of drift and deals with big streams of real-time data. It also works and integrates well with Weka.

It is available as a GNU license and can be downloaded from `https://moa.cms.waikato.ac.nz/`. The following are its main packages:

- `moa.classifiers`: Contains the algorithms for classification
- `moa.clusters`: Contains the algorithms for clustering
- `moa.streams`: Contains the classes related to working with streams
- `moa.evaluation`: Used for evaluating

Comparing libraries

The following table summarizes all of the presented libraries. The table is, by no means, exhaustive—there are many more libraries that cover specific problem domains. This review should serve as an overview of the big names in the Java machine learning world:

Libraries	Problem domains	License	Architecture	Algorithms
Weka	General purpose	GNU GPL	Single machine	Decision trees, Naive Bayes, neural network, random forest, AdaBoost, hierarchical clustering, and so on
Java-ML	General purpose	GNU GPL	Single machine	K-means clustering, self-organizing maps, Markov chain clustering, Cobweb, random forest, decision trees, bagging, distance measures, and so on

Mahout	Classification, recommendation and clustering	Apache 2.0 License	Distributed single machine	Logistic regression, Naive Bayes, random forest, HMM, multilayer perceptron, k-means clustering, and so on
Spark	General purpose	Apache 2.0 License	Distributed	SVM, logistic regression, decision trees, Naive Bayes, k-means clustering, linear least squares, Lasso, ridge regression, and so on
DL4J	Deep learning	Apache 2.0 License	Distributed single machine	RBM, deep belief networks, deep autoencoders, recursive neural tensor networks, convolutional neural network, and stacked denoising autoencoders
MALLET	Text mining	Common Public License 1.0	Single machine	Naive Bayes, decision trees, maximum entropy, HMM, and conditional random fields
Encog	Machine Learning Framework	Apache 2.0 License	Cross Platform	SVM, Neural Network, Bayesian Networks, HMMs, Genetic Programming, and Genetic Algorithms
ELKI	Data Mining	AGPL	Distributed single machine	Cluster Detection, Anomaly Detection, Evaluation, Index
MOA	Machine Learning	GNU GPL	Distributed single machine	Classification, Regression, Clustering, Outlier Detection, Recommender System, Frequent Pattern Mining

Building a machine learning application

Machine learning applications, especially those focused on classification, usually follow the same high-level workflow that's shown in the following diagram. The workflow is comprised of two phases—training the classifier and the classification of new instances. Both phases share common steps, as shown here:

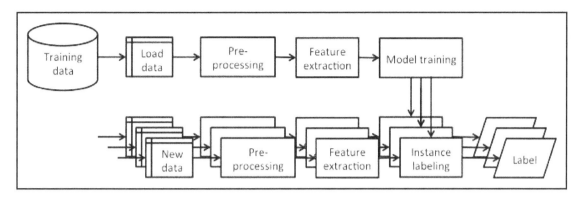

First, we use a set of training data, select a representative subset as the training set, preprocess the missing data, and extract its features. A selected supervised learning algorithm is used to train a model, which is deployed in the second phase. The second phase puts a new data instance through the same preprocessing and feature extraction procedure and applies the learned model to obtain the instance label. If you are able to collect new labelled data, periodically rerun the learning phase to retrain the model and replace the old one with the retrained one in the classification phase.

Traditional machine learning architecture

Structured data, such as transactional, customers, analytical, and market data, usually resides within a local relational database. Given a query language, such as SQL, we can query the data used for processing, as shown in the workflow in the preceding diagram. Usually, all the data can be stored in memory and further processed with a machine learning library such as Weka, Java-ML, or MALLET.

A common practice in the architecture design is to create data pipelines, where different steps in the workflow are split. For instance, in order to create a client data record, we might have to scrap the data from different data sources. The record can be then saved in an intermediate database for further processing.

To understand how the high-level aspects of big data architecture differ, let's first clarify when data is considered big.

Dealing with big data

Big data existed long before the phrase was invented. For instance, banks and stock exchanges have been processing billions of transactions daily for years and airline companies have worldwide real-time infrastructures for operational management of passenger booking, and so on. So, what is big data really? Doug Laney (2001) suggested that big data is defined by three Vs: volume, velocity, and variety. Therefore, to answer the question of whether your data is big, we can translate this into the following three sub-questions:

- **Volume**: Can you store your data in memory?
- **Velocity**: Can you process new incoming data with a single machine?
- **Variety**: Is your data from a single source?

If you answered all of these questions with yes, then your data is probably not big, and you have just simplified your application architecture.

If your answer to all of these questions was no, then your data is big! However, if you have mixed answers, then it's complicated. Some may argue that one V is important; others may say that the other Vs are more important. From a machine learning point of view, there is a fundamental difference in algorithm implementation in order process the data in memory or from distributed storage. Therefore, a rule of thumb is: if you cannot store your data in memory, then you should look into a big data machine learning library.

The exact answer depends on the problem that you are trying to solve. If you're starting a new project, I suggest that you start off with a single-machine library and prototype your algorithm, possibly with a subset of your data if the entire data does not fit into the memory. Once you've established good initial results, consider moving to something more heavy duty such as Mahout or Spark.

Big data application architecture

Big data, such as documents, web blogs, social networks, sensor data, and others, are stored in a NoSQL database, such as MongoDB, or a distributed filesystem, such as HDFS. In case we deal with structured data, we can deploy database capabilities using systems such as Cassandra or HBase, which are built atop Hadoop. Data processing follows the MapReduce paradigm, which breaks data processing problems into smaller sub problems and distributes tasks across processing nodes. Machine learning models are finally trained with machine learning libraries such as Mahout and Spark.

MongoDB is a NoSQL database, which stores documents in a JSON-like format. You can read more about it at `https://www.mongodb.org`. Hadoop is a framework for the distributed processing of large datasets across a cluster of computers. It includes its own filesystem format, HDFS, job scheduling framework, YARD, and implements the MapReduce approach for parallel data processing. We can learn more about Hadoop at `http://hadoop.apache.org/`. Cassandra is a distributed database management system that was built to provide fault-tolerant, scalable, and decentralized storage. More information is available at `http://cassandra.apache.org/`. HBase is another database that focuses on random read/write access for distributed storage. More information is available at `https://hbase.apache.org/`.

Summary

Selecting a machine learning library has an important impact on your application architecture. The key is to consider your project requirements. What kind of data do you have? What kind of problem are you trying to solve? Is your data big? Do you need distributed storage? What kind of algorithm are you planning to use? Once you figure out what you need to solve your problem, pick a library that best fits your needs.

In the next chapter, we will cover how to complete basic machine learning tasks such as classification, regression, and clustering by using some of the presented libraries.

3
Basic Algorithms – Classification, Regression, and Clustering

In the previous chapter, we reviewed the key Java libraries that are used for machine learning and what they bring to the table. In this chapter, we will finally get our hands dirty. We will take a closer look at the basic machine learning tasks, such as classification, regression, and clustering. Each of the topics will introduce basic algorithms for classification, regression, and clustering. The example datasets will be small, simple, and easy to understand.

The following topics will be covered in this chapter:

- Loading data
- Filtering attributes
- Building classification, regression, and clustering models
- Evaluating models

Before you start

Before you start, download the latest stable version of Weka (Weka 3.8 at the time of writing) from http://www.cs.waikato.ac.nz/ml/weka/downloading.html.

There are multiple download options available. You'll want to use Weka as a library in your source code, so make sure that you skip the self-extracting executables and download the ZIP archive, as shown in the following screenshot. Unzip the archive and locate `weka.jar` within the extracted archive:

○ Other platforms (Linux, etc.)

Click **here** to download a zip archive containing Weka
(weka-3-7-11.zip; 33.2 MB)

First unzip the zip file. This will create a new directory called weka-3-7-11. To run Weka, change into that directory and type

```
java -Xmx1000M -jar weka.jar
```

Note that Java needs to be installed on your system for this to work. Also note, that using `-jar` will override your current CLASSPATH variable and only use the `weka.jar`.

We'll use the Eclipse IDE to show examples; follow these steps:

1. Start a new Java project.
2. Right-click on the project properties, select **Java Build Path**, click on the **Libraries** tab, and select **Add External JARs**.
3. Navigate to extract the Weka archive and select the `weka.jar` file.

That's it; we are ready to implement the basic machine learning techniques!

Classification

We will start with the most commonly used machine learning technique: classification. As we reviewed in the first chapter, the main idea is to automatically build a mapping between the input variables and the outcome. In the following sections, we will look at how to load the data, select features, implement a basic classifier in Weka, and evaluate its performance.

Data

For this task, we will take a look at the `zoo` database. The database contains 101 data entries of animals described with 18 attributes, as shown in the following table:

animal	aquatic	fins
hair	predator	legs

---

feathers	toothed	tail
eggs	backbone	domestic
milk	breathes	cat size
airborne	venomous	type

An example entry in the dataset is a lion, with the following attributes:

- `animal`: lion
- `hair`: true
- `feathers`: false
- `eggs`: false
- `milk`: true
- `airborne`: false
- `aquatic`: false
- `predator`: true
- `toothed`: true
- `backbone`: true
- `breathes`: true
- `venomous`: false
- `fins`: false
- `legs`: 4
- `tail`: true
- `domestic`: false
- `catsize`: true
- `type`: mammal

Our task will be to build a model to predict the outcome variable, `animal`, given all of the other attributes as input.

Loading data

Before we start the analysis, we will load the data in Weka's **Attribute-Relation File Format** (**ARFF**) and print the total number of loaded instances. Each data sample is held within a `DataSource` object, while the complete dataset, accompanied by meta-information, is handled by the `Instances` object.

To load the input data, we will use the `DataSource` object that accepts a variety of file formats and converts them into `Instances`:

```
DataSource source = new DataSource("data/zoo.arff");
Instances data = source.getDataSet();
System.out.println(data.numInstances() + " instances loaded.");
System.out.println(data.toString());
```

This will provide the number of loaded instances as output, as follows:

```
101 instances loaded.
```

We can also print the complete dataset by calling the `data.toString()` method.

Our task is to learn a model that is able to predict the `animal` attribute in the future examples for which we know the other attributes, but do not know the `animal` label. Hence, we will remove the `animal` attribute from the training set. We will accomplish this by filtering out the animal attribute, using the `Remove()` filter.

First, we set a string table of parameters, specifying that the first attribute must be removed. The remaining attributes are used as our dataset for training a classifier:

```
Remove remove = new Remove();
String[] opts = new String[]{ "-R", "1"};
```

Finally, we call the `Filter.useFilter(Instances, Filter)` static method to apply the filter on the selected dataset:

```
remove.setOptions(opts);
remove.setInputFormat(data);
data = Filter.useFilter(data, remove);
System.out.println(data.toString());
```

Feature selection

As introduced in `Chapter 1`, *Applied Machine Learning Quick Start*, one of the preprocessing steps is focused on feature selection, also known as **attribute selection**. The goal is to select a subset of relevant attributes that will be used in a learned model. Why is feature selection important? A smaller set of attributes simplifies the models and makes them easier for users to interpret. This usually requires shorter training and reduces overfitting.

Attribute selection can take the class value into account or it cannot. In the first case, an attribute selection algorithm evaluates the different subsets of features and calculates a score that indicates the quality of selected attributes. We can use different searching algorithms, such as exhaustive search and best-first search, and different quality scores, such as information gain, the Gini index, and so on.

Weka supports this process with an `AttributeSelection` object, which requires two additional parameters: an evaluator, which computes how informative an attribute is, and a ranker, which sorts the attributes according to the score assigned by the evaluator.

We will use the following steps to perform selection:

1. In this example, we will use information gain as an evaluator, and we will rank the features by their information gain score:

```
InfoGainAttributeEval eval = new InfoGainAttributeEval();
Ranker search = new Ranker();
```

2. We will initialize an `AttributeSelection` object and set the evaluator, ranker, and data:

```
AttributeSelection attSelect = new AttributeSelection();
attSelect.setEvaluator(eval);
attSelect.setSearch(search);
attSelect.SelectAttributes(data);
```

3. We will print an order list of attribute `indices`, as follows:

```
int[] indices = attSelect.selectedAttributes();
System.out.println(Utils.arrayToString(indices));
```

This process will provide the following result as output:

```
12,3,7,2,0,1,8,9,13,4,11,5,15,10,6,14,16
```

The most informative attributes are 12 (fins), 3 (eggs), 7 (aquatic), 2 (hair), and so on. Based on this list, we can remove additional, non-informative features in order to help the learning algorithms achieve more accurate and faster learning models.

What would make the final decision about the number of attributes to keep? There's no rule of thumb related to an exact number; the number of attributes depends on the data and the problem. The purpose of attribute selection is to choose attributes that serve your model better, so it is best to focus on whether the attributes are improving the model.

Learning algorithms

We have loaded our data and selected the best features, and we are ready to learn some classification models. Let's begin with basic decision trees.

In Weka, a decision tree is implemented within the J48 class, which is a reimplementation of Quinlan's famous C4.5 decision tree learner (Quinlan, 1993).

We will make a decision tree by using the following steps:

1. We initialize a new J48 decision tree learner. We can pass additional parameters with a string table—for instance, the tree pruning that controls the model complexity (refer to Chapter 1, *Applied Machine Learning Quick Start*). In our case, we will build an un-pruned tree; hence, we will pass a single -U parameter, as follows:

   ```
   J48 tree = new J48();
   String[] options = new String[1];
   options[0] = "-U";

   tree.setOptions(options);
   ```

2. We will call the buildClassifier(Instances) method to initialize the learning process:

   ```
   tree.buildClassifier(data);
   ```

3. The built model is now stored in a tree object. We can provide the entire J48 unpruned tree by calling the toString() method:

   ```
   System.out.println(tree);
   ```

The output will be as follows:

```
J48 unpruned tree
------------------
feathers = false
|   milk = false
|   |   backbone = false
|   |   |   airborne = false
|   |   |   |   predator = false
|   |   |   |   |   legs <= 2: invertebrate (2.0)
|   |   |   |   |   legs > 2: insect (2.0)
|   |   |   |   predator = true: invertebrate (8.0)
|   |   |   airborne = true: insect (6.0)
|   |   backbone = true
|   |   |   fins = false
|   |   |   |   tail = false: amphibian (3.0)
|   |   |   |   tail = true: reptile (6.0/1.0)
|   |   |   fins = true: fish (13.0)
|   milk = true: mammal (41.0)
feathers = true: bird (20.0)
Number of Leaves  : 9
Size of the tree : 17
```

The tree in the output has 17 nodes in total and 9 of them are terminal (Leaves).

Another way to present the tree is to leverage the built-in TreeVisualizer tree viewer, as follows:

```
TreeVisualizer tv = new TreeVisualizer(null, tree.graph(), new
PlaceNode2());
JFrame frame = new javax.swing.JFrame("Tree Visualizer");
frame.setSize(800, 500);
frame.setDefaultCloseOperation(JFrame.EXIT_ON_CLOSE);
frame.getContentPane().add(tv);
frame.setVisible(true);
tv.fitToScreen();
```

The preceding code results in the following output frame:

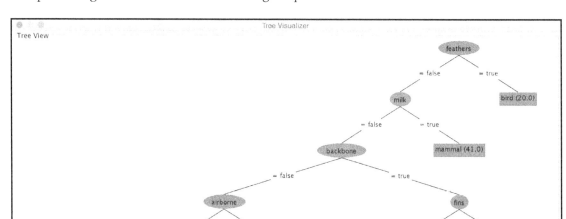

The decision process starts at the top node, also known as the root node. The node label specifies the attribute value that will be checked. In our example, first, we check the value of the feathers attribute. If the feather is present, we follow the right-hand branch, which leads us to the leaf labeled bird, indicating that there are 20 examples supporting this outcome. If the feather is not present, we follow the left-hand branch, which leads us to the milk attribute. We check the value of the attribute again, and we follow the branch that matches the attribute value. We repeat the process until we reach a leaf node.

We can build other classifiers by following the same steps: initialize a classifier, pass the parameters controlling the model complexity, and call the buildClassifier(Instances) method.

In the next section, you will learn how to use a trained model to assign a class label to a new example whose label is unknown.

Classifying new data

Suppose that we record attributes for an animal whose label we do not know; we can predict its label from the learned classification model. We will use the following animal for this process:

First, we construct a feature vector describing the new specimen, as follows:

```
double[] vals = new double[data.numAttributes()];
vals[0] = 1.0; //hair {false, true}
vals[1] = 0.0;  //feathers {false, true}
vals[2] = 0.0;  //eggs {false, true}
vals[3] = 1.0;  //milk {false, true}
vals[4] = 0.0;  //airborne {false, true}
vals[5] = 0.0;  //aquatic {false, true}
vals[6] = 0.0;  //predator {false, true}
vals[7] = 1.0;  //toothed {false, true}
vals[8] = 1.0;  //backbone {false, true}
vals[9] = 1.0;  //breathes {false, true}
vals[10] = 1.0;  //venomous {false, true}
vals[11] = 0.0;  //fins {false, true}
vals[12] = 4.0;  //legs INTEGER [0,9]
vals[13] = 1.0;  //tail {false, true}
vals[14] = 1.0;  //domestic {false, true}
vals[15] = 0.0;  //catsize {false, true}
DenseInstance myUnicorn = new DenseInstance(1.0, vals);
myUnicorn.setDataset(data);
```

Then, we call the `classify(Instance)` method on the model, in order to obtain the class value. The method returns the label index, as follows:

```
double result = tree.classifyInstance(myUnicorn);
System.out.println(data.classAttribute().value((int) result));
```

This will provide the `mammal` class label as output.

Evaluation and prediction error metrics

We built a model, but we do not know if it can be trusted. To estimate its performance, we can apply a cross-validation technique that was explained in `Chapter 1`, *Applied Machine Learning Quick Start*.

Weka offers an `Evaluation` class for implementing cross-validation. We pass the model, data, number of folds, and an initial random seed, as follows:

```
Classifier cl = new J48();
Evaluation eval_roc = new Evaluation(data);
eval_roc.crossValidateModel(cl, data, 10, new Random(1), new Object[] {});
System.out.println(eval_roc.toSummaryString());
```

The evaluation results are stored in the `Evaluation` object.

A mix of the most common metrics can be invoked by calling the `toString()` method. Note that the output does not differentiate between regression and classification, so make sure to pay attention to the metrics that make sense, as follows:

```
Correctly Classified Instances          93              92.0792 %
Incorrectly Classified Instances         8               7.9208 %
Kappa statistic                          0.8955
Mean absolute error                      0.0225
Root mean squared error                  0.14
Relative absolute error                 10.2478 %
Root relative squared error             42.4398 %
Coverage of cases (0.95 level)          96.0396 %
Mean rel. region size (0.95 level)      15.4173 %
Total Number of Instances              101
```

In the classification, we are interested in the number of correctly/incorrectly classified instances.

The confusion matrix

Furthermore, we can inspect where a particular misclassification has been made by examining the confusion matrix. The confusion matrix shows how a specific class value was predicted:

```
double[][] confusionMatrix = eval_roc.confusionMatrix();
System.out.println(eval_roc.toMatrixString());
```

The resulting confusion matrix is as follows:

```
=== Confusion Matrix ===
  a  b  c  d  e  f  g   <-- classified as
 41  0  0  0  0  0  0 |  a = mammal
  0 20  0  0  0  0  0 |  b = bird
  0  0  3  1  0  1  0 |  c = reptile
  0  0  0 13  0  0  0 |  d = fish
  0  0  1  0  3  0  0 |  e = amphibian
  0  0  0  0  0  5  3 |  f = insect
  0  0  0  0  0  2  8 |  g = invertebrate
```

The column names in the first row correspond to the labels assigned by the classification node. Each additional row then corresponds to an actual true class value. For instance, the second row corresponds to instances with the mammal true class label. In the column line, we read that all mammals were correctly classified as mammals. In the fourth row, reptiles, we notice that three were correctly classified as reptiles, while one was classified as fish and one as insect. The confusion matrix gives us insight into the kinds of errors that our classification model can make.

Choosing a classification algorithm

Naive Bayes is one of the most simple, efficient, and effective inductive algorithms in machine learning. When features are independent, which is rarely true in the real world, it is theoretically optimal and, even with dependent features, its performance is amazingly competitive (Zhang, 2004). The main disadvantage is that it cannot learn how features interact with each other; for example, despite the fact that you like your tea with lemon or milk, you hate a tea that has both of them at the same time.

The main advantage of the decision tree is that it is a model that is easy to interpret and explain, as we studied in our example. It can handle both nominal and numeric features, and you don't have to worry about whether the data is linearly separable.

Some other examples of classification algorithms are as follows:

- `weka.classifiers.rules.ZeroR`: This predicts the majority class and is considered a baseline; that is, if your classifier's performance is worse than the average value predictor, it is not worth considering it.
- `weka.classifiers.trees.RandomTree`: This constructs a tree that considers *K* randomly chosen attributes at each node.
- `weka.classifiers.trees.RandomForest`: This constructs a set (forest) of random trees and uses majority voting to classify a new instance.
- `weka.classifiers.lazy.IBk`: This is the k-nearest neighbors classifier that is able to select an appropriate value of neighbors, based on cross-validation.
- `weka.classifiers.functions.MultilayerPerceptron`: This is a classifier based on neural networks that uses backpropagation to classify instances. The network can be built by hand, or created by an algorithm, or both.
- `weka.classifiers.bayes.NaiveBayes`: This is a Naive Bayes classifier that uses estimator classes, where numeric estimator precision values are chosen based on the analysis of the training data.
- `weka.classifiers.meta.AdaBoostM1`: This is the class for boosting a nominal class classifier by using the `AdaBoost M1` method. Only nominal class problems can be tackled. This often dramatically improves the performance, but sometimes, it overfits.
- `weka.classifiers.meta.Bagging`: This is the class for bagging a classifier to reduce the variance. This can perform classification and regression, depending on the base learner.

Classification using Encog

In the previous section, you saw how to use a Weka library for classification. In this section, we will quickly look at how the same can be achieved by using the Encog library. Encog requires us to build a model to do the classification. Download the Encog library from `https://github.com/encog/encog-java-core/releases`. Once downloaded, add the `.jar` file in the Eclipse project, as explained at the beginning of the chapter.

For this example, we will use the `iris` dataset, which is available in `.csv` format; it can be downloaded from `https://archive.ics.uci.edu/ml/datasets/Iris`. From the download path, copy the `iris.data.csv` file into your data directory. This file contains the data of 150 different flowers. It contains four different measurements about the flowers, and the last column is a label.

We will now perform the classification, using the following steps:

1. We will use the `VersatileMLDataSet` method to load the file and define all four columns. The next step is to call the `analyze` method that will read the entire file and find the statistical parameters, such as the mean, the standard deviation, and many more:

```
File irisFile = new File("data/iris.data.csv");
VersatileDataSource source = new CSVDataSource(irisFile, false,
CSVFormat.DECIMAL_POINT);

VersatileMLDataSet data = new VersatileMLDataSet(source);
data.defineSourceColumn("sepal-length", 0, ColumnType.continuous);
data.defineSourceColumn("sepal-width", 1, ColumnType.continuous);
data.defineSourceColumn("petal-length", 2, ColumnType.continuous);
data.defineSourceColumn("petal-width", 3, ColumnType.continuous);
ColumnDefinition outputColumn = data.defineSourceColumn("species",
4, ColumnType.nominal);
data.analyze();
```

2. The next step is to define the output column. Then, it's time to normalize the data; but before that, we need to decide on the model type according to which the data will be normalized, as follows:

```
data.defineSingleOutputOthersInput(outputColumn);

EncogModel model = new EncogModel(data);
model.selectMethod(data, MLMethodFactory.TYPE_FEEDFORWARD);

model.setReport(new ConsoleStatusReportable());
data.normalize();
```

3. The next step is to fit the model on a training set, leaving a test set aside. We will hold 30% of the data, as specified by the first argument, `0.3`; the next argument specifies that we want to shuffle the data in randomly. `1001` says that there is a seed value of 1001, so we use a `holdBackValidation` model:

```
model.holdBackValidation(0.3, true, 1001);
```

4. Now, it's time to train the model and classify the data, according to the measurements and labels. The cross-validation breaks the training dataset into five different combinations:

```
model.selectTrainingType(data);
MLRegression bestMethod = (MLRegression)model.crossvalidate(5,
true);
```

5. The next step is to display the results of each fold and the errors:

```
System.out.println( "Training error: " +
EncogUtility.calculateRegressionError(bestMethod,
model.getTrainingDataset()));
System.out.println( "Validation error: " +
EncogUtility.calculateRegressionError(bestMethod,
model.getValidationDataset()));
```

6. Now, we will start to use the model to predict the values, using the following code block:

```
while(csv.next()) {
        StringBuilder result = new StringBuilder();
        line[0] = csv.get(0);
        line[1] = csv.get(1);
        line[2] = csv.get(2);
        line[3] = csv.get(3);
        String correct = csv.get(4);
helper.normalizeInputVector(line,input.getData(),false);
        MLData output = bestMethod.compute(input);
        String irisChosen =
helper.denormalizeOutputVectorToString(output)[0];
        result.append(Arrays.toString(line));
        result.append(" -> predicted: ");
        result.append(irisChosen);
        result.append("(correct: ");
        result.append(correct);
        result.append(")");
        System.out.println(result.toString());
    }
```

This will yield an output similar to the following:

```
5/5 : Fold #5/5: Iteration #116, Training Error: 0.00316917, Validation Error: 0.03959239
5/5 : Fold #5/5: Iteration #117, Training Error: 0.00306926, Validation Error: 0.03959239
5/5 : Fold #5/5: Iteration #118, Training Error: 0.00295826, Validation Error: 0.03959239
5/5 : Fold #5/5: Iteration #119, Training Error: 0.00283791, Validation Error: 0.03959239
5/5 : Fold #5/5: Iteration #120, Training Error: 0.00285336, Validation Error: 0.03959239
5/5 : Fold #5/5: Iteration #121, Training Error: 0.00283003, Validation Error: 0.04615343
5/5 : Fold #5/5: Iteration #122, Training Error: 0.00278216, Validation Error: 0.04615343
5/5 : Fold #5/5: Iteration #123, Training Error: 0.00274684, Validation Error: 0.04615343
5/5 : Fold #5/5: Iteration #124, Training Error: 0.00269973, Validation Error: 0.04615343
5/5 : Fold #5/5: Iteration #125, Training Error: 0.00263623, Validation Error: 0.04615343
5/5 : Fold #5/5: Iteration #126, Training Error: 0.00256257, Validation Error: 0.04615343
5/5 : Fold #5/5: Iteration #127, Training Error: 0.00247902, Validation Error: 0.04821044
5/5 : Fold #5/5: Iteration #128, Training Error: 0.00238564, Validation Error: 0.04821044
5/5 : Fold #5/5: Iteration #129, Training Error: 0.00228351, Validation Error: 0.04821044
5/5 : Fold #5/5: Iteration #130, Training Error: 0.00219218, Validation Error: 0.04821044
5/5 : Fold #5/5: Iteration #131, Training Error: 0.00214636, Validation Error: 0.04821044
5/5 : Fold #5/5: Iteration #132, Training Error: 0.00215036, Validation Error: 0.04821044
5/5 : Fold #5/5: Iteration #133, Training Error: 0.00209383, Validation Error: 0.05149271
5/5 : Fold #5/5: Iteration #134, Training Error: 0.00202164, Validation Error: 0.05149271
5/5 : Fold #5/5: Iteration #135, Training Error: 0.00193870, Validation Error: 0.05149271
5/5 : Fold #5/5: Iteration #136, Training Error: 0.00184413, Validation Error: 0.05149271
5/5 : Fold #5/5: Iteration #137, Training Error: 0.00173880, Validation Error: 0.05149271
5/5 : Fold #5/5: Iteration #138, Training Error: 0.00169552, Validation Error: 0.05149271
5/5 : Fold #5/5: Iteration #139, Training Error: 0.00175292, Validation Error: 0.05322542
5/5 : Fold #5/5: Iteration #140, Training Error: 0.00169372, Validation Error: 0.05322542
5/5 : Fold #5/5: Iteration #141, Training Error: 0.00163858, Validation Error: 0.05322542
5/5 : Fold #5/5: Iteration #142, Training Error: 0.00157472, Validation Error: 0.05322542
5/5 : Fold #5/5: Iteration #143, Training Error: 0.00157964, Validation Error: 0.05322542
5/5 : Fold #5/5: Iteration #144, Training Error: 0.00152719, Validation Error: 0.05322542
5/5 : Fold #5/5: Iteration #145, Training Error: 0.00147310, Validation Error: 0.05566345
5/5 : Cross-validated score:0.09367002840811614
Training error: 0.014938424036306448
Validation error: 0.061569949736656415
[NormalizationHelper:
[ColumnDefinition:sepal-length(continuous);low=4.300000,high=7.900000,mean=5.843333,sd=0.825301]
[ColumnDefinition:sepal-width(continuous);low=2.000000,high=4.400000,mean=3.054000,sd=0.432147]
[ColumnDefinition:petal-length(continuous);low=1.000000,high=6.900000,mean=3.758667,sd=1.758529]
[ColumnDefinition:petal-width(continuous);low=0.100000,high=2.500000,mean=1.198667,sd=0.760613]
[ColumnDefinition:species(nominal);[Iris-setosa, Iris-versicolor, Iris-virginica]]
]
Final model: [BasicNetwork: Layers=3]
[5.1, 3.5, 1.4, 0.2] -> predicted: Iris-setosa(correct: Iris-setosa)
[4.9, 3.0, 1.4, 0.2] -> predicted: Iris-setosa(correct: Iris-setosa)
[4.7, 3.2, 1.3, 0.2] -> predicted: Iris-setosa(correct: Iris-setosa)
[4.6, 3.1, 1.5, 0.2] -> predicted: Iris-setosa(correct: Iris-setosa)
[5.0, 3.6, 1.4, 0.2] -> predicted: Iris-setosa(correct: Iris-setosa)
[5.4, 3.9, 1.7, 0.4] -> predicted: Iris-setosa(correct: Iris-setosa)
[4.6, 3.4, 1.4, 0.3] -> predicted: Iris-setosa(correct: Iris-setosa)
[5.0, 3.4, 1.5, 0.2] -> predicted: Iris-setosa(correct: Iris-setosa)
[4.4, 2.9, 1.4, 0.2] -> predicted: Iris-setosa(correct: Iris-setosa)
[4.9, 3.1, 1.5, 0.1] -> predicted: Iris-setosa(correct: Iris-setosa)
```

Encog supports many other options in `MLMethodFactory`, such as SVM, PNN, and so on.

Classification using massive online analysis

Massive Online Analysis (**MOA**), as discussed in Chapter 2, *Java Libraries and Platforms for Machine Learning,* is another library that can be used to achieve classification. It is mainly designed to work with the stream. If it is working with the stream, a lot of data will be there; so, how do we evaluate the model? In the traditional batch learning mode, we usually divide the data into training and test sets and cross-validation is preferred if the data is limited. In stream processing, where the data seems to be unlimited, cross-validation proves to be expensive. Two approaches that we can use are as follows:

- **Holdout**: This is useful when the data is already divided into two parts, which are predefined. It gives the estimation of the current classifier, if it is similar to the current data. This similarity is hard to guarantee between the holdout set and the current data.

- **Interleaved test-then-train, or prequential**: In this method, the model is tested on the example before it is used for training. So, the model is always tested for the data that it has never seen. In this, no holdout scheme is needed. It uses the available data. Over time, this approach will improve the accuracy of classification.

MOA provides various ways to generate the stream of data. First, download the MOA library from https://moa.cms.waikato.ac.nz/downloads/. Add the downloaded .jar files to Eclipse, like we did for Weka at the beginning of this chapter. We will be using the GUI tool provided by MOA to see how to use MOA for streams. To launch the GUI, make sure moa.jar and sizeofag.jar are in the current path; then, run the following command in Command Prompt:

```
$ java -cp moa.jar -javaagent:sizeofag.jar moa.gui.GUI
```

It will display the following output:

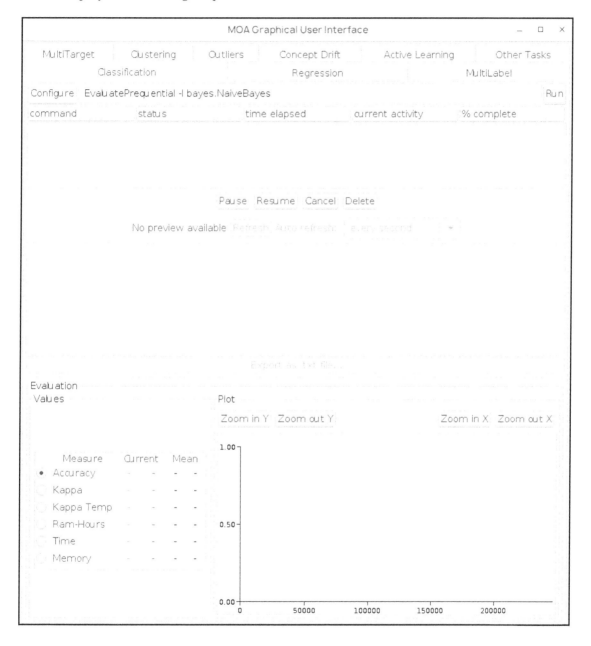

We can see that it has options for classification, regression, clustering, outliers, and more. Clicking on the **Configure** button will display the screen used to make your classifier. It provides various learners and streams to work with, as shown in the following screenshot:

The following is an example of running `RandomTreeGenerator` with `NaiveBayes` and `HoeffdingTree`:

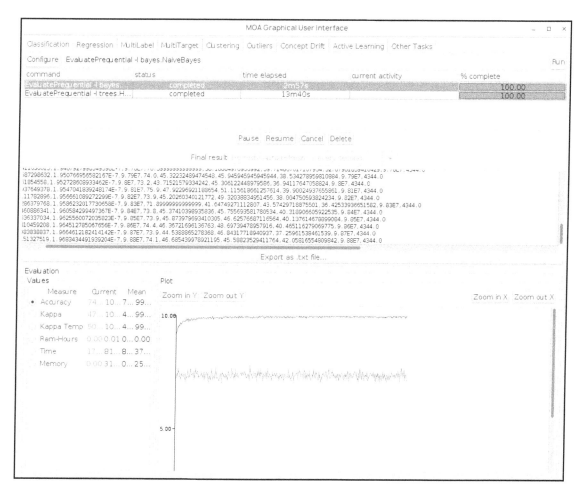

Evaluation

Evaluation is the next important task, after the model has been developed. It lets you decide whether the model is performing on the given dataset well and ensures that it will be able to handle data that it has never seen. The evaluation framework mostly uses the following features:

- **Error estimation**: This uses holdout or interleaved test-and-train methods to estimate the errors. K-fold cross-validation is also used.

- **Performance measures**: The **Kappa** statistics are used, which are more sensitive towards streaming classifiers.
- **Statistical validation**: When comparing evaluating classifiers, we must look at the differences in random and non-random experiments. The McNemar's test is the most popular test in streaming, used to access the statistical significance of differences in two classifiers. If we are working with one classifier, the confidence intervals of parameter estimates indicate the reliability.
- **The cost measure of the process**: As we are dealing with streaming data, which may require access to third-party or cloud-based solutions to get and process the data, the cost per hour of usage and memory is considered for evaluation purposes.

Baseline classifiers

Batch learning has led to the development of many classifiers in different paradigms, such as divide and conquer, lazy learners, kernel methods, graphics models, and so on. Now, if we move to a stream for the same, we need to understand how to make them incremental and fast for the large datasets in the streams. We have to think in terms of the complexity of the model versus the speed of the model update, and this is the main trade-off that needs to be taken care of.

The **majority class algorithm** is one of the simplest classifiers, and it is used as a baseline. It is also used as a default classifier for decision tree leaves. Another is the **no-change classifier**, which predicts the labels for new instances. The Naive Bayes algorithm is known for its low cost in terms of computational power and simplicity. It's an incremental algorithm and is best suited for streams.

Decision tree

The decision tree is a very popular classifier technique, making it easy to interpret and visualize the models. It is based on trees. It divides or splits the nodes on the basis of the attribute value and the leaves of the tree usually fall to the majority class classifier. In streaming data, the Hoeffding tree is a very fast algorithm for decision trees; it waits for new instances, instead of reusing instances. It builds a tree for large data. The **Concept-adapting Very Fast Decision Tree** (**CVFDT**) deals with the concept of drift, which maintains a model consistency with the instances in a sliding window. The other trees are the **Ultra Fast Forest of Trees** (**UFFT**), the Hoeffding adaptive tree, the exhaustive binary tree, and so on.

Lazy learning

In the streaming context, **k-nearest neighbor** (**KNN**) is the most convenient batch method. A sliding window is used to determine the KNN for a new instance that is not yet classified. It normally uses the 1,000 most recent instances for the sliding window. As the sliding window slides, it handles the concept drift, too.

Active learning

We all know that classifiers work well with labeled data, but that is not always the case with stream data. For example, the data from a stream may come unlabeled. Labeling data is costly, because it requires human intervention to label the unlabeled data. We understand that the streams generate large amounts of data. Active learning algorithms only do the labeling for selective data. The data to be labeled is decided on from historical data suited for pool-based settings. Regular retraining is required to decide whether a label is required for incoming instances. A simple strategy for labeling data is to use a random strategy. It is also called a baseline strategy, and it asks for a label for each incoming instance with probability of a budget for labelling. Another strategy is to ask for a label for the instance for which the current classifier is least confident. This may work fine, but soon, the classifier will exhaust its budget or reach its threshold.

Regression

We will explore basic regression algorithms through an analysis of an energy efficiency dataset (Tsanas and Xifara, 2012). We will investigate the heating and cooling load requirements of the buildings based on their construction characteristics, such as surface, wall, and roof area; height; glazing area; and compactness. The researchers have used a simulator to design 12 different house configurations, while varying 18 building characteristics. In total, 768 different buildings were simulated.

Our first goal is to systematically analyze the impact that each building characteristic has on the target variable, that is, the heating or cooling load. The second goal is to compare the performance of a classical linear regression model against other methods, such as SVM regression, random forests, and neural networks. For this task, we will use the Weka library.

Loading the data

Download the energy efficiency dataset from `https://archive.ics.uci.edu/ml/datasets/Energy+efficiency`.

The dataset is in Excel's XLSX format, which cannot be read by Weka. We can convert it into a **comma-separated value** (**CSV**) format by clicking on **File** | **Save As** and picking `.csv` in the saving dialog, as shown in the following screenshot. Confirm to save only the active sheet (since all of the others are empty), and confirm to continue, to lose some formatting features. Now, the file is ready to be loaded by Weka:

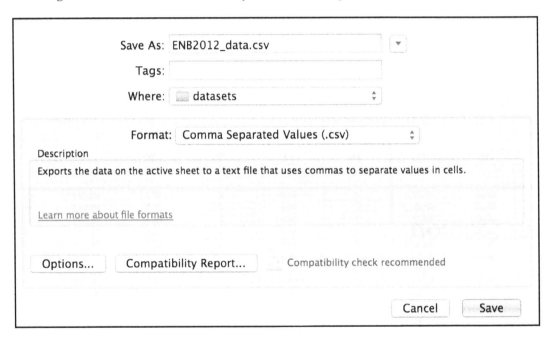

Open the file in a text editor and inspect whether the file was correctly transformed. There might be some minor issues that could cause problems. For instance, in my export, each line ended with a double semicolon, as follows:

```
X1;X2;X3;X4;X5;X6;X7;X8;Y1;Y2;;
0,98;514,50;294,00;110,25;7,00;2;0,00;0;15,55;21,33;;
0,98;514,50;294,00;110,25;7,00;3;0,00;0;15,55;21,33;;
```

To remove the doubled semicolon, you can use the **Find and Replace** function: find ; ; and replace it with ; .

The second problem was that my file had a long list of empty lines at the end of the document, which can be deleted, as follows:

```
0,62;808,50;367,50;220,50;3,50;5;0,40;5;16,64;16,03;;
;;;;;;;;;;;
;;;;;;;;;;;
```

Now, we are ready to load the data. Let's open a new file and write a simple data import function by using Weka's converter for reading files in a CSV format, as follows:

```
import weka.core.Instances;
import weka.core.converters.CSVLoader;
import java.io.File;
import java.io.IOException;

public class EnergyLoad {

  public static void main(String[] args) throws IOException {

    // load CSV
    CSVLoader loader = new CSVLoader();
    loader.setFieldSeparator(",");
    loader.setSource(new File("data/ENB2012_data.csv"));
    Instances data = loader.getDataSet();

    System.out.println(data);
  }
}
```

The data is loaded! Let's move on.

Analyzing attributes

Before we analyze the attributes, let's try to understand what we are dealing with. In total, there are eight attributes describing building characteristics, and there are also two target variables, the heating and cooling load, as shown in the following table:

Attribute	Attribute name
X1	Relative compactness
X2	Surface area
X3	Wall area

X4	Roof area
X5	Overall height
X6	Orientation
X7	Glazing area
X8	Glazing area distribution
Y1	Heating load
Y2	Cooling load

Building and evaluating the regression model

We will start by learning a model for the heating load by setting the class attribute at the feature position:

```
data.setClassIndex(data.numAttributes() - 2);
```

The second target variable, the cooling load, can now be removed:

```
//remove last attribute Y2
Remove remove = new Remove();
remove.setOptions(new String[]{"-R", data.numAttributes()+""});
remove.setInputFormat(data);
data = Filter.useFilter(data, remove);
```

Linear regression

We will start with a basic linear regression model, implemented with the `LinearRegression` class. Similar to the classification example, we will initialize a new model instance, pass the parameters and data, and invoke the `buildClassifier(Instances)` method, as follows:

```
import weka.classifiers.functions.LinearRegression;
...
data.setClassIndex(data.numAttributes() - 2);
LinearRegression model = new LinearRegression();
model.buildClassifier(data);
System.out.println(model);
```

The learned model, which is stored in the object, can be provided by calling the `toString()` method, as follows:

```
Y1 =
    -64.774  * X1 +
    -0.0428  * X2 +
     0.0163  * X3 +
    -0.089   * X4 +
     4.1699  * X5 +
    19.9327  * X7 +
     0.2038  * X8 +
    83.9329
```

The linear regression model constructs a function that linearly combines the input variables to estimate the heating load. The number in front of the feature explains the feature's impact on the target variable: the sign corresponds to the positive/negative impact, while the magnitude corresponds to its significance. For instance, the relative compactness of the feature X1 is negatively correlated with heating load, while the glazing area is positively correlated. These two features also significantly impact the final heating load estimate. The model's performance can similarly be evaluated with the cross-validation technique.

The ten-fold cross-validation is as follows:

```
Evaluation eval = new Evaluation(data);
eval.crossValidateModel(model, data, 10, new Random(1), new String[]{});
System.out.println(eval.toSummaryString());
```

We can provide the common evaluation metrics, including the correlation, the mean absolute error, the relative absolute error, and so on, as output, as follows:

```
Correlation coefficient              0.956
Mean absolute error                  2.0923
Root mean squared error              2.9569
Relative absolute error             22.8555 %
Root relative squared error         29.282  %
Total Number of Instances         768
```

Linear regression using Encog

Now, we will quickly look at how Encog can be used to make a regression model. We will be using the dataset that we used in a previous section, *Loading the data*. The following steps show how to make the model:

1. To load the data, we will use the `VersatileMLDataSet` function, as follows:

```
File datafile = new File("data/ENB2012_data.csv");
VersatileDataSource source = new CSVDataSource(datafile, true,
CSVFormat.DECIMAL_POINT);
VersatileMLDataSet data = new VersatileMLDataSet(source);
data.defineSourceColumn("X1", 0, ColumnType.continuous);
data.defineSourceColumn("X2", 1, ColumnType.continuous);
data.defineSourceColumn("X3", 2, ColumnType.continuous);
data.defineSourceColumn("X4", 3, ColumnType.continuous);
data.defineSourceColumn("X5", 4, ColumnType.continuous);
data.defineSourceColumn("X6", 5, ColumnType.continuous);
data.defineSourceColumn("X7", 6, ColumnType.continuous);
data.defineSourceColumn("X8", 7, ColumnType.continuous);
```

2. As we have two pieces of output, `Y1` and `Y2`, they can be added by using the `defineMultipleOutputsOthersInput` function, as follows:

```
ColumnDefinition outputColumn1 = data.defineSourceColumn("Y1", 8,
ColumnType.continuous);
ColumnDefinition outputColumn2 = data.defineSourceColumn("Y2", 9,
ColumnType.continuous);
ColumnDefinition outputscol [] = {outputColumn1, outputColumn2};
data.analyze();

data.defineMultipleOutputsOthersInput(outputscol);
```

3. The next step is to develop a simple regression model by using the `FEEDFORWARD` instance:

```
EncogModel model = new EncogModel(data);
model.selectMethod(data, MLMethodFactory.TYPE_FEEDFORWARD);
model.setReport(new ConsoleStatusReportable());
data.normalize();
model.holdBackValidation(0.3, true, 1001);
model.selectTrainingType(data);
MLRegression bestMethod = (MLRegression)model.crossvalidate(5,
true);
NormalizationHelper helper = data.getNormHelper();
System.out.println(helper.toString());
System.out.println("Final model: " + bestMethod);
```

Now, our regression model is ready. The last few lines of the output are given in the following screenshot:

```
EncogRegressionDemo [Java Application] /usr/lib/jvm/java-8-oracle/bin/java (04-Oct-2018, 2:01:44 PM)
5/5 : Fold #5/5: Iteration #1384, Training Error: 0.00281073, Validation Error: 0.00354880
5/5 : Fold #5/5: Iteration #1385, Training Error: 0.00281052, Validation Error: 0.00354880
5/5 : Fold #5/5: Iteration #1386, Training Error: 0.00281029, Validation Error: 0.00354880
5/5 : Fold #5/5: Iteration #1387, Training Error: 0.00281003, Validation Error: 0.00354669
5/5 : Cross-validated score:0.004556173292848932
[NormalizationHelper:
[ColumnDefinition:X1(continuous);low=0.620000,high=0.980000,mean=0.764167,sd=0.105709]
[ColumnDefinition:X2(continuous);low=514.500000,high=808.500000,mean=671.708333,sd=88.028750]
[ColumnDefinition:X3(continuous);low=245.000000,high=416.500000,mean=318.500000,sd=43.598070]
[ColumnDefinition:X4(continuous);low=110.250000,high=220.500000,mean=176.604167,sd=45.136536]
[ColumnDefinition:X5(continuous);low=3.500000,high=7.000000,mean=5.250000,sd=1.750000]
[ColumnDefinition:X6(continuous);low=2.000000,high=5.000000,mean=3.500000,sd=1.118034]
[ColumnDefinition:X7(continuous);low=0.000000,high=0.400000,mean=0.234375,sd=0.133134]
[ColumnDefinition:X8(continuous);low=0.000000,high=5.000000,mean=2.812500,sd=1.549950]
[ColumnDefinition:Y1(continuous);low=6.010000,high=43.100000,mean=22.307201,sd=10.083624]
[ColumnDefinition:Y2(continuous);low=10.900000,high=48.030000,mean=24.587760,sd=9.507110]
]
Final model: [BasicNetwork: Layers=3]
```

Regression using MOA

Using MOA for regression requires us to use the GUI. You can download the dataset from `http://www.cs.waikato.ac.nz/~bernhard/halifax17/census.arff.gz`.

The following steps show how to perform regression:

1. Launch the MOA GUI by using the following command:

```
$ java -cp moa.jar -javaagent:sizeofag-1.0.4.jar moa.gui.GUI
```

2. Select the **Regression** tab and click on **Configure,** as shown in the following screenshot:

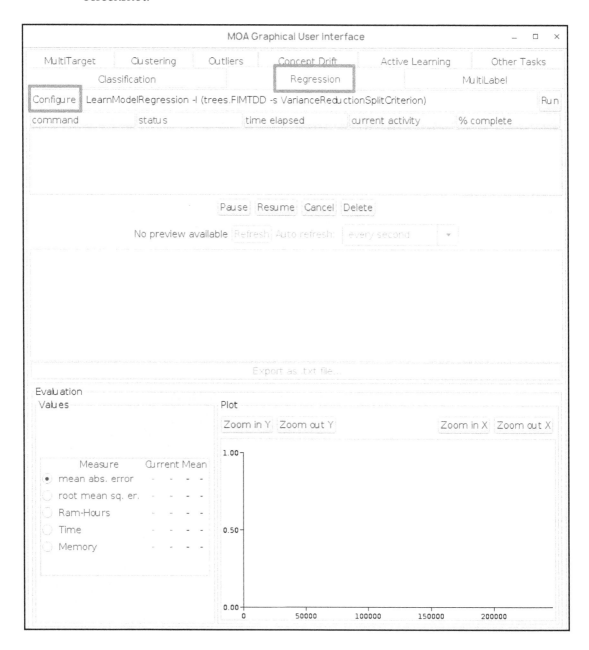

3. We will use the downloaded `.arff` file for regression. When we click on **Configure** in the preceding step, it will display the **Configure task** window, as shown in the following screenshot:

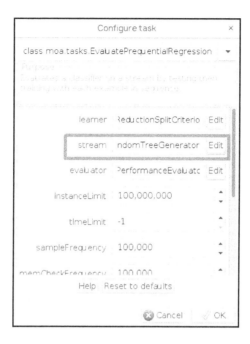

4. In the **stream** option, click on **Edit** and select the **ArffFileStream**; select the `.arff` file that we downloaded, as shown in the following screenshot:

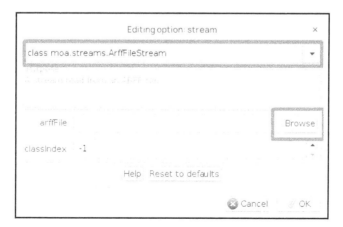

5. In **classIndex**, specify −1, which sets the first attribute as the target. Click on **OK** in all pop-up windows and click on **Run**. It will take some time, as the census file has a large amount of data to process, as shown in the following screenshot:

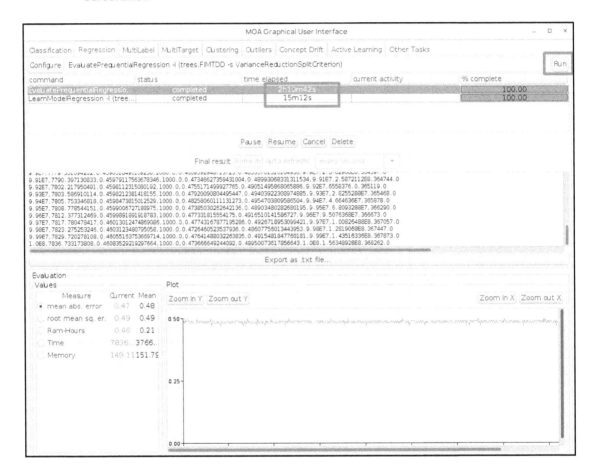

Regression trees

Another approach is to construct a set of regression models, each on its own part of the data. The following diagram shows the main difference between a regression model and a regression tree. A regression model constructs a single model that best fits all of the data. A regression tree, on the other hand, constructs a set of regression models, each modeling a part of the data, as shown on the right-hand side. Compared to the regression model, the regression tree can better fit the data, but the function is a piece-wise linear plot, with jumps between modeled regions, as seen in the following diagram:

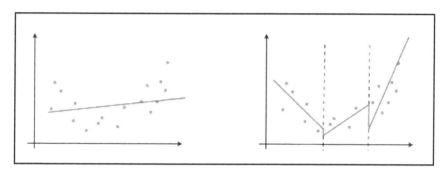

A regression tree in Weka is implemented within the M5 class. The model construction follows the same paradigm: initialize the model, pass the parameters and data, and invoke the buildClassifier(Instances) method, as follows:

```
import weka.classifiers.trees.M5P;
...
M5P md5 = new M5P();
md5.setOptions(new String[]{""});
md5.buildClassifier(data);
System.out.println(md5);
```

The induced model is a tree with equations in the leaf nodes, as follows:

```
M5 pruned model tree:
(using smoothed linear models)
X1 <= 0.75 :
|   X7 <= 0.175 :
|   |   X1 <= 0.65 : LM1 (48/12.841%)
|   |   X1 >  0.65 : LM2 (96/3.201%)
|   X7 >  0.175 :
|   |   X1 <= 0.65 : LM3 (80/3.652%)
|   |   X1 >  0.65 : LM4 (160/3.502%)
X1 >  0.75 :
|   X1 <= 0.805 : LM5 (128/13.302%)
|   X1 >  0.805 :
|   |   X7 <= 0.175 :
|   |   |   X8 <= 1.5 : LM6 (32/20.992%)
|   |   |   X8 >  1.5 :
|   |   |   |   X1 <= 0.94 : LM7 (48/5.693%)
|   |   |   |   X1 >  0.94 : LM8 (16/1.119%)
|   |   X7 >  0.175 :
|   |   |   X1 <= 0.84 :
|   |   |   |   X7 <= 0.325 : LM9 (20/5.451%)
|   |   |   |   X7 >  0.325 : LM10 (20/5.632%)
|   |   |   X1 >  0.84 :
|   |   |   |   X7 <= 0.325 : LM11 (60/4.548%)
|   |   |   |   X7 >  0.325 :
|   |   |   |   |   X3 <= 306.25 : LM12 (40/4.504%)
|   |   |   |   |   X3 >  306.25 : LM13 (20/6.934%)
LM num: 1
Y1 =
   72.2602 * X1
   + 0.0053 * X3
   + 11.1924 * X7
   + 0.429 * X8
   - 36.2224
...
LM num: 13
Y1 =
   5.8829 * X1
   + 0.0761 * X3
   + 9.5464 * X7
   - 0.0805 * X8
   + 2.1492
Number of Rules : 13
```

The tree has 13 leaves, each corresponding to a linear equation. The preceding output is visualized in the following diagram:

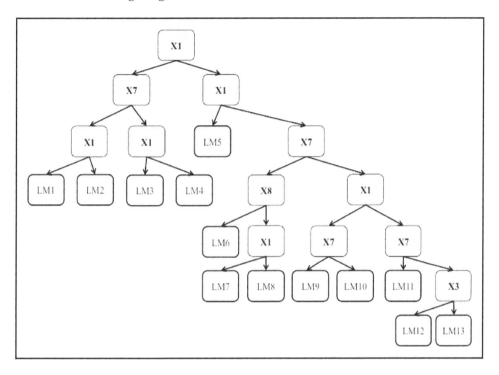

The tree can be read similarly to a classification tree. The most important features are at the top of the tree. The terminal node, the leaf, contains a linear regression model explaining the data that reaches this part of the tree.

An evaluation will provide the following results as output:

```
Correlation coefficient               0.9943
Mean absolute error                   0.7446
Root mean squared error               1.0804
Relative absolute error               8.1342 %
Root relative squared error          10.6995 %
Total Number of Instances           768
```

Tips to avoid common regression problems

First, we have to use prior studies and domain knowledge to figure out which features to include in regression. Check literature, reports, and previous studies on what kinds of features work and some reasonable variables for modeling your problem. Suppose that you have a large set of features with random data; it is highly likely that several features will be correlated to the target variable (even though the data is random).

We have to keep the model simple, in order to avoid overfitting. The Occam's razor principle states that you should select a model that best explains your data, with the least assumptions. In practice, the model can be as simple as having two to four predictor features.

Clustering

Compared to a supervised classifier, the goal of clustering is to identify intrinsic groups in a set of unlabeled data. It can be applied to identifying representative examples of homogeneous groups, finding useful and suitable groupings, or finding unusual examples, such as outliers.

We'll demonstrate how to implement clustering by analyzing a bank dataset. The dataset consists of 11 attributes, describing 600 instances, with age, sex, region, income, marital status, children, car ownership status, saving activity, current activity, mortgage status, and PEP. In our analysis, we will try to identify the common groups of clients by applying the **expectation maximization** (**EM**) clustering.

EM works as follows: given a set of clusters, EM first assigns each instance with a probability distribution of belonging to a particular cluster. For example, if we start with three clusters—namely, A, B, and C—an instance might get the probability distribution of 0.70, 0.10, and 0.20, belonging to the A, B, and C clusters, respectively. In the second step, EM re-estimates the parameter vector of the probability distribution of each class. The algorithm iterates these two steps until the parameters converge or the maximum number of iterations is reached.

The number of clusters to be used in EM can be set either manually or automatically by cross-validation. Another approach to determining the number of clusters in a dataset includes the elbow method. This method looks at the percentage of variance that is explained with a specific number of clusters. The method suggests increasing the number of clusters until the additional cluster does not add much information, that is, it explains little additional variance.

Clustering algorithms

The process of building a cluster model is quite similar to the process of building a classification model, that is, loading the data and building a model. Clustering algorithms are implemented in the `weka.clusterers` package, as follows:

```java
import java.io.BufferedReader;
import java.io.FileReader;

import weka.core.Instances;
import weka.clusterers.EM;

public class Clustering {

  public static void main(String args[]) throws Exception{
    //load data
    Instances data = new Instances(new BufferedReader
        (new FileReader("data/bank-data.arff")));
    // new instance of clusterer
    EM model = new EM();
    // build the clusterer
    model.buildClusterer(data);
    System.out.println(model);

  }
}
```

The model identified the following six clusters:

```
EM
==
Number of clusters selected by cross validation: 6
                  Cluster
Attribute               0       1       2       3       4       5
                      (0.1)  (0.13)  (0.26)  (0.25)  (0.12)  (0.14)
==================================================================
age
   0_34                10.0535 51.8472 122.2815 12.6207  3.1023  1.0948
```

```
   35_51              38.6282  24.4056  29.6252  89.4447  34.5208   3.3755
   52_max             13.4293   6.693    6.3459  50.8984  37.861   81.7724
   [total]            62.1111  82.9457 158.2526 152.9638  75.4841  86.2428
sex
   FEMALE             27.1812  32.2338  77.9304  83.5129  40.3199  44.8218
   MALE               33.9299  49.7119  79.3222  68.4509  34.1642  40.421
   [total]            61.1111  81.9457 157.2526 151.9638  74.4841  85.2428
region
   INNER_CITY         26.1651  46.7431  73.874   60.1973  33.3759  34.6445
   TOWN               24.6991  13.0716  48.4446  53.1731  21.617   17.9946
   ...
```

The table can be read as follows: the first line indicates six clusters, while the first column shows the attributes and their ranges. For example, the attribute `age` is split into three ranges: `0-34`, `35-51`, and `52-max`. The columns on the left indicate how many instances fall into the specific range in each cluster; for example, clients in the `0-34` years age group are mostly in cluster 2 (122 instances).

Evaluation

A clustering algorithm's quality can be estimated by using the `logLikelihood` measure, which measures how consistent the identified clusters are. The dataset is split into multiple folds, and clustering is run with each fold. The motivation is that, if the clustering algorithm assigns a high probability to similar data that wasn't used to fit parameters, then it has probably done a good job of capturing the data structure. Weka offers the `CluterEvaluation` class to estimate it, as follows:

```
double logLikelihood = ClusterEvaluation.crossValidateModel(model, data,
10, new Random(1));
System.out.println(logLikelihood);
```

It provides the following output:

```
-8.773410259774291
```

Clustering using Encog

Encog supports k-means clustering. Let's consider a very simple example, with the data shown in the following code block:

```
DATA = { { 28, 15, 22 }, { 16, 15, 32 }, { 32, 20, 44 }, { 1, 2, 3 }, { 3,
2, 1 } };
```

To make `BasicMLDataSet` from this data, a simple `for` loop is used, which will add data to the dataset:

```
BasicMLDataSet set = new BasicMLDataSet();

for (final double[] element : DATA) {
    set.add(new BasicMLData(element));
}
```

Using the `KMeansClustering` function, let's clusters the dataset into two clusters, as follows:

```
KMeansClustering kmeans = new KMeansClustering(2, set);

kmeans.iteration(100);

// Display the cluster
int i = 1;
for (MLCluster cluster : kmeans.getClusters()) {
    System.out.println("*** Cluster " + (i++) + " ***");
    final MLDataSet ds = cluster.createDataSet();
    final MLDataPair pair = BasicMLDataPair.createPair(ds.getInputSize(),
ds.getIdealSize());
    for (int j = 0; j < ds.getRecordCount(); j++) {
        ds.getRecord(j, pair);
        System.out.println(Arrays.toString(pair.getInputArray()));
        }
    }
```

This will generate the following output:

```
*** Cluster 1 ***
[16.0, 15.0, 32.0]
[1.0, 2.0, 3.0]
[3.0, 2.0, 1.0]
*** Cluster 2 ***
[28.0, 15.0, 22.0]
*** Cluster 3 ***
[32.0, 20.0, 44.0]
```

Clustering using ELKI

ELKI supports many clustering algorithms. A few are listed as follows:

- **Affinity propagation clustering algorithm**: This is a cluster analysis that uses affinity propagation.
- **DBSCAN**: This is density based clustering especially for the applications with noise; it finds the sets in the database on the basis of density.
- **EM**: This algorithm creates clusters based on the expectation maximization algorithm.
- **AGNES**: **Hierarchical agglomerative clustering (HAC),** or **agglomerative nesting (AGNES),** is a classic hierarchical clustering algorithm.
- **SLINK**: This is the single link algorithm.
- **CLINK**: This is used for complete linkage.
- **HDBSCAN**: This is an extracting cluster hierarchy.

Also, KMeansSort, KMeansCompare, KMedianLloyd, KMediodsEM, KMeansBisecting, and so on, are some examples from the family of KMean.

A detailed list of clustering algorithms, with all of the algorithms supported by ELKI, can be found at `https://elki-project.github.io/algorithms/`.

We need to get the required `.jar` file from `https://elki-project.github.io/releases/`. Download the executable archive, and download the mouse dataset from `https://elki-project.github.io/datasets/`.

From the Terminal or Command Prompt, run the following command:

```
$ java -jar elki-bundle-0.7.1.jar
```

The preceding command generates the following output:

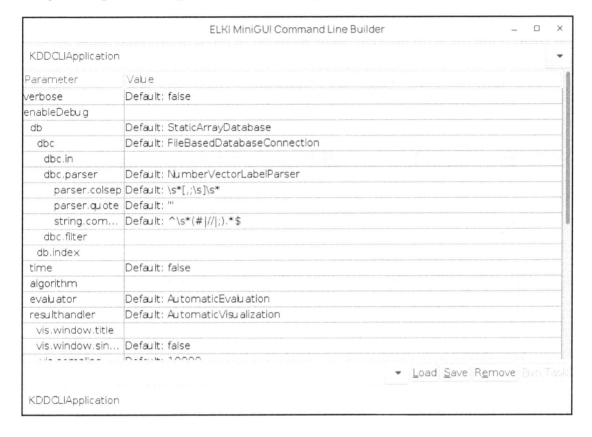

We can see two options, in an orange color: `dbc.in` and `algorithm`. We need to specify the value. In `dbc.in`, click on the dots (...) to select the `mouse.csv` file that we downloaded. In `algorithm`, select `k-Mean Clustering algorithm` by clicking on the plus sign (+), find `kmean.k`, and fill it with the value 3. Click on the **Run Task** button, which is now enabled. It will generate the following output:

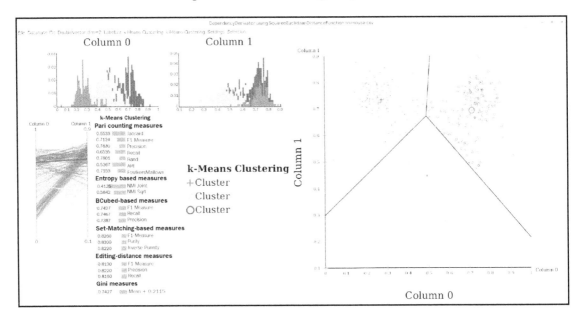

Summary

In this chapter, you learned how to implement basic machine learning tasks with Weka: classification, regression, and clustering. We briefly discussed the attribute selection process and trained models and evaluated their performance.

The next chapter will focus on how to apply these techniques to solving real-life problems, such as customer retention.

4
Customer Relationship Prediction with Ensembles

Any type of company that offers a service, product, or experience needs a solid understanding of their relationship with their customers; therefore, **customer relationship management** (**CRM**) is a key element of modern marketing strategies. One of the biggest challenges that businesses face is the need to understand exactly what causes a customer to buy new products.

In this chapter, we will work on a real-world marketing database provided by the French telecom company, Orange. The task will be to estimate the likelihood of the following customer actions:

- Switch provider (churn)
- Buy new products or services (appetency)
- Buy upgrades or add-ons proposed to them to make the sale more profitable (upselling)

We will tackle the **Knowledge Discovery and Data Mining** (**KDD**) Cup 2009 challenge and show the steps to process the data using Weka. First, we will parse and load the data and implement the basic baseline models. Later, we will address advanced modeling techniques, including data preprocessing, attribute selection, model selection, and evaluation.

 The KDD Cup is the leading data mining competition in the world. It is organized annually by the ACM **Special Interest Group on Knowledge Discovery and Data Mining**. The winners are announced at the Conference on Knowledge Discovery and Data Mining, which is usually held in August. Yearly archives, including all of the corresponding datasets, are available at http://www.kdd.org/kdd-cup.

The customer relationship database

The most practical way to build knowledge on customer behavior is to produce scores that explain a target variable, such as churn, appetency, or upselling. The score is computed by a model using input variables that describe customers; for example, their current subscription, purchased devices, consumed minutes, and so on. The scores are then used by the information system for things like providing relevant personalized marketing actions.

A customer is the main entity in most of the customer-based relationship databases; getting to know the customer's behavior is important. The customer's behavior produces a score in relation to the churn, appetency, or upselling. The basic idea is to produce a score using a computational model, which may use different parameters, such as the current subscription of the customer, devices purchased, minutes consumed, and so on. Once the score is formed, it is used by the information system to decide on the next strategy, which is especially designed for the customer, based on his or her behavior.

In 2009, the conference on KDD organized a machine learning challenge on customer relationship prediction.

Challenge

Given a large set of customer attributes, the task in the challenge was to estimate the following target variables:

- **Churn probability**: This is the likelihood that a customer will switch providers. The churn rate is also known as the attrition rate or the participant turnover rate, and is a measure used to find the number of individuals, objects, terms, or items moving into or out of a given collection, over a given time period. The term is heavily used in industries that are driven by customers and use subscriber-based models; for example, the cell phone industry and cable TV operators.
- **Appetency probability**: This is the propensity to buy a service or product.
- **Upselling probability**: This is the likelihood that a customer will buy an add-on or upgrade. Upselling implies selling something in addition to what the customer is already using. Consider it like the value-added services that are provided by most cell phone operators. Using sales techniques, salesmen try to make customers opt for value-added services, which will bring more revenue. Many times, customers are not aware of other options, and the salesmen convince them to use or consider those options.

The challenge was to beat the in-house system developed by Orange Labs. This was an opportunity for the participants to prove that they could handle a large database, including heterogeneous, noisy data, and unbalanced class distributions.

Dataset

For the challenge, Orange released a large dataset of customer data, containing about one million customers, described in ten tables with hundreds of fields. In the first step, they resampled the data to select a less unbalanced subset, containing 100,000 customers. In the second step, they used an automatic feature construction tool that generated 20,000 features describing the customers, which was then narrowed down to 15,000 features. In the third step, the dataset was anonymized by randomizing the order of features, discarding the attribute names, replacing the nominal variables with randomly generated strings, and multiplying the continuous attributes by a random factor. Finally, all of the instances were split randomly into training and testing datasets.

The KDD Cup provided two sets of data, a large set and a small set, corresponding to fast and slow challenges, respectively. Both the training and testing sets contained 50,000 examples, and the data was split similarly, but the samples were ordered differently for each set.

In this chapter, we will work with the small dataset, consisting of 50,000 instances, each described with 230 variables. Each of the 50,000 rows of data corresponds to a client, and they are associated with three binary outcomes, one for each of the three challenges (upselling, churn, and appetency).

To make this clearer, the following table illustrates the dataset:

230 numeric and nominal attributes										Three binary classes		
Var85	Var123	Var125	Var126	Var132	Var133	Var134	Var225	Var229	Var230	Label Churn	Label Appetency	Label Upselling
12	6	720	8	0	1212385	69134				-1	-1	-1
2	72	0		8	4136430	357038				1	-1	-1
58	114	5967	-28	0	3478905	248932	kG3k	am7c		-1	-1	-1
0	0	0	-14	0	0	0				-1	-1	-1
0	0	15111	58	0	150650	66046	kG3k	mj86		-1	-1	-1
10	0	1935		8	641020	43684		am7c		-1	-1	-1
16	24	13194	-24	0	1664450	104978	kG3k	am7c		-1	-1	-1
2	12	0	-8	8	3839825	1284128				-1	-1	-1
2	90	2754		0	3830510	203586	kG3k	am7c		-1	-1	-1
24	66	6561		32	2577245	210014	kG3k			-1	-1	-1
6	12	5823	58	0	0	7134	kG3k	mj86		-1	-1	-1
28	24	66825	52	8	134105	15166	kG3k			-1	-1	-1
0	0	44154	10	0	0	0		mj86		-1	-1	-1
22	54	5202		0	2772010	1095062	xG3x			-1	-1	-1
0	102	31104	8	0	2170355	57596				-1	-1	1
0	0	2574		0	0	0	ELof	oJmt		-1	-1	-1
14	186	8019		48	3571845	587392	kG3k	am7c		-1	-1	-1
0	30	5319		8	500295	31436		am7c		-1	-1	-1
2	0	13788	4	0	918350	0	kG3k			-1	-1	-1
14	0	7110		0	2055150	392138				1	-1	-1
8	66	0	-8	0	3258940	1121306				-1	-1	-1
0	18	0	-10	0	0	0				-1	-1	-1
12	0	531	36	0	491345	56742	ELof	mj86		-1	-1	-1
0	12	16803	12	0	201110	1693090				1	-1	-1
14	0	25740		0	2932660	313200	xG3x			-1	-1	1

The table depicts the first 25 instances, that is, customers, each described with 250 attributes. For this example, only a selected subset of 10 attributes is shown. The dataset contains many missing values, and even empty or constant attributes. The last three columns of the table correspond to the three distinct class labels involving the ground truth, that is, if the customer indeed switched providers (churn), bought a service (appetency), or bought an upgrade (upsell). However, note that the labels are provided separately from the data in three distinct files, hence it is essential to retain the order of the instances and the corresponding class labels to ensure proper correspondence.

Evaluation

The submissions were evaluated according to the arithmetic mean of the area under the ROC curve for the three tasks (churn, appetency, and upselling). The ROC curve shows the performance of the model as a curve obtained by plotting the sensitivity against specificity for various threshold values used to determine the classification result (refer to `Chapter 1`, *Applied Machine Learning Quick Start*, in the section *ROC curves*). Now, the **area under the ROC curve** (**AUC**) is related to the area under this curve – the larger the area, the better the classifier). Most toolboxes, including Weka, provide an API to calculate the AUC score.

Basic Naive Bayes classifier baseline

As per the rules of the challenge, the participants had to outperform the basic Naive Bayes classifier in order to qualify for prizes, which makes an assumption that features are independent (refer to `Chapter 1`, *Applied Machine Learning Quick Start*).

The KDD Cup organizers ran the vanilla Naive Bayes classifier, without any feature selection or hyperparameter adjustments. For the large dataset, the overall scores of the Naive Bayes on the test set were as follows:

- **Churn problem**: AUC = 0.6468
- **Appetency problem**: AUC = 0.6453
- **Upselling problem**: AUC=0.7211

Note that the baseline results are only reported for the large dataset. Moreover, while both the training and testing datasets are provided at the KDD Cup site, the actual true labels for the test set are not provided. Therefore, when we process the data with our models, there is no way to know how well the models will perform on the test set. What we will do is only use the training data, and evaluate our models with cross-validation. The results will not be directly comparable, but nevertheless, we will have an idea about what a reasonable magnitude of the AUC score should be.

Getting the data

At the KDD Cup web page (`http://kdd.org/kdd-cup/view/kdd-cup-2009/Data`), you should see a page that looks similar to the following screenshot. First, under the **Small version (230 var.)** header, download `orange_small_train.data.zip`. Next, download the three sets of true labels associated with this training data. The following files are found under the **Real binary targets (small)** header:

- `orange_small_train_appentency.labels`
- `orange_small_train_churn.labels`
- `orange_small_train_upselling.labels`

Save and unzip all of the files marked in the red boxes, as shown in the screenshot:

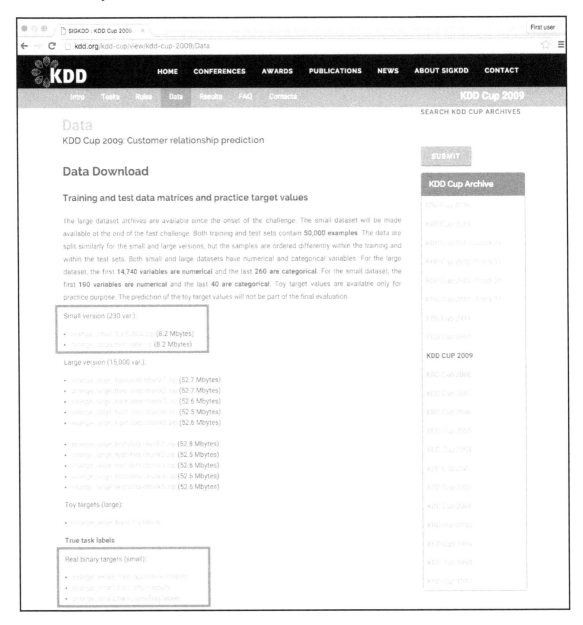

In the following sections, first, we will load the data into Weka and apply basic modeling with the Naive Bayes classifier, in order to obtain our own baseline AUC scores. Later, we will look at more advanced modeling techniques and tricks.

Loading the data

We will load the data to Weka directly from the `.csv` format. For this purpose, we will write a function that accepts the path to the data file and the true labels file. The function will load and merge both datasets and remove empty attributes. We will begin with the following code block:

```
public static Instances loadData(String pathData, String
  pathLabeles) throws Exception {
```

First, we load the data using the `CSVLoader()` class. Additionally, we specify the `\t` tab as a field separator and force the last 40 attributes to be parsed as nominal:

```
// Load data
CSVLoader loader = new CSVLoader();
loader.setFieldSeparator("\t");
loader.setNominalAttributes("191-last");
loader.setSource(new File(pathData));
Instances data = loader.getDataSet();
```

 The `CSVLoader` class accepts many additional parameters, specifying the column separator, string enclosures, whether a header row is present, and so on. The complete documentation is available at `http://weka.sourceforge.net/doc.dev/weka/core/converters/CSVLoader.html`.

Some of the attributes do not contain a single value, and Weka automatically recognizes them as `String` attributes. We actually do not need them, so we can safely remove them by using the `RemoveType` filter. Additionally, we specify the `-T` parameters, which removes an attribute of a specific type and specifies the attribute type that we want to remove:

```
// remove empty attributes identified as String attribute
RemoveType removeString = new RemoveType();
removeString.setOptions(new String[]{"-T", "string"});
removeString.setInputFormat(data);
Instances filteredData = Filter.useFilter(data, removeString);
```

Alternatively, we could use the `void deleteStringAttributes()` method, implemented within the `Instances` class, which has the same effect; for example, `data.removeStringAttributes()`.

Now, we will load and assign class labels to the data. We will utilize `CVSLoader` again, where we specify that the file does not have any header line, that is, `setNoHeaderRowPresent(true)`:

```
// Load labeles
loader = new CSVLoader();
loader.setFieldSeparator("\t");
loader.setNoHeaderRowPresent(true);
loader.setNominalAttributes("first-last");
loader.setSource(new File(pathLabeles));
Instances labels = loader.getDataSet();
```

Once we have loaded both files, we can merge them together by calling the `Instances.mergeInstances (Instances, Instances)` static method. The method returns a new dataset that has all of the attributes from the first dataset, plus the attributes from the second set. Note that the number of instances in both datasets must be the same:

```
// Append label as class value
Instances labeledData = Instances.mergeInstances(filteredData,
    labeles);
```

Finally, we set the last attribute, that is, the label attribute that we just added, as a target variable, and return the resulting dataset:

```
// set the label attribute as class
labeledData.setClassIndex(labeledData.numAttributes() - 1);

System.out.println(labeledData.toSummaryString());
return labeledData;
}
```

The function provides a summary as output, as shown in the following code block, and returns the labeled dataset:

```
    Relation Name:  orange_small_train.data-
weka.filters.unsupervised.attribute.RemoveType-
Tstring_orange_small_train_churn.labels.txt
    Num Instances:  50000
    Num Attributes: 215
    Name           Type   Nom  Int Real      Missing       Unique  Dist
    1 Var1         Num    0%   1%   0% 49298 / 99%     8 /   0%     18
    2 Var2         Num    0%   2%   0% 48759 / 98%     1 /   0%      2
    3 Var3         Num    0%   2%   0% 48760 / 98%   104 /   0%    146
    4 Var4         Num    0%   3%   0% 48421 / 97%     1 /   0%      4
    . . .
```

Basic modeling

In this section, we will implement our own baseline model by following the approach that the KDD Cup organizers took. However, before we get to the model, let's first implement the evaluation engine that will return the AUC on all three problems.

Evaluating models

Now, let's take a closer look at the evaluation function. The evaluation function accepts an initialized model, cross-validates the model on all three problems, and reports the results as an area under the ROC curve (AUC), as follows:

```
public static double[] evaluate(Classifier model)
    throws Exception {

  double results[] = new double[4];

  String[] labelFiles = new String[]{
    "churn", "appetency", "upselling"};

  double overallScore = 0.0;
  for (int i = 0; i < labelFiles.length; i++) {
```

First, we call the `Instance loadData(String, String)` function that we implemented earlier to load the training data and merge it with the selected labels:

```
// Load data
Instances train_data = loadData(
 path + "orange_small_train.data",
  path+"orange_small_train_"+labelFiles[i]+".labels.txt");
```

Next, we initialize the `weka.classifiers.Evaluation` class and pass our dataset. (The dataset is only used to extract data properties; the actual data is not considered.) We call the `void crossValidateModel(Classifier, Instances, int, Random)` method to begin cross-validation, and we create five folds. As validation is done on random subsets of the data, we need to pass a random seed, as well:

```
// cross-validate the data
Evaluation eval = new Evaluation(train_data);
eval.crossValidateModel(model, train_data, 5,
new Random(1));
```

After the evaluation completes, we read the results by calling the `double areUnderROC(int)` method. As the metric depends on the target value that we are interested in, the method expects a class value index, which can be extracted by searching the index of the "1" value in the class attribute, as follows:

```
// Save results
results[i] = eval.areaUnderROC(
    train_data.classAttribute().indexOfValue("1"));
overallScore += results[i];
}
```

Finally, the results are averaged and returned:

```
// Get average results over all three problems
results[3] = overallScore / 3;
return results;
}
```

Implementing the Naive Bayes baseline

Now, when we have all of the ingredients, we can replicate the Naive Bayes approach that we are expected to outperform. This approach will not include any additional data preprocessing, attribute selection, or model selection. As we do not have true labels for the test data, we will apply five-fold cross-validation to evaluate the model on a small dataset.

First, we initialize a Naive Bayes classifier, as follows:

```
Classifier baselineNB = new NaiveBayes();
```

Next, we pass the classifier to our evaluation function, which loads the data and applies cross-validation. The function returns an area under the ROC curve score for all three problems, and the overall results:

```
double resNB[] = evaluate(baselineNB);
System.out.println("Naive Bayes\n" +
"\tchurn:     " + resNB[0] + "\n" +
"\tappetency: " + resNB[1] + "\n" +
"\tup-sell:   " + resNB[2] + "\n" +
"\toverall:   " + resNB[3] + "\n");
```

In our case, the model returns the following results:

```
Naive Bayes
    churn:     0.5897891153549814
    appetency: 0.630778394752436
```

```
up-sell:   0.6686116692438094
overall:   0.6297263931170756
```

These results will serve as a baseline when we tackle the challenge with more advanced modeling. If we process the data with significantly more sophisticated, time-consuming, and complex techniques, we expect the results to be much better. Otherwise, we are simply wasting resources. In general, when solving machine learning problems, it is always a good idea to create a simple baseline classifier that serves us as an orientation point.

Advanced modeling with ensembles

In the previous section, we implemented an orientation baseline; now, let's focus on heavy machinery. We will follow the approach taken by the KDD Cup 2009 winning solution, developed by the IBM research team (Niculescu-Mizil and others).

To address this challenge, they used the ensemble selection algorithm (Caruana and Niculescu-Mizil, 2004). This is an ensemble method, which means it constructs a series of models and combines their output in a specific way, in order to provide the final classification. It has several desirable properties that make it a good fit for this challenge, as follows:

- It was proven to be robust, yielding excellent performance.
- It can be optimized for a specific performance metric, including AUC.
- It allows for different classifiers to be added to the library.
- It is an anytime method, meaning that if we run out of time, we have a solution available.

In this section, we will loosely follow the steps as they are described in their report. Note that this is not an exact implementation of their approach, but rather a solution overview that will include the necessary steps to dive deeper.

A general overview of the steps is as follows:

1. First, we will preprocess the data by removing attributes that clearly do not bring any value – for example, all of the missing or constant values; fixing missing values, in order to help machine learning algorithms, which cannot deal with them; and converting categorical attributes to numerical attributes.
2. Next, we will run the attribute selection algorithm to select only a subset of attributes that can help in the prediction of tasks.
3. In the third step, we will instantiate the ensemble selection algorithms with a wide variety of models, and finally, we will evaluate the performance.

Before we start

For this task, we will need an additional Weka package, `ensembleLibrary`. Weka 3.7.2 and higher versions support external packages, mainly developed by the academic community. A list of **WEKA Packages** is available at `http://weka.sourceforge.net/packageMetaData`, as shown in the following screenshot:

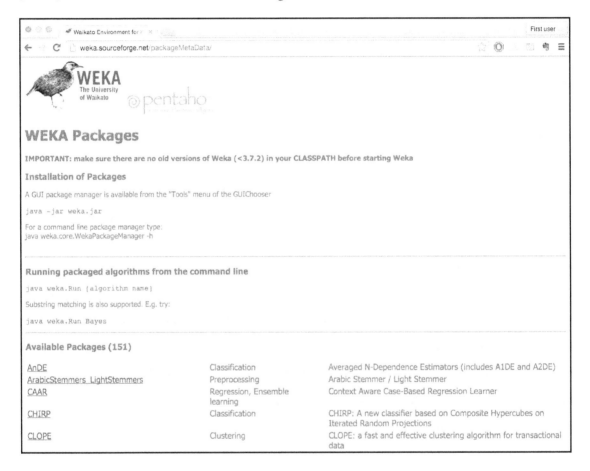

Find and download the latest available version of the `ensembleLibrary` package at `http://prdownloads.sourceforge.net/weka/ensembleLibrary1.0.5.zip?download`.

After you unzip the package, locate `ensembleLibrary.jar` and import it into your code, as follows:

```
import weka.classifiers.meta.EnsembleSelection;
```

Data preprocessing

First, we will utilize Weka's built-in `weka.filters.unsupervised.attribute.RemoveUseless` filter, which works exactly as its name suggests. It removes the attributes that do not vary much, for instance, all constant attributes are removed. The maximum variance, which is only applied to nominal attributes, is specified with the `-M` parameter. The default parameter is 99%, which means that if more than 99% of all instances have unique attribute values, the attribute is removed, as follows:

```
RemoveUseless removeUseless = new RemoveUseless();
removeUseless.setOptions(new String[] { "-M", "99" });// threshold
removeUseless.setInputFormat(data);
data = Filter.useFilter(data, removeUseless);
```

Next, we will replace all of the missing values in the dataset with the modes (nominal attributes) and means (numeric attributes) from the training data, by using the `weka.filters.unsupervised.attribute.ReplaceMissingValues` filter. In general, missing value replacement should be proceeded with caution, while taking into consideration the meaning and context of the attributes:

```
ReplaceMissingValues fixMissing = new ReplaceMissingValues();
fixMissing.setInputFormat(data);
data = Filter.useFilter(data, fixMissing);
```

Finally, we will discretize numeric attributes, that is, we will transform numeric attributes into intervals by using the `weka.filters.unsupervised.attribute.Discretize` filter. With the `-B` option, we set splitting numeric attributes into four intervals, and the `-R` option specifies the range of attributes (only numeric attributes will be discretized):

```
Discretize discretizeNumeric = new Discretize();
discretizeNumeric.setOptions(new String[] {
    "-B",  "4",  // no of bins
    "-R",  "first-last"}); //range of attributes
fixMissing.setInputFormat(data);
data = Filter.useFilter(data, fixMissing);
```

Attribute selection

In the next step, we will select only informative attributes, that is, attributes that are more likely to help with prediction. A standard approach to this problem is to check the information gain carried by each attribute. We will use the `weka.attributeSelection.AttributeSelection` filter, which requires two additional methods: an evaluator (how attribute usefulness is calculated) and search algorithms (how to select a subset of attributes).

In our case, first, we initialize `weka.attributeSelection.InfoGainAttributeEval`, which implements the calculation of information gain:

```
InfoGainAttributeEval eval = new InfoGainAttributeEval();
Ranker search = new Ranker();
```

To only select the top attributes above a threshold, we initialize `weka.attributeSelection.Ranker`, in order to rank the attributes with information gain above a specific threshold. We specify this with the `-T` parameter, while keeping the value of the threshold low, in order to keep the attributes with at least some information:

```
search.setOptions(new String[] { "-T", "0.001" });
```

 The general rule for setting this threshold is to sort the attributes by information gain and pick the threshold where the information gain drops to a negligible value.

Next, we can initialize the `AttributeSelection` class, set the evaluator and ranker, and apply the attribute selection to our dataset, as follows:

```
AttributeSelection attSelect = new AttributeSelection();
attSelect.setEvaluator(eval);
attSelect.setSearch(search);

// apply attribute selection
attSelect.SelectAttributes(data);
```

Finally, we remove the attributes that were not selected in the last run by calling the `reduceDimensionality(Instances)` method:

```
// remove the attributes not selected in the last run
data = attSelect.reduceDimensionality(data);
```

In the end, we are left with 214 out of 230 attributes.

Model selection

Over the years, practitioners in the field of machine learning have developed a wide variety of learning algorithms and improvements for existing ones. There are so many unique supervised learning methods that it is challenging to keep track of all of them. As the characteristics of the datasets vary, no one method is the best in all of the cases, but different algorithms are able to take advantage of the different characteristics and relationships of a given dataset.

First, we need to create the model library by initializing the `weka.classifiers.EnsembleLibrary` class, which will help us define the models:

```
EnsembleLibrary ensembleLib = new EnsembleLibrary();
```

Next, we add the models and their parameters to the library as string values; for example, we can add three decision tree learners with different parameters, as follows:

```
ensembleLib.addModel("weka.classifiers.trees.J48 -S -C 0.25 -B -M
    2");
ensembleLib.addModel("weka.classifiers.trees.J48 -S -C 0.25 -B -M
    2 -A");
```

If you are familiar with the Weka graphical interface, you can also explore the algorithms and their configurations there and copy the configuration, as shown in the following screenshot. Right-click on the algorithm name and navigate to **Edit configuration** | **Copy configuration string**:

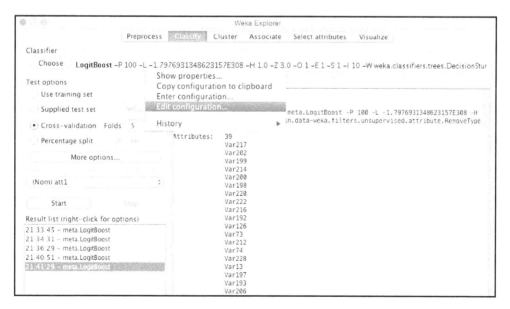

To complete this example, we added the following algorithms and their parameters:

- The Naive Bayes that was used as the default baseline:

```
ensembleLib.addModel("weka.classifiers.bayes.NaiveBayes");
```

- The k-nearest neighbors, based on lazy models:

```
ensembleLib.addModel("weka.classifiers.lazy.IBk");
```

- Logistic regression as a simple logistic with default parameters:

```
ensembleLib.addModel("weka.classifiers.functions.SimpleLogi
    stic");
```

- Support vector machines with default parameters:

```
ensembleLib.addModel("weka.classifiers.functions.SMO");
```

- AdaBoost, which is, in itself, an ensemble method:

```
ensembleLib.addModel("weka.classifiers.meta.AdaBoostM1");
```

- LogitBoost, an ensemble method based on logistic regression:

```
ensembleLib.addModel("weka.classifiers.meta.LogitBoost");
```

- DecisionStump, an ensemble method based on one-level decision trees:

```
ensembleLib.addModel("classifiers.trees.DecisionStump");
```

As the EnsembleLibrary implementation is primarily focused on GUI and console users, we have to save the models into a file by calling the saveLibrary(File, EnsembleLibrary, JComponent) method, as follows:

```
EnsembleLibrary.saveLibrary(new
    File(path+"ensembleLib.model.xml"), ensembleLib, null);
System.out.println(ensembleLib.getModels());
```

Next, we can initialize the ensemble selection algorithm by instantiating the `weka.classifiers.meta.EnsembleSelection` class. First, let's review the following method options:

- `-L </path/to/modelLibrary>`: This specifies the `modelLibrary` file, continuing the list of all models.
- `-W </path/to/working/directory>`: This specifies the working directory, where all models will be stored.
- `-B <numModelBags>`: This sets the number of bags, that is, the number of iterations to run the ensemble selection algorithm.
- `-E <modelRatio>`: This sets the ratio of library models that will be randomly chosen to populate each bag of models.
- `-V <validationRatio>`: This sets the ratio of the training dataset that will be reserved for validation.
- `-H <hillClimbIterations>`: This sets the number of hill climbing iterations to be performed on each model bag.
- `-I <sortInitialization>`: This sets the ratio of the ensemble library that the sort initialization algorithm will be able to choose from, while initializing the ensemble for each model bag.
- `-X <numFolds>`: This sets the number of cross-validation folds.
- `-P <hillclimbMetric>`: This specifies the metric that will be used for model selection during the hill climbing algorithm. Valid metrics include the accuracy, rmse, roc, precision, recall, fscore, and all.
- `-A <algorithm>`: This specifies the algorithm to be used for ensemble selection. Valid algorithms include forward (default) for forward selection, backward for backward elimination, both for both forward and backward elimination, best to simply print the top performer from the ensemble library, and library to only train the models in the ensemble library.
- `-R`: This flags whether the models can be selected more than once for an ensemble.
- `-G`: This states whether the sort initialization greedily stops adding models when the performance degrades.
- `-O`: This is a flag for verbose output. This prints the performance of all of the selected models.
- `-S <num>`: This is a random number seed (the default is 1).
- `-D`: If set, the classifier is run in debug mode, and may provide additional information to the console as output.

We initialize the algorithm with the following initial parameters, where we specify optimizing the ROC metric:

```
EnsembleSelection ensambleSel = new EnsembleSelection();
ensambleSel.setOptions(new String[]{
  "-L", path+"ensembleLib.model.xml", // </path/to/modelLibrary>
    "-W", path+"esTmp", // </path/to/working/directory> -
"-B", "10", // <numModelBags>
  "-E", "1.0", // <modelRatio>.
  "-V", "0.25", // <validationRatio>
  "-H", "100", // <hillClimbIterations>
"-I", "1.0", // <sortInitialization>
  "-X", "2", // <numFolds>
  "-P", "roc", // <hillclimbMettric>
  "-A", "forward", // <algorithm>
  "-R", "true", // - Flag to be selected more than once
  "-G", "true", // - stops adding models when performance degrades
  "-O", "true", // - verbose output.
  "-S", "1", // <num> - Random number seed.
  "-D", "true" // - run in debug mode
});
```

Performance evaluation

The evaluation is heavy, both computationally and memory-wise, so make sure that you initialize the JVM with extra heap space (for instance, `java -Xmx16g`). The computation can take a couple of hours or days, depending on the number of algorithms that you include in the model library. This example took 4 hours and 22 minutes on a 12-core Intel Xeon E5-2420 CPU with 32 GB of memory and utilizing 10% CPU and 6 GB of memory on average.

We call our evaluation method and provide the results as output, as follows:

```
double resES[] = evaluate(ensambleSel);
System.out.println("Ensemble Selection\n"
+ "\tchurn:    " + resES[0] + "\n"
+ "\tappetency: " + resES[1] + "\n"
+ "\tup-sell:   " + resES[2] + "\n"
+ "\toverall:   " + resES[3] + "\n");
```

The specific set of classifiers in the model library achieved the following result:

```
Ensamble
  churn:     0.7109874158176481
  appetency: 0.786325687118347
  up-sell:   0.8521363243575182
  overall:   0.7831498090978378
```

Overall, the approach has brought us to a significant improvement of more than 15 percentage points, compared to the initial baseline that we designed at the beginning of this chapter. While it is hard to give a definite answer, the improvement was mainly due to three factors: data preprocessing and attribute selection, the exploration of a large variety of learning methods, and the use of an ensemble-building technique that is able to take advantage of the variety of base classifiers without overfitting. However, the improvement requires a significant increase in processing time, as well as working memory.

Ensemble methods – MOA

To ensemble, as the word suggests, is to view together, or at the same time. It is used to combine multiple learner algorithms, in order to obtain better results and performance. There are various techniques that you can use for an ensemble. Some commonly used ensemble techniques or classifiers include bagging, boosting, stacking, a bucket of models, and so on.

Massive Online Analysis (**MOA**) supports ensemble classifiers, such as accuracy weighted ensembles, accuracy updated ensembles, and many more. In this section, we will show you how to use the leveraging bagging algorithm:

1. Open the Terminal and execute the following command:

```
java -cp moa.jar -javaagent:sizeofag-1.0.4.jar moa.gui.GUI
```

2. Select the **Classification** tab and click on the **Configure** button:

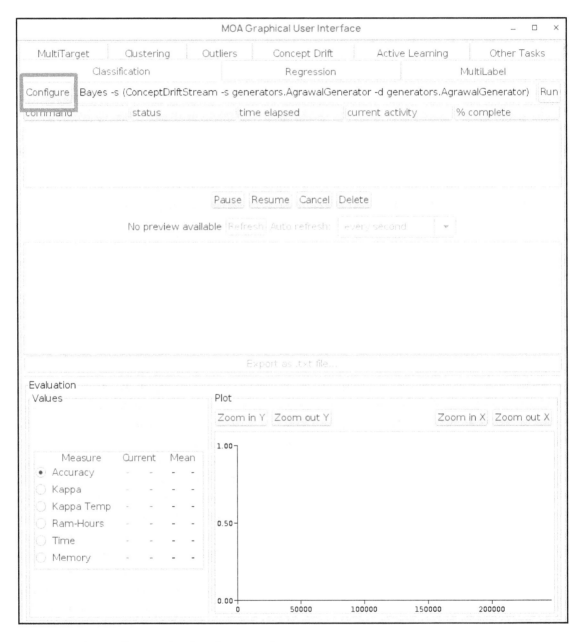

This will open the **Configure task** option.

3. In the **learner** option, select **bayes.NaiveBayes**, and then, in the **stream** option, click on **Edit**, as shown in the following screenshot:

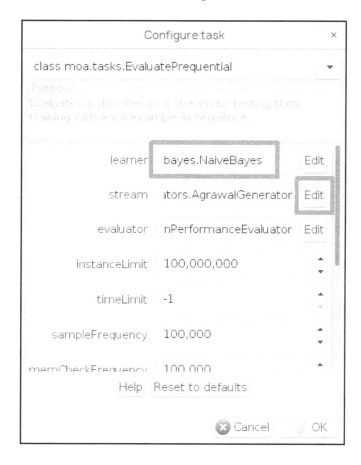

4. Select **ConceptDriftStream**, and, in **stream** and **driftstream**, select the
   AgrawalGenerator; it will use the Agrawal dataset for the stream generator:

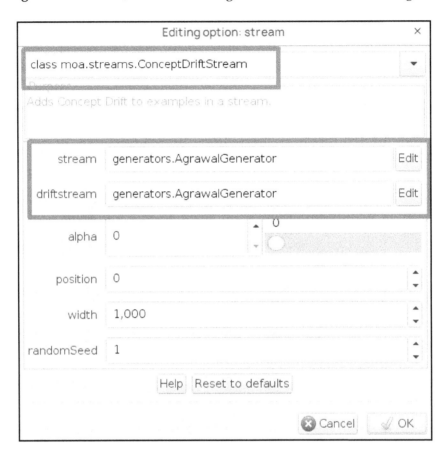

5. Close all of the windows and click on the **Run** button:

MOA Graphical User Interface — □ ×

MultiTarget	Clustering	Outliers	Concept Drift	Active Learning	Other Tasks

Classification	Regression	MultiLabel

Configure ｜ ngBag -s (ConceptDriftStream -s generators.AgrawalGenerator -d generators.AgrawalGenerator) ｜ Run

command	status	time elapsed	current activity	% complete

Pause   Resume   Cancel   Delete

No preview available

Export as txt file...

Evaluation
Values

Plot

Zoom in Y   Zoom out Y   Zoom in X   Zoom out X

Measure	Current	Mean
• Accuracy	-	-
Kappa	-	-
Kappa Temp	-	-
Ram-Hours	-	-
Time	-	-
Memory	-	-

1.00

0.50

0.00
  0   50000   100000   150000   200000

This will run the task and generate the following output:

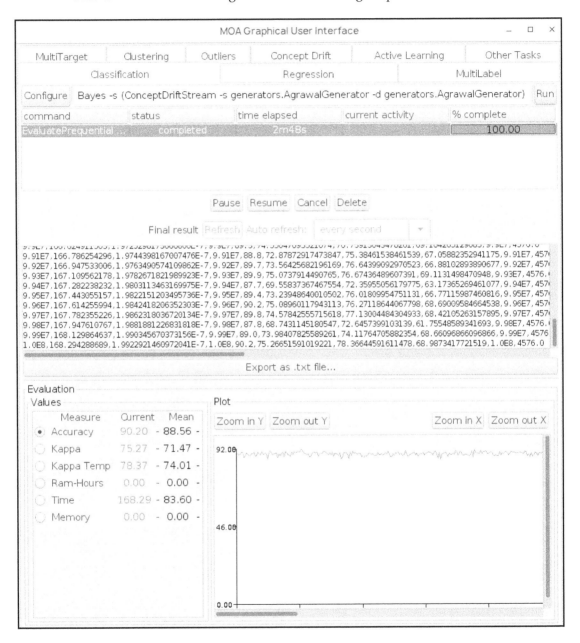

6. Let's use the **LeveragingBag** option. For this, open the **Configure task** window and select the **Edit** option in **baseLearner**, which will show the following; select **LeveragingBag** from the first drop-down box. You can find other options, such as boosting and average weight ensembles, in the first drop-down box:

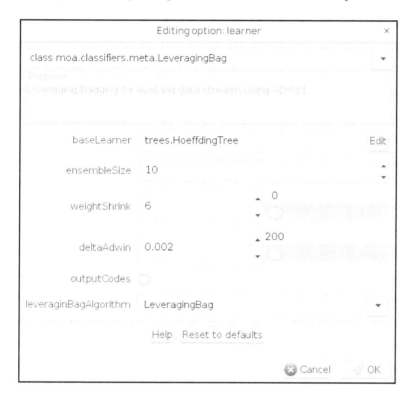

Leave the **stream** as **AgrawalGenerator**, as shown in the following screenshot:

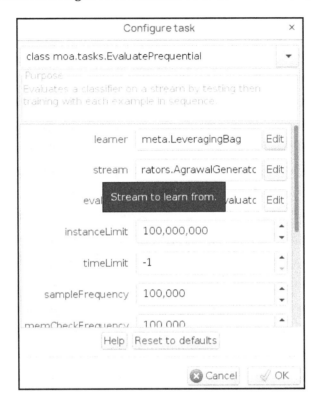

7. Close the **Configure task** window and click on the **Run** button; this will take some time to complete:

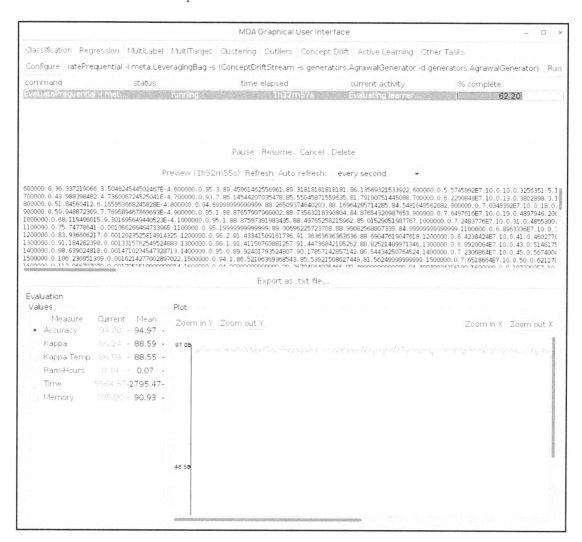

The output shows the evaluation after every 10,000 instances, how much RAM time is taken with classification correctness, as well as Kappa statistics. As you can see, over time, the classification correctness increases, along with the increasing instances. The graph in the preceding screenshot shows the correctness and the number of instances.

Summary

In this chapter, we tackled the KDD Cup 2009 challenge on customer relationship predictions, implementing the data preprocessing steps and addressing the missing values and redundant attributes. We followed the winning KDD Cup solution and studied how to leverage ensemble methods by using a basket of learning algorithms, which can significantly boost classification performance.

In the next chapter, we will tackle another problem concerning customer behavior: purchasing behavior. You will learn how to use algorithms that detect frequently occurring patterns.

5
Affinity Analysis

Affinity analysis is the heart of **Market Basket Analysis** (**MBA**). It can discover co-occurring relationships among activities performed by specific users or groups. In retail, affinity analysis can help you understand the purchasing behavior of customers. These insights can drive revenue through smart cross-selling and upselling strategies and can assist you in developing loyalty programs, sales promotions, and discount plans.

In this chapter, we will look into the following topics:

- MBA
- Association rule learning
- Other applications in various domains

First, we will revise the core association rule-learning concepts and algorithms, such as support and lift Apriori algorithms and the FP-Growth algorithm. Next, we will use Weka to perform our first affinity analysis on a supermarket dataset and study how to interpret the resulting rules. We will conclude this chapter by analyzing how association rule learning can be applied in other domains, such as IT operations analytics, and medicine.

Market basket analysis

Since the introduction of electronic points of sale, retailers have been collecting an incredible amount of data. To leverage this data in to produce business value, they first developed a way to consolidate and aggregate the data to understand the basics of the business.

Recently, the focus shifted to the lowest level of granularity—the market basket transaction. At this level of detail, the retailers have direct visibility into the market basket of each customer who shopped at their store, understanding not only the quantity of the purchased items in that particular basket, but also how these items were bought in conjunction with one another. This can be used to drive decisions about how to differentiate store assortment and merchandise, as well as to effectively combine offers of multiple products, within and across categories, to drive higher sales and profits. These decisions can be implemented across an entire retail chain, by channel, at the local store level, and even for a specific customer, with so-called personalized marketing, where a unique product offering is made for each customer:

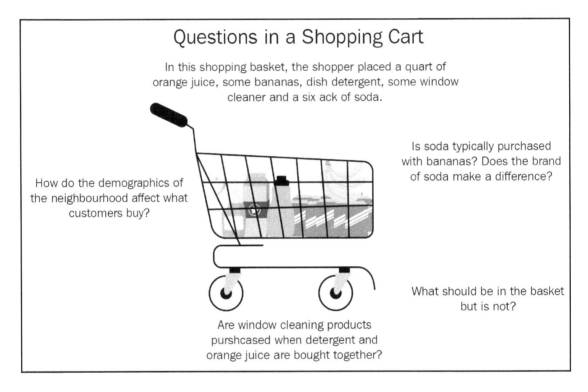

MBA covers a wide variety of analysis:

- **Item affinity**: This defines the likelihood of two (or more) items being purchased together.
- **Identification of driver items**: This enables the identification of the items that drive people to the store and always need to be in stock.
- **Trip classification**: This analyzes the content of the basket and classifies the shopping trip into a category: weekly grocery trip, special occasion, and so on.

- **Store-to-store comparison**: Understanding the number of baskets allows any metric to be divided by the total number of baskets, effectively creating a convenient and easy way to compare the stores to different characteristics (units sold per customer, revenue per transaction, number of items per basket, and so on).
- **Revenue optimization**: This helps in determining the magic price points for this store, increasing the size and the value of the market basket.
- **Marketing**: This helps in identifying more profitable advertising and promotions, targeting offers more precisely to improve ROI, generating better loyalty card promotions with longitudinal analysis and attracting more traffic to the store.
- **Operations optimization**: This helps in matching the inventory to the requirement by customizing the store and assortment to trade area demographics, and optimizing store layout.

Predictive models help retailers to direct the right offer to the right customer segments or profiles, as well as to gain an understanding of what is valid for which customer, predict the probability score of customers responding to this offer, and understand the customer value gain from the offer acceptance.

Affinity analysis

Affinity analysis is used to determine the likelihood that a set of items will be bought together. In retail, there are natural product affinities; for example, it is very typical for people who buy hamburger patties to buy hamburger rolls, along with ketchup, mustard, tomatoes, and other items that make up the burger experience.

While there are some product affinities that might seem trivial, there are some affinities that are not very obvious. A classic example is toothpaste and tuna. It seems that people who eat tuna are more prone to brushing their teeth right after finishing their meal. So, why it is important for retailers to get a good grasp of product affinities? This information is critical to appropriately plan promotions, as reducing the price for some items may cause a spike on related high-affinity items without the need to further promote these related items.

In the following section, we'll look into the algorithms for association rule learning: Apriori and FP-Growth.

Association rule learning

Association rule learning has been a popular approach to discover interesting relationships among items in large databases. It is most commonly applied in retail to reveal regularities between products.

Association rule learning approaches find patterns as interesting strong rules in the database using different measures of interestingness. For example, the following rule would indicate, that if a customer buys onions and potatoes together, they are likely to also buy hamburger meat: {onions, potatoes} -> {burger}.

Another classic story probably told in every machine-learning class is the beer and diaper story. An analysis of supermarket shoppers' behavior showed that customers, presumably young men, who buy diapers also tend to buy beer. It immediately became a popular example of how an unexpected association rule might be found from everyday data; however, there are varying opinions as to how much of the story is true. In *DSS News 2002*, Daniel Powers says this:

> *"In 1992, Thomas Blischok, manager of a retail consulting group at Teradata, and his staff prepared an analysis of 1.2 million market baskets from about 25 Osco Drug stores. Database queries were developed to identify affinities. The analysis did discover that between 5:00 and 7:00 pm, consumers bought beer and diapers. Osco managers did not exploit the beer and diapers relationship by moving the products closer together on the shelves."*

In addition to the preceding example from MBA, association rules are today employed in many application areas, including web usage mining, intrusion detection, continuous production, and bioinformatics. We'll take a closer look at these areas later in this chapter.

Basic concepts

Before we dive into algorithms, let's first review the basic concepts.

Database of transactions

In association rule mining, the dataset is structured a bit differently than the approach presented in the first chapter. First, there is no class value, as this is not required for learning association rules. Next, the dataset is presented as a transactional table, where each supermarket item corresponds to a binary attribute. Hence, the feature vector could be extremely large.

Consider the following example. Suppose we have four receipts, as shown next. Each receipt corresponds to a purchasing transaction:

To write these receipts in the form of a transactional database, we first identify all of the possible items that appear in the receipts. These items are **onions**, **potatoes**, **burger**, **beer**, and **dippers**. Each purchase, that is, transaction, is presented in a row, and there is *1* if an item was purchased within the transaction and *0* otherwise, as shown in the following table:

Transaction ID	Onions	Potatoes	Burger	Beer	Dippers
1	0	1	1	0	0
2	1	1	1	1	0
3	0	0	0	1	1
4	1	0	1	1	0

This example is really small. In practical applications, the dataset often contains thousands or millions of transactions, which allow the learning algorithm the discovery of statistically significant patterns.

Itemset and rule

Itemset is simply a set of items, for example, {onions, potatoes, burger}. A rule consists of two itemsets, X and Y, in the following format:

$$X \rightarrow Y$$

This indicates a pattern that when the X itemset is observed, Y is also observed. To select interesting rules, various measures of significance can be used.

Support

Support, for an itemset, is defined as the proportion of transactions that contain the itemset. The `{potatoes, burger}` itemset in the previous table has the following support, as it occurs in 50% of transactions (two out of four transactions): supp({potatoes, burger}) = 2/4 = 0.5.

Intuitively, it indicates the share of transactions that support the pattern.

Lift

Lift is a measure of the performance of a targeting model (association rule) at predicting or classifying cases as having an enhanced response (with respect to the population as a whole), measured against a random choice targeting model. It is defined using the following formula:

$$lift = \frac{P(A \bigcap B)}{P(A) \times P(B)}$$

Confidence

The confidence of a rule indicates its accuracy. It is defined using the following formula:

$$Conf(X \geq Y) = (X \bigcup Y)/supp(X)$$

For example, the {onions, burger} -> {beer} rule has the confidence *0.5/0.5 = 1.0* in the previous table, which means that 100% of the time when onions and burger are bought together, beer is bought as well.

Apriori algorithm

The **Apriori algorithm** is a classic algorithm used for frequent pattern mining and association rule learning over transactional. By identifying the frequent individual items in a database and extending them to larger itemsets, Apriori can determine the association rules, which highlight general trends about a database.

The Apriori algorithm constructs a set of itemsets, for example, itemset1= {Item A, Item B}, and calculates support, which counts the number of occurrences in the database. Apriori then uses a bottom up approach, where frequent itemsets are extended, one item at a time, and it works by eliminating the largest sets as candidates by first looking at the smaller sets and recognizing that a large set cannot be frequent unless all of its subsets are. The algorithm terminates when no further successful extensions are found.

Although the Apriori algorithm is an important milestone in machine learning, it suffers from a number of inefficiencies and tradeoffs. In the following section, we'll look into a more recent FP-Growth technique.

FP-Growth algorithm

FP-Growth (where FP is frequent patterns) represents the transaction database as a suffix tree. First, the algorithm counts the occurrence of items in the dataset. In the second pass, it builds a suffix tree, an ordered tree data structure commonly used to store a string. An example of a suffix tree based on the previous example is shown in the following diagram:

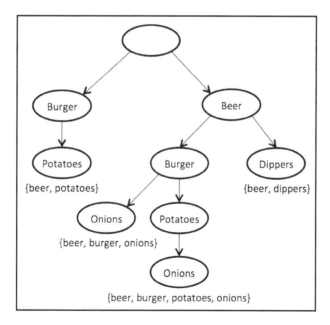

If many transactions share the most frequent items, the suffix tree provides high compression close to the tree root. Large itemsets are grown directly, instead of generating candidate items and testing them against the entire database. Growth starts at the bottom of the tree, by finding all of the itemsets matching minimal support and confidence. Once the recursive process has completed, all large itemsets with minimum coverage have been found and association rule creation begins.

An FP-Growth algorithm has several advantages. First, it constructs an FP-tree, which encodes the original dataset in a substantially compact presentation. Second, it efficiently builds frequent itemsets, leveraging the FP-tree structure and the divide-and-conquer strategy.

The supermarket dataset

The supermarket dataset, located in `data/supermarket.arff`, describes the shopping habits of supermarket customers. Most of the attributes stand for a particular item group, for example, diary foods, beef, and potatoes; or they stand for a department, for example, department 79, department 81, and so on. The following table shows an excerpt of the database, where the value is *t* if the customer had bought an item and missing otherwise. There is one instance per customer. The dataset contains no class attribute, as this is not required to learn association rules. A sample of data is shown in the following table:

coffee	sauces-gravy-pkle	confectionary	puddings-deserts	dishcloths-scour	deod-disinfectan1	frozen foods	razor blades	fuels-garden aids	spices	jams-spreads
1	1	1	0	1	0	1	1	0	0	0
0	1	0	0	0	1	1	0	0	0	0
0	1	0	1	0	0	0	0	0	0	0
0	0	0	0	0	0	1	0	0	0	1
1	1	0	0	0	0	1	0	0	0	1
0	0	1	0	0	0	1	0	0	1	0
0	1	0	0	0	0	0	0	0	0	0
1	1	0	0	0	0	1	0	0	0	0
0	0	0	0	0	0	0	0	0	0	0
0	1	0	1	0	0	0	0	0	0	1
1	0	0	0	1	0	1	0	0	0	0
0	0	0	1	0	0	0	0	0	0	1
1	1	0	0	0	0	1	0	0	0	1
0	0	0	1	0	0	0	0	0	0	1
0	1	0	0	0	0	0	0	0	0	0
0	1	0	0	1	0	1	0	1	0	0
0	0	0	0	0	1	1	0	0	0	0
0	0	0	0	0	0	0	0	0	0	0
1	1	0	0	0	0	0	0	0	0	0
0	1	1	0	0	0	1	0	0	0	0
0	1	0	0	0	0	1	0	0	0	0
0	1	1	1	1	0	1	0	0	0	1
0	1	1	0	0	0	1	0	0	0	0
1	1	0	0	0	0	1	0	0	0	0
0	1	0	0	0	0	0	0	0	0	0
0	0	0	1	1	0	1	0	0	0	0
0	0	0	0	0	0	1	0	0	0	0
0	1	1	1	1	1	1	0	0	0	0

Discover patterns

To discover shopping patterns, we will use the two algorithms that we have looked into before: Apriori and FP-Growth.

Apriori

We will use the `Apriori` algorithm as implemented in Weka. It iteratively reduces the minimum support until it finds the required number of rules with the given minimum confidence. We'll implement the algorithm using the following steps:

1. We'll import the required libraries using the following lines of code:

```
import java.io.BufferedReader;
import java.io.FileReader;
import weka.core.Instances;
import weka.associations.Apriori;
```

2. First, we'll load the `supermarket.arff` dataset:

```
Instances data = new Instances(new BufferedReader(new
FileReader("data/supermarket.arff")));
```

3. We'll initialize an `Apriori` instance and call the `buildAssociations(Instances)` function to start frequent pattern mining, as follows:

```
Apriori model = new Apriori();
model.buildAssociations(data);
```

4. We can output the discovered itemsets and rules, as shown in the following code:

```
System.out.println(model);
```

The output is as follows:

```
Apriori
=======
Minimum support: 0.15 (694 instances)
Minimum metric <confidence>: 0.9
Number of cycles performed: 17
Generated sets of large itemsets:
Size of set of large itemsets L(1): 44
Size of set of large itemsets L(2): 380
Size of set of large itemsets L(3): 910
```

```
        Size of set of large itemsets L(4): 633
        Size of set of large itemsets L(5): 105
        Size of set of large itemsets L(6): 1
        Best rules found:
        1. biscuits=t frozen foods=t fruit=t total=high 788 ==> bread and
cake=t 723      <conf:(0.92)> lift:(1.27) lev:(0.03) [155] conv:(3.35)
        2. baking needs=t biscuits=t fruit=t total=high 760 ==> bread and
cake=t 696      <conf:(0.92)> lift:(1.27) lev:(0.03) [149] conv:(3.28)
        3. baking needs=t frozen foods=t fruit=t total=high 770 ==> bread
and cake=t 705      <conf:(0.92)> lift:(1.27) lev:(0.03) [150]
conv:(3.27)
        . . .
```

The algorithm outputs the ten best rules according to confidence. Let's look at the first rule and interpret the output, as follows:

```
biscuits=t frozen foods=t fruit=t total=high 788 ==> bread and cake=t 723
<conf:(0.92)> lift:(1.27) lev:(0.03) [155] conv:(3.35)
```

It says that when `biscuits`, `frozen foods`, and `fruits` are bought together and the total purchase price is high, it is also very likely that `bread` and `cake` are purchased as well. The `{biscuits, frozen foods, fruit, total high}` itemset appears in `788` transactions, while the `{bread, cake}` itemset appears in `723` transactions. The confidence of this rule is `0.92`, meaning that the rule holds true in 92% of transactions where the `{biscuits, frozen foods, fruit, total high}` itemset is present.

The output also reports additional measures such as lift, leverage, and conviction, which estimate the accuracy against our initial assumptions; for example, the `3.35` conviction value indicates that the rule would be incorrect `3.35` times as often if the association was purely a random chance. Lift measures the number of times X and Y occur together than expected if they were statistically independent (`lift=1`). The `2.16` lift in the X -> Y rule means that the probability of X is `2.16` times greater than the probability of Y.

FP-Growth

Now, let's try to get the same results with the more efficient FP-Growth algorithm. FP-Growth is also implemented in the `weka.associations` package:

```
import weka.associations.FPGrowth;
```

The FP-Growth algorithm is initialized similarly, as we did earlier:

```
FPGrowth fpgModel = new FPGrowth();
fpgModel.buildAssociations(data);
System.out.println(fpgModel);
```

The output reveals that FP-Growth discovered `16 rules`:

```
FPGrowth found 16 rules (displaying top 10)
     1. [fruit=t, frozen foods=t, biscuits=t, total=high]: 788 ==> [bread
and cake=t]: 723    <conf:(0.92)> lift:(1.27) lev:(0.03) conv:(3.35)
     2. [fruit=t, baking needs=t, biscuits=t, total=high]: 760 ==> [bread
and cake=t]: 696    <conf:(0.92)> lift:(1.27) lev:(0.03) conv:(3.28)
     ...
```

We can observe that FP-Growth found the same set of rules as Apriori; however, the time required to process larger datasets can be significantly shorter.

Other applications in various areas

We looked into affinity analysis to demystify shopping behavior patterns in supermarkets. Although the roots of association rule learning are in analyzing point-of-sale transactions, they can be applied outside the retail industry to find relationships among other types of baskets. The notion of a basket can easily be extended to services and products, for example, to analyze items purchased using a credit card, such as rental cars and hotel rooms, and to analyze information on value-added services purchased by telecom customers (call waiting, call forwarding, DSL, speed call, and so on), which can help the operators determine the ways to improve their bundling of service packages.

Additionally, we will look into the following examples of potential cross industry applications:

- Medical diagnosis
- Protein sequences
- Census data
- Customer relationship management
- IT operations analytics

Medical diagnosis

Applying association rules in medical diagnosis can be used to assist physicians while curing patients. The general problem of the induction of reliable diagnostic rules is hard as, theoretically, no induction process can guarantee the correctness of induced hypotheses by itself. Practically, diagnosis is not an easy process, as it involves unreliable diagnosis tests and the presence of noise in training examples.

Nevertheless, association rules can be used to identify likely symptoms appearing together. A transaction, in this case, corresponds to a medical case, while symptoms correspond to items. When a patient is treated, a list of symptoms is recorded as one transaction.

Protein sequences

A lot of research has gone into understanding the composition and nature of proteins; yet, many things remain to be understood satisfactorily. It is now generally believed that amino acid sequences of proteins are not random.

With association rules, it is possible to identify associations between different amino acids that are present in a protein. A protein is a sequence made up of 20 types of amino acids. Each protein has a unique three-dimensional structure, which depends on the amino-acid sequence; a slight change in the sequence may change the functioning of protein. To apply association rules, a protein corresponds to a transaction, while amino acids and their structure correspond to the items.

Such association rules are desirable for enhancing our understanding of protein composition and hold the potential to give clues regarding the global interactions among some particular sets of amino acids occurring in the proteins. Knowledge of these association rules or constraints is highly desirable for the synthesis of artificial proteins.

Census data

Censuses make a huge variety of general statistical information about a society available to both researchers and general public. The information related to population and economic censuses can be forecasted in planning public services (education, health, transport, and funds) as well as in business (for setting up new factories, shopping malls, or banks and even marketing particular products).

To discover frequent patterns, each statistical area (for example, municipality, city, and neighborhood) corresponds to a transaction, and the collected indicators correspond to the items.

Customer relationship management

The **Customer Relationship Management** (**CRM**), as we briefly discussed in the previous chapters, is a rich source of data through which companies hope to identify the preference of different customer groups, products, and services in order to enhance the cohesion among their products and services and their customers.

Association rules can reinforce the knowledge management process and allow the marketing personnel to know their customers well to provide better quality services. For example, association rules can be applied to detect a change of customer behavior at different time snapshots from customer profiles and sales data. The basic idea is to discover changes from two datasets and generate rules from each dataset to carry out rule matching.

IT operations analytics

Based on records of a large number of transactions, association rule learning is well-suited to be applied to the data that is routinely collected in day-to-day IT operations, enabling IT operations analytics tools to detect frequent patterns and identify critical changes. IT specialists need to see the big picture and understand, for example, how a problem on a database could impact an application server.

For a specific day, IT operations may take in a variety of alerts, presenting them in a transactional database. Using an association rule-learning algorithm, IT operations analytics tools can correlate and detect the frequent patterns of alerts appearing together. This can lead to a better understanding about how one component impacts another.

With identified alert patterns, it is possible to apply predictive analytics. For example, a particular database server hosts a web application and suddenly an alert about a database is triggered. By looking into frequent patterns identified by an association rule-learning algorithm, this means that the IT staff need to take action before the web application is impacted.

Association rule learning can also discover alert events originating from the same IT event. For example, every time a new user is added, six changes in the Windows operating system are detected. Next, in **Application Portfolio Management** (**APM**), IT may face multiple alerts, showing that the transactional time in a database as high. If all of these issues originate from the same source (such as getting hundreds of alerts about changes that are all due to a Windows update), this frequent pattern mining can help to quickly cut through a number of alerts, allowing the IT operators to focus on truly critical changes.

Summary

In this chapter, you learned how to leverage association rule learning on transactional datasets to gain insight about frequent patterns. We performed an affinity analysis in Weka and learned that the hard work lies in the analysis of results—careful attention is required when interpreting rules, as association (that is, correlation) is not the same as causation.

In the next chapter, we'll look at how to take the problem of item recommendation to the next level using a scalable machine-learning library, Apache Mahout, which is able to handle big data.

Recommendation Engines with Apache Mahout 6

Recommendation engines are one of the most applied data science approaches in startups today. There are two principal techniques for building a recommendation system: content-based filtering and collaborative filtering. The content-based algorithm uses the properties of the items to find items with similar properties. Collaborative filtering algorithms take user ratings, or other user behaviors, and make recommendations based on what users with similar behaviors liked or purchased.

In this chapter, we will first explain the basic concepts required to understand recommendation engine principles, and then we will demonstrate how to utilize Apache Mahout's implementation of various algorithms in order to quickly get a scalable recommendation engine.

This chapter will cover the following topics:

- How to build a recommendation engine
- Getting Apache Mahout ready
- The content-based approach
- The collaborative filtering approach

By the end of this chapter, you will have learned about the kind of recommendation engine that is appropriate for our problem and how to quickly implement that engine.

Basic concepts

Recommendation engines aim at showing users items of interest. What makes them different from search engines is the relevant content usually appears on a website without having been requested, and users don't have to build queries, as recommendation engines observe the users' actions and construct the queries for users without their knowledge.

Arguably, the most well-known example of a recommendation engine is www.amazon.com, which provides personalized recommendation in a number of ways. The following screenshot shows an example of **Customers Who Bought This Item Also Bought**. As you will see later on, this is an example of collaborative item-based recommendation, where items similar to a particular item are recommended:

In this section, we will introduce key concepts related to understanding and building recommendation engines.

Key concepts

Recommendation engines require the following pieces of input in order to make recommendations:

- Item information, described with attributes
- A user profile, such as age range, gender, location, friends, and so on
- User interactions, in the form of rating, browsing, tagging, comparing, saving, and emailing
- The context where the items will be displayed; for example, the item's category and the item's geographical location

This input is then combined by the recommendation engine to help obtain the following:

- Users who bought, watched, viewed, or bookmarked this item also bought, watched, viewed, or bookmarked
- Items similar to this item
- Other users you may know
- Other users who are similar to you

Now, let's take a closer look at how this combination works.

User-based and item-based analysis

Building a recommendation engine depends on whether the engine searches for related items or users when trying to recommend a particular item.

In item-based analysis, the engine focuses on identifying items that are similar to a particular item, while in user-based analysis, users similar to the particular user are determined first. For example, users with the same profile information (age, gender, and so on) or action history (bought, watched, viewed, and so on) are determined, and then the same items are recommended to other, similar users.

Both approaches require us to compute a similarity matrix, depending on whether we're analyzing item attributes or user actions. Let's take a deeper look at how this is done.

Calculating similarity

There are three fundamental approaches to calculating similarity, as follows:

- Collaborative filtering algorithms take user ratings or other user behaviors and make recommendations based on what users with similar behaviors liked or purchased
- The content-based algorithm uses the properties of the items to find items with similar properties
- A hybrid approach combines collaborative and content-based filtering

Let's take a look at each approach in detail in the following sections.

Collaborative filtering

Collaborative filtering is based solely on user ratings or other user behaviors, making recommendations based on what users with similar behaviors liked or purchased.

A key advantage of collaborative filtering is that it does not rely on item content, and therefore, it is capable of accurately recommending complex items, such as movies, without understanding the item itself. The underlying assumption is that people that agreed in the past will agree in the future, and that they will like similar kinds of items to what they liked in the past.

A major disadvantage of this approach is the so-called cold start, meaning that if we want to build an accurate collaborative filtering system, the algorithm often needs a large amount of user ratings. This usually takes collaborative filtering out of the first version of the product, and it is introduced later, when a decent amount of data has been collected.

Content-based filtering

Content-based filtering, on the other hand, is based on a description of items and a profile of a user's preferences, which is combined as follows. First, the items are described with attributes, and to find similar items, we measure the distances between items using a distance measure, such as the cosine distance or Pearson coefficient (there is more about distance measures in Chapter 1, *Applied Machine Learning Quick Start*). Now, the user profile enters the equation. Given the feedback about the kinds of items the user likes, we can introduce weights, specifying the importance of a specific item attribute. For instance, the Pandora Radio streaming service applies content-based filtering to create stations, using more than 400 attributes. A user initially picks a song with specific attributes, and, by providing feedback, important song attributes are emphasized.

Initially, this approach needs very little information on user feedback; thus, it effectively avoids the cold start issue.

Hybrid approach

Now, between collaborative and content-based, which one should you choose? Collaborative filtering is able to learn user preferences from a user's actions regarding one content source, and use them across other content types. Content-based filtering is limited to recommending content of the same type that the user is already using. This provides value in certain use cases; for example, recommending news articles based on news browsing is useful, but it is much more useful if different sources, such as books and movies, can be recommended based on news browsing.

Collaborative filtering and content-based filtering are not mutually exclusive; they can be combined to be more effective in some cases. For example, Netflix uses collaborative filtering to analyze the searching and watching patterns of similar users, as well as content-based filtering to offer movies that share characteristics with films that the user has rated highly.

There is a wide variety of hybridization techniques: weighted, switching, and mixed, feature combination, feature augmentation, cascade, meta-level, and so on. Recommendation systems are an active area in the machine learning and data mining community, with special tracks on data science conferences. A good overview of techniques is summarized in the paper *Toward the Next Generation of Recommender Systems: A Survey of the State-of-the-Art and Possible Extensions,* by Adomavicius and Tuzhilin (2005), where the authors discuss different approaches and underlying algorithms, and provide references to further papers. To get more technical and understand all of the tiny details when a particular approach makes sense, you should look at the book edited by Ricci, et al.: *Recommender Systems Handbook* (First Edition, 2010, Springer-Verlag, New York).

Exploitation versus exploration

In recommendation systems, there is always a trade-off between recommending items that fall into the user's sweet spot, based on what we already know about the user (**exploitation**), and recommending items that don't fall into the user's sweet spot, with the aim to expose the user to some novelties (**exploration**). Recommendation systems with little exploration will only recommend items that are consistent with the previous user ratings, thus preventing showing items outside of their current bubble. In practice, the serendipity of getting new items out of the user's sweet spot is often desirable, leading to a pleasant surprise, and potentially, the discovery of new sweet spots.

In this section, we discussed the essential concepts required to start building recommendation engines. Now, let's take a look at how to actually build one with Apache Mahout.

Getting Apache Mahout

Mahout was introduced in `Chapter 2`, *Java Libraries and Platforms for Machine Learning*, as a scalable machine learning library. It provides a rich set of components with which you can construct a customized recommendation system from a selection of algorithms. The creators of Mahout say that it is designed to be enterprise-ready; it's designed for performance, scalability, and flexibility.

Mahout can be configured to run in two flavors: with or without Hadoop, and for a single machine and distributed processing, respectively. We will focus on configuring Mahout without Hadoop. For more advanced configurations and further uses of Mahout, I would recommend two recent books: *Learning Apache Mahout,* by Chandramani Tiwary, Packt Publishing, and *Learning Apache Mahout Classification,* by Ashish Gupta, Packt Publishing.

As Apache Mahout's build and release system is based on Maven, you will need to learn how to install it. We will look at the most convenient approach; using Eclipse with the Maven plugin.

Configuring Mahout in Eclipse with the Maven plugin

You will need a recent version of Eclipse, which can be downloaded from its home page (https://www.eclipse.org/downloads/). In this book, we will use Eclipse Luna. Open Eclipse and start a new **Maven Project** with the default settings, as shown in the following screenshot:

The **New Maven project** screen will appear, as shown in the following screenshot:

Now, we need to tell the project to add the Mahout JAR file and its dependencies to the project. Locate the `pom.xml` file and open it with the text editor (left-click on **Open With | Text Editor**), as shown in the following screenshot:

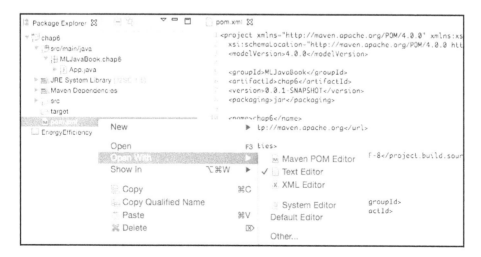

Locate the line starting with `<dependencies>` and add the following code in the next line:

```
<dependency>
  <groupId>org.apache.mahout</groupId>
    <artifactId>mahout-mr</artifactId>
    <version>0.10.0</version>
</dependency>
```

That's it; Mahout has been added, and we are ready to begin.

Building a recommendation engine

To demonstrate both the content-based filtering and collaborative filtering approaches, we'll build a book recommendation engine.

Book ratings dataset

In this chapter, we will work with a book ratings dataset (Ziegler et al., 2005) that was collected in a four-week crawl. It contains data on 278,858 members of the Book-Crossing website and 1,157,112 ratings, both implicit and explicit, referring to 271,379 distinct ISBNs. User data is anonymized, but with demographic information. The dataset is taken from `Improving Recommendation Lists Through Topic Diversification`, Cai-Nicolas Ziegler, Sean M. McNee, Joseph A. Konstan, Georg Lausen: *Proceedings of the 14th International World Wide Web Conference* (WWW '05), May 10-14, 2005, Chiba, Japan (`http://www2.informatik.uni-freiburg.de/~cziegler/BX/`).

The Book-Crossing dataset is comprised of three files, as follows:

* `BX-Users`: This contains the users. Note that user IDs (**User-ID**) have been anonymized and mapped to integers. Demographic data is provided (**Location** and **Age**) if available. Otherwise, these fields contain null values.
* `BX-Books`: Books are identified by their respective ISBNs. Invalid ISBNs have already been removed from the dataset. Moreover, some content-based information is given (**Book-Title**, **Book-Author**, **Year-Of-Publication**, and **Publisher**), which has been obtained from Amazon Web Services. Note that in the case of several authors, only the first author is provided. URLs linking to cover images are also given, appearing in three different flavors (**Image-URL-S**, **Image-URL-M**, and **Image-URL-L**), referring to small, medium, and large URLs. These URLs point to the Amazon website.

- `BX-Book-Ratings`: This contains the book rating information. Ratings (**Book-Rating**) are either explicit, expressed on a scale of 1-10 (with higher values denoting higher appreciation), or implicit, expressed by 0.

Loading the data

There are two approaches to loading the data, according to where the data is stored: a file or database. First, we will take a detailed look at how to load the data from a file, including how to deal with custom formats. At the end, we will quickly take a look at how to load the data from a database.

Loading data from a file

Loading data from a file can be achieved with the `FileDataModel` class. We will be expecting a comma-delimited file, where each line contains a `userID`, an `itemID`, an optional `preference` value, and an optional `timestamp`, in the same order, as follows:

```
userID,itemID[,preference[,timestamp]]
```

An optional preference accommodates applications with binary preference values, that is, the user either expresses a preference for an item or not, without a degree of preference; for example, with a like or dislike.

A line that begins with a hash (#) or an empty line will be ignored. It is also acceptable for the lines to contain additional fields, which will be ignored.

The `DataModel` class assumes the following types:

- The `userID` and `itemID` can be parsed as `long`
- The `preference` value can be parsed as `double`
- The `timestamp` can be parsed as `long`

If you are able to provide the dataset in the preceding format, you can simply use the following line to load the data:

```
DataModel model = new FileDataModel(new File(path));
```

This class is not intended to be used for very large amounts of data; for example, tens of millions of rows. For that, a JDBC-backed `DataModel` and a database are more appropriate.

In the real world, however, we cannot always ensure that the input data supplied to us contains only integer values for `userID` and `itemID`. For example, in our case, `itemID` corresponds to ISBN book numbers, which uniquely identify items, but these are not integers, and the `FileDataModel` default won't be suitable to process our data.

Now, let's consider how to deal with a case where our `itemID` is a string. We will define our custom data model by extending `FileDataModel` and overriding the long `readItemIDFromString(String)` method in order to read the `itemID` as a string and convert it into `long`, and return a unique `long` value. To convert a `String` into a unique `long`, we'll extend another Mahout `AbstractIDMigrator` helper class, which is designed exactly for this task.

Now, let's look at how `FileDataModel` is extended:

```
class StringItemIdFileDataModel extends FileDataModel {

  //initialize migrator to covert String to unique long
  public ItemMemIDMigrator memIdMigtr;

  public StringItemIdFileDataModel(File dataFile, String regex)
     throws IOException {
    super(dataFile, regex);
  }

  @Override
  protected long readItemIDFromString(String value) {
    if (memIdMigtr == null) {
      memIdMigtr = new ItemMemIDMigrator();
    }
    // convert to long
    long retValue = memIdMigtr.toLongID(value);
    //store it to cache
    if (null == memIdMigtr.toStringID(retValue)) {
      try {
        memIdMigtr.singleInit(value);
      } catch (TasteException e) {
        e.printStackTrace();
      }
    }
    return retValue;
  }
  // convert long back to String
  String getItemIDAsString(long itemId) {
    return memIdMigtr.toStringID(itemId);
  }
}
```

Other useful methods that can be overridden are as follows:

- readUserIDFromString(String value), if user IDs are not numeric
- readTimestampFromString(String value), to change how timestamp is parsed

Now, let's take a look at how AbstractIDMigrator is extended:

```
class ItemMemIDMigrator extends AbstractIDMigrator {

  private FastByIDMap<String> longToString;

  public ItemMemIDMigrator() {
    this.longToString = new FastByIDMap<String>(10000);
  }

  public void storeMapping(long longID, String stringID) {
    longToString.put(longID, stringID);
  }

  public void singleInit(String stringID) throws TasteException {
    storeMapping(toLongID(stringID), stringID);
  }

  public String toStringID(long longID) {
    return longToString.get(longID);
  }
}
```

Now, we have everything in place, and we can load our dataset with the following code:

```
StringItemIdFileDataModel model = new StringItemIdFileDataModel(
  new File("datasets/chap6/BX-Book-Ratings.csv"), ";");
System.out.println(
"Total items: " + model.getNumItems() +
"\nTotal users: " +model.getNumUsers());
```

This provides the total number of users and items as output:

```
Total items: 340556
Total users: 105283
```

We are ready to move on and start making recommendations.

Loading data from a database

Alternatively, we can load the data from a database using one of the JDBC data models. In this chapter, we will not dive into the detailed instructions of how to set up a database, connections, and so on, but we will give a sketch of how this can be done.

Database connectors have been moved to a separate package, mahout-integration; hence, we have to add the package to our dependency list. Open the pom.xml file and add the following dependency:

```
<dependency>
  <groupId>org.apache.mahout</groupId>
  <artifactId>mahout-integration</artifactId>
  <version>0.7</version>
</dependency>
```

Consider that we want to connect to a MySQL database. In this case, we will also need a package that handles database connections. Add the following to the pom.xml file:

```
<dependency>
  <groupId>mysql</groupId>
  <artifactId>mysql-connector-java</artifactId>
  <version>5.1.35</version>
</dependency>
```

Now, we have all of the packages, so we can create a connection. First, let's initialize a DataSource class with connection details, as follows:

```
MysqlDataSource dbsource = new MysqlDataSource();
  dbsource.setUser("user");
  dbsource.setPassword("pass");
  dbsource.setServerName("hostname.com");
  dbsource.setDatabaseName("db");
```

Mahout integration implements JDBCDataModel to various databases that can be accessed via JDBC. By default, this class assumes that there is a DataSource available under the JNDI name, jdbc/taste, which gives access to a database with a taste_preferences table, with the following schema:

```
CREATE TABLE taste_preferences (
  user_id BIGINT NOT NULL,
  item_id BIGINT NOT NULL,
  preference REAL NOT NULL,
  PRIMARY KEY (user_id, item_id)
)
CREATE INDEX taste_preferences_user_id_index ON taste_preferences
```

```
    (user_id);
CREATE INDEX taste_preferences_item_id_index ON taste_preferences
    (item_id);
```

A database-backed data model is initialized as follows. In addition to the DB connection object, we can specify the custom table name and the table column names, as follows:

```
DataModel dataModel = new MySQLJDBCDataModel(dbsource,
    "taste_preferences",
    "user_id", "item_id", "preference", "timestamp");
```

In-memory databases

Last, but not least, the data model can be created on the fly and held in memory. A database can be created from an array of preferences, which will hold user ratings for a set of items.

We can proceed as follows. First, we create a `FastByIdMap` hash map of preference arrays, `PreferenceArray`, which stores an array of preferences:

```
FastByIDMap <PreferenceArray> preferences = new FastByIDMap
    <PreferenceArray> ();
```

Next, we can create a new preference array for a user that will hold their ratings. The array must be initialized with a size parameter that reserves that many slots in the memory:

```
PreferenceArray prefsForUser1 =
    new GenericUserPreferenceArray (10);
```

Next, we set the user ID for the current preference at the position 0. This will actually set the user ID for all preferences:

```
prefsForUser1.setUserID (0, 1L);
```

Set an `itemID` for the current preference at the position 0, as follows:

```
prefsForUser1.setItemID (0, 101L);
```

Set the preference value for the preference at 0, as follows:

```
prefsForUser1.setValue (0, 3.0f);
```

Continue for other item ratings, as follows:

```
prefsForUser1.setItemID (1, 102L);
prefsForUser1.setValue (1, 4.5F);
```

Finally, add the user `preferences` to the hash map:

```
preferences.put (1L, prefsForUser1); // use userID as the key
```

The preference hash map can now be used to initialize `GenericDataModel`:

```
DataModel dataModel = new GenericDataModel(preferences);
```

This code demonstrates how to add two preferences for a single user; in a practical application, you'll want to add multiple preferences for multiple users.

Collaborative filtering

The recommendation engines in Mahout can be built with the `org.apache.mahout.cf.taste` package, which was formerly a separate project called `Taste`, and has continued to be developed in Mahout.

A Mahout-based collaborative filtering engine takes the users' preferences for items (tastes) and returns the estimated preferences for other items. For example, a site that sells books or CDs could easily use Mahout to figure out the CDs that a customer might be interested in listening to, with the help of previous purchase data.

Top-level packages define the Mahout interfaces to the following key abstractions:

- **DataModel**: This represents a repository of information about users and their preferences for items
- **UserSimilarity**: This defines a notion of similarity between two users
- **ItemSimilarity**: This defines a notion of similarity between two items
- **UserNeighborhood**: This computes neighboring users for a given user
  - **Recommender**: This recommends items for the user

A general structure of the preceding concepts is shown in the following diagram:

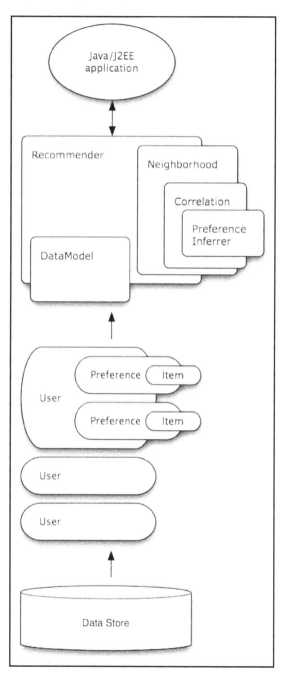

User-based filtering

The most basic user-based collaborative filtering can be implemented by initializing the previously described components, as follows:

First, load the data model:

```
StringItemIdFileDataModel model = new StringItemIdFileDataModel(
    new File("/datasets/chap6/BX-Book-Ratings.csv", ";");
```

Next, define how to calculate how the users are correlated; for example, using the Pearson correlation:

```
UserSimilarity similarity =
  new PearsonCorrelationSimilarity(model);
```

Next, define how to tell which users are similar, that is, the users that are close to each other, according to their ratings:

```
UserNeighborhood neighborhood =
  new ThresholdUserNeighborhood(0.1, similarity, model);
```

Now, we can initialize a `GenericUserBasedRecommender` default engine with the data for `model`, `neighborhood`, and similar objects, as follows:

```
UserBasedRecommender recommender =
new GenericUserBasedRecommender(model, neighborhood, similarity);
```

That's it. Our first basic recommendation engine is ready. Let's discuss how to invoke recommendations. First, let's print the items that the user has already rated, along with ten recommendations for that user:

```
long userID = 80683;
int noItems = 10;

List<RecommendedItem> recommendations = recommender.recommend(
  userID, noItems);

System.out.println("Rated items by user:");
for(Preference preference : model.getPreferencesFromUser(userID)) {
  // convert long itemID back to ISBN
  String itemISBN = model.getItemIDAsString(
  preference.getItemID());
  System.out.println("Item: " + books.get(itemISBN) +
    " | Item id: " + itemISBN +
    " | Value: " + preference.getValue());
}
```

```
System.out.println("\nRecommended items:");
for (RecommendedItem item : recommendations) {
  String itemISBN = model.getItemIDAsString(item.getItemID());
  System.out.println("Item: " + books.get(itemISBN) +
    " | Item id: " + itemISBN +
    " | Value: " + item.getValue());
}
```

This will provide the following recommendations, along with their scores, as output:

```
    Rated items:
    Item: The Handmaid's Tale | Item id: 0395404258 | Value: 0.0
    Item: Get Clark Smart : The Ultimate Guide for the Savvy Consumer |
Item id: 1563526298 | Value: 9.0
    Item: Plum Island | Item id: 0446605409 | Value: 0.0
    Item: Blessings | Item id: 0440206529 | Value: 0.0
    Item: Edgar Cayce on the Akashic Records: The Book of Life | Item id:
0876044011 | Value: 0.0
    Item: Winter Moon | Item id: 0345386108 | Value: 6.0
    Item: Sarah Bishop | Item id: 059032120X | Value: 0.0
    Item: Case of Lucy Bending | Item id: 0425060772 | Value: 0.0
    Item: A Desert of Pure Feeling (Vintage Contemporaries) | Item id:
0679752714 | Value: 0.0
    Item: White Abacus | Item id: 0380796155 | Value: 5.0
    Item: The Land of Laughs : A Novel | Item id: 0312873115 | Value: 0.0
    Item: Nobody's Son | Item id: 0152022597 | Value: 0.0
    Item: Mirror Image | Item id: 0446353957 | Value: 0.0
    Item: All I Really Need to Know | Item id: 080410526X | Value: 0.0
    Item: Dreamcatcher | Item id: 0743211383 | Value: 7.0
    Item: Perplexing Lateral Thinking Puzzles: Scholastic Edition | Item
id: 0806917695 | Value: 5.0
    Item: Obsidian Butterfly | Item id: 0441007813 | Value: 0.0
    Recommended items:
    Item: Keeper of the Heart | Item id: 0380774933 | Value: 10.0
    Item: Bleachers | Item id: 0385511612 | Value: 10.0
    Item: Salem's Lot | Item id: 0451125452 | Value: 10.0
    Item: The Girl Who Loved Tom Gordon | Item id: 0671042858 | Value: 10.0
    Item: Mind Prey | Item id: 0425152898 | Value: 10.0
    Item: It Came From The Far Side | Item id: 0836220730 | Value: 10.0
    Item: Faith of the Fallen (Sword of Truth, Book 6) | Item id:
081257639X | Value: 10.0
    Item: The Talisman | Item id: 0345444884 | Value: 9.86375
    Item: Hamlet | Item id: 067172262X | Value: 9.708363
    Item: Untamed | Item id: 0380769530 | Value: 9.708363
```

Item-based filtering

The `ItemSimilarity` attribute is the most important point to discuss here. Item-based recommenders are useful, as they can take advantage of something very fast; they base their computations on item similarity, not user similarity, and item similarity is relatively static. It can be precomputed, instead of recomputed in real time.

Thus, it's strongly recommended that you use `GenericItemSimilarity` with precomputed similarities, if you're going to use this class. You can use `PearsonCorrelationSimilarity`, too, which computes similarities in real time, but you will probably find this painfully slow for large amounts of data:

```
StringItemIdFileDataModel model = new StringItemIdFileDataModel(
  new File("datasets/chap6/BX-Book-Ratings.csv"), ";");

ItemSimilarity itemSimilarity = new
  PearsonCorrelationSimilarity(model);

ItemBasedRecommender recommender = new
  GenericItemBasedRecommender(model, itemSimilarity);

String itemISBN = "0395272238";
long itemID = model.readItemIDFromString(itemISBN);
int noItems = 10;
List<RecommendedItem> recommendations =
  recommender.mostSimilarItems(itemID, noItems);

System.out.println("Recommendations for item:
  "+books.get(itemISBN));

System.out.println("\nMost similar items:");
for (RecommendedItem item : recommendations) {
  itemISBN = model.getItemIDAsString(item.getItemID());
  System.out.println("Item: " + books.get(itemISBN) + " | Item id:
    " + itemISBN + " | Value: " + item.getValue());
}
```
```
Recommendations for item: Close to the BoneMost similar items:Item: Private
Screening | Item id: 0345311396 | Value: 1.0Item: Heartstone | Item id:
0553569783 | Value: 1.0Item: Clockers / Movie Tie In | Item id: 0380720817
| Value: 1.0Item: Rules of Prey | Item id: 0425121631 | Value: 1.0Item: The
Next President | Item id: 0553576666 | Value: 1.0Item: Orchid Beach (Holly
Barker Novels (Paperback)) | Item id: 0061013412 | Value: 1.0Item: Winter
Prey | Item id: 0425141233 | Value: 1.0Item: Night Prey | Item id:
0425146413 | Value: 1.0Item: Presumed Innocent | Item id: 0446359866 |
Value: 1.0Item: Dirty Work (Stone Barrington Novels (Paperback)) | Item id:
  0451210158 | Value: 1.0
```

The resulting list returns a set of items that are similar to a particular item that we selected.

Adding custom rules to recommendations

It often happens that some business rules require us to boost the score of the selected items. In the book dataset, for example, if a book is recent, we want to give it a higher score. That's possible by using the IDRescorer interface, as follows:

- rescore(long, double) takes the itemId and original score as an argument and returns a modified score
- isFiltered(long) returns true to exclude a specific item from the recommendations, or false, otherwise

Our example can be implemented as follows:

```
class MyRescorer implements IDRescorer {

  public double rescore(long itemId, double originalScore) {
    double newScore = originalScore;
    if(bookIsNew(itemId)){
      originalScore *= 1.3;
    }
    return newScore;
  }

  public boolean isFiltered(long arg0) {
    return false;
  }

}
```

An instance of IDRescorer is provided when invoking recommender.recommend:

```
IDRescorer rescorer = new MyRescorer();
List<RecommendedItem> recommendations =
recommender.recommend(userID, noItems, rescorer);
```

Evaluation

You might be wondering how to make sure that the returned recommendations make any sense. The only way to really be sure about how effective recommendations are is to use A/B testing in a live system, with real users. For example, the A group receives a random item as a recommendation, while the B group receives an item that's recommended by our engine.

As this is not always possible (nor practical), we can get an estimate with offline statistical evaluation. One way to proceed is to use k-fold cross-validation, which was introduced in Chapter 1, *Applied Machine Learning Quick Start*. We partition a dataset into multiple sets; some are used to train our recommendation engine, and the rest are used to test how well it recommends items to unknown users.

Mahout implements the RecommenderEvaluator class, which splits a dataset in two parts. The first part (90%, by default) is used to produce recommendations, while the rest of the data is compared against estimated preference values in order to test the match. The class does not accept a recommender object directly; you need to build a class that's implementing the RecommenderBuilder interface instead, which builds a recommender object for a given DataModel object that is then used for testing. Let's take a look at how this is implemented.

First, we create a class that implements the RecommenderBuilder interface. We need to implement the buildRecommender method, which will return a recommender, as follows:

```
public class BookRecommender implements RecommenderBuilder {
  public Recommender buildRecommender(DataModel dataModel) {
    UserSimilarity similarity =
      new PearsonCorrelationSimilarity(model);
    UserNeighborhood neighborhood =
      new ThresholdUserNeighborhood(0.1, similarity, model);
    UserBasedRecommender recommender =
      new GenericUserBasedRecommender(
        model, neighborhood, similarity);
    return recommender;
  }
}
```

Now that we have a class that returns a recommender object, we can initialize a RecommenderEvaluator instance. The default implementation of this class is the AverageAbsoluteDifferenceRecommenderEvaluator class, which computes the average absolute difference between the predicted and actual ratings for users. The following code shows how to put the pieces together and run a hold-out test:

First, load a data model, as follows:

```
DataModel dataModel = new FileDataModel(
  new File("/path/to/dataset.csv"));
```

Next, initialize an evaluator instance, as follows:

```
RecommenderEvaluator evaluator =
  new AverageAbsoluteDifferenceRecommenderEvaluator();
```

Initialize the `BookRecommender` object, implementing the `RecommenderBuilder` interface, as follows:

```
RecommenderBuilder builder = new MyRecommenderBuilder();
```

Finally, call the `evaluate()` method, which accepts the following parameters:

- `RecommenderBuilder`: This is the object implementing the `RecommenderBuilder` that can build the `recommender` to test
- `DataModelBuilder`: This indicates the `DataModelBuilder` to use; if null, a default `DataModel` implementation will be used
- `DataModel`: This is the dataset that will be used for testing
- `trainingPercentage`: This indicates the percentage of each user's preferences to use to produce recommendations; the rest are compared to estimated preference values in order to evaluate the performance of the `recommender`
- `evaluationPercentage`: This is the percentage of users to be used in the evaluation

The method is called as follows:

```
double result = evaluator.evaluate(builder, null, model, 0.9,
    1.0);
System.out.println(result);
```

The method returns a `double`, where 0 represents the best possible evaluation, meaning that the recommender perfectly matches user preferences. In general, the lower the value, the better the match.

Online learning engine

In any online platform, the new users will continue increasing. The previously discussed approach works well for the existing user. It is expensive to create a recommendation instance for every new user that's added. We cannot ignore the users that have been added to the system after the recommendation engine is made. To cope with situations that are similar to this, Apache Mahout has the ability of adding a temporary user to a data model. The general setup is as follows:

- Periodically recreate the whole recommendation using current data (for example, each day or hour, depending on how long it takes)
- Always check whether the user exists in the system before going for a recommendation

- If the user exists, then complete the recommendations
- If the user does not exist, create a temporary user, fill in the preferences, and do the recommendation

The first step seems to be tricky, in regards to how frequently the whole recommendation is to be generated using the current data. If the system is huge, memory constraints will be there, because when the new recommender is being generated, the old, working recommender should be held in memory, so the request is being served from the old copy until the new recommender is ready.

As for the temporary users, we can wrap our data model with a PlusAnonymousConcurrentUserDataModel instance. This class allows us to obtain a temporary user ID; the ID must later be released so that it can be reused (there's a limited number of such IDs). After obtaining the ID, we have to fill in the preferences, and then we can proceed with the recommendation, as always:

```
class OnlineRecommendation{

  Recommender recommender;
  int concurrentUsers = 100;
  int noItems = 10;

  public OnlineRecommendation() throws IOException {
    DataModel model = new StringItemIdFileDataModel(
      new File /chap6/BX-Book-Ratings.csv"), ";");
    PlusAnonymousConcurrentUserDataModel plusModel = new
        PlusAnonymousConcurrentUserDataModel
          (model, concurrentUsers);
    recommender = ...;
  }
  public List<RecommendedItem> recommend(long userId,
      PreferenceArray preferences){
    if(userExistsInDataModel(userId)){
      return recommender.recommend(userId, noItems);
    }
    else{
      PlusAnonymousConcurrentUserDataModel plusModel =
        (PlusAnonymousConcurrentUserDataModel)
          recommender.getDataModel();
      // Take an available anonymous user form the poll
      Long anonymousUserID = plusModel.takeAvailableUser();
      // Set temporary preferences
      PreferenceArray tempPrefs = preferences;
      tempPrefs.setUserID(0, anonymousUserID);
      tempPrefs.setItemID(0, itemID);
       plusModel.setTempPrefs(tempPrefs, anonymousUserID);
```

```
    List<RecommendedItem> results =
        recommender.recommend(anonymousUserID, noItems);
    // Release the user back to the poll
    plusModel.releaseUser(anonymousUserID);
    return results;


  }
 }
}
```

Content-based filtering

Content-based filtering is out of the scope of the Mahout framework, mainly because it is up to you to decide how to define similar items. If we want to do a content-based item similarity, we need to implement our own `ItemSimilarity`. For instance, in our book's dataset, we might want to make up the following rule for book similarity:

- If the genres are the same, add `0.15` to `similarity`
- If the author is the same, add `0.50` to `similarity`

We can now implement our own `similarity` measure, as follows:

```
class MyItemSimilarity implements ItemSimilarity {
 ...
 public double itemSimilarity(long itemID1, long itemID2) {
  MyBook book1 = lookupMyBook (itemID1);
  MyBook book2 = lookupMyBook (itemID2);
  double similarity = 0.0;
  if (book1.getGenre().equals(book2.getGenre())
   similarity += 0.15;
  }
  if (book1.getAuthor().equals(book2. getAuthor ())) {
   similarity += 0.50;
  }
  return similarity;
 }
 ...
}
```

We can then use this `ItemSimilarity`, instead of something like `LogLikelihoodSimilarity`, or other implementations with a `GenericItemBasedRecommender`. That's about it. This is as far as we have to go to perform content-based recommendations in the Mahout framework.

What we saw here is one of the simplest forms of content-based recommendation. Another approach would be to create a content-based profile of users, based on a weighted vector of item features. The weights denote the importance of each feature to the user, and can be computed from individually-rated content vectors.

Summary

In this chapter, you learned about the basic concept of recommendation engines, the differences between collaborative and content-based filtering, and how to use Apache Mahout, which is a great basis for creating recommenders, as it is very configurable and provides many extension points. We looked at how to pick the right configuration parameter values, set up rescoring, and evaluate the recommendation results.

With this chapter, we have completed our overview of the data science techniques that are used to analyze customer behavior, which started with customer relationship prediction in Chapter 4, *Customer Relationship Prediction with Ensembles*, and continued with affinity analytics in Chapter 5, *Affinity Analysis*. In the next chapter, we will move on to other topics, such as fraud and anomaly detection.

Fraud and Anomaly Detection

7

Outlier detection is used to identify exceptions, rare events, and other anomalous situations. Such anomalies may be needles in a haystack, but their consequences can nonetheless be quite dramatic; for instance, credit card fraud detection, identifying network intrusions, faults in manufacturing processes, clinical trials, voting activities, and criminal activities in e-commerce. Therefore, anomalies represent a high value when they are found and high costs if they are not. Applying machine learning to outlier detection problems can bring new insights and better detection of outlier events. Machine learning can take into account many disparate sources of data, and can find correlations that are too obscure for human analysis to identify.

Take the example of e-commerce fraud detection. With machine learning algorithms in place, the purchaser's online behavior, that is, website browsing history, becomes a part of the fraud detection algorithm, rather than simply the history of purchases made by the cardholder. This involves analyzing a variety of data sources, but it is also a far more robust approach to e-commerce fraud detection.

In this chapter, we will cover the following topics:

- Problems and challenges
- Suspicious pattern detection
- Anomalous pattern detection
- Working with unbalanced datasets
- Anomaly detection in time series

Suspicious and anomalous behavior detection

The problem of learning patterns from sensor data arises in many applications, including e-commerce, smart environments, video surveillance, network analysis, human-robot interaction, ambient assisted living, and so on. We focus on detecting patterns that deviate from regular behaviors and might represent a security risk, health problem, or any other abnormal behavior contingency.

In other words, deviant behavior is a data pattern that either does not conform to the expected behavior (anomalous behavior) or matches a previously defined unwanted behavior (suspicious behavior). Deviant behavior patterns are also referred to as outliers, exceptions, peculiarities, surprises, misuse, and so on. Such patterns occur relatively infrequently; however, when they do occur, their consequences can be quite dramatic, and often negatively so. Typical examples include credit card fraud, cyber intrusions, and industrial damage. In e-commerce, fraud is estimated to cost merchants more than $200 billion a year; in healthcare, fraud is estimated to cost taxpayers $60 billion a year; for banks, the cost is over $12 billion.

Unknown unknowns

When Donald Rumsfeld, US Secretary of Defense, had a news briefing on February 12, 2002, about the lack of evidence linking the government of Iraq to the supply of weapons of mass destruction to terrorist groups, it immediately became a subject of much commentary. Rumsfeld stated the following (*DoD News*, 2012):

> *"Reports that say that something hasn't happened are always interesting to me, because as we know, there are known knowns; there are things we know we know. We also know there are known unknowns; that is to say we know there are some things we do not know. But there are also unknown unknowns-the ones we don't know we don't know. And if one looks throughout the history of our country and other free countries, it is the latter category that tend to be the difficult ones."*

This statement might seem confusing at first, but the idea of unknown unknowns was well studied among scholars dealing with risk, NSA, and other intelligence agencies. What the statement basically implies is the following:

- **Known knowns**: These are well-known problems or issues; we know how to recognize them and how deal with them

- **Known unknowns**: These are expected or foreseeable problems, which can be reasonably anticipated, but have not occurred before
- **Unknown unknowns**: These are unexpected and unforeseeable problems, which pose significant risk, as they cannot be anticipated, based on previous experience

In the following sections, we will look into two fundamental approaches dealing with the first two types of knowns and unknowns: suspicious pattern detection dealing with known knowns, and anomalous pattern detection targeting known unknowns.

Suspicious pattern detection

The first approach involves a behavior library that encodes negative patterns, shown as red minus signs in the following diagram, and recognizes that observed behavior corresponds to identifying a match in the library. If a new pattern can be matched against negative patterns, then it is considered suspicious:

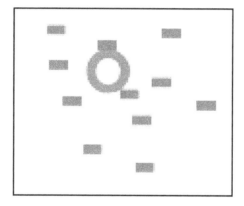

For example, when you visit a doctor, he/she inspects various health symptoms (body temperature, pain levels, affected areas, and so on) and matches the symptoms to a known disease. In machine learning terms, the doctor collects attributes and performs classifications.

An advantage of this approach is that we immediately know what is wrong; for example, assuming that we know the disease, we can select an appropriate treatment procedure.

A major disadvantage of this approach is that it can only detect suspicious patterns that are known in advance. If a pattern is not inserted into a negative pattern library, then we will not be able to recognize it. This approach is, therefore, appropriate for modeling known knowns.

Anomalous pattern detection

The second approach uses the pattern library in an inverse fashion, meaning that the library encodes only the positive patterns, which are marked with green plus signs in the following diagram. When an observed behavior (the blue circle) cannot be matched against the library, it is considered anomalous:

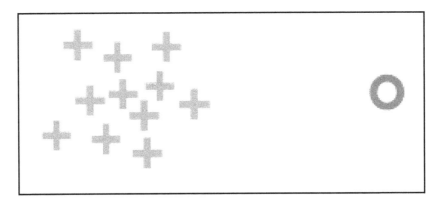

This approach requires us to model only what we have seen in the past, that is, normal patterns. If we return to the doctor example, the main reason that we visited the doctor in the first place was because we did not feel well. Our perceived state of feelings (for example, a headache and sore skin) did not match our usual feelings, and therefore, we decided to seek a doctor. We don't know which disease caused this state, nor do we know the treatment, but we were able to observe that it doesn't match the usual state.

A major advantage of this approach is that it does not require us to say anything about abnormal patterns; hence, it is appropriate for modeling known unknowns and unknown unknowns. On the other hand, it does not tell us exactly what is wrong.

Analysis types

Several approaches have been proposed to tackle this problem. We broadly classify anomalous and suspicious behavior detection in the following three categories: pattern analysis, transaction analysis, and plan recognition. In the following sections, we will quickly look at some real-life applications.

Pattern analysis

An active area of anomalous and suspicious behavior detection from patterns is based on visual modalities, such as a camera. Zhang, et al. (2007) proposed a system for a visual human motion analysis from a video sequence, which recognizes unusual behavior based on walking trajectories; Lin, et al. (2009) described a video surveillance system based on color features, distance features, and a count feature, where evolutionary techniques are used to measure observation similarity. The system tracks each person and classifies their behavior by analyzing their trajectory patterns. The system extracts a set of visual low-level features in different parts of the image, and performs a classification with SVMs in order to detect aggressive, cheerful, intoxicated, nervous, neutral, and tired behavior.

Transaction analysis

Transaction analysis assumes discrete states/transactions, in contrast to continuous observations. A major research area is **intrusion detection** (**ID**), which aims to detect attacks against information systems, in general. There are two types of ID systems, signature-based and anomaly-based, that broadly follow the suspicious and anomalous pattern detection that was described in the previous sections. A comprehensive review of ID approaches was published by Gyanchandani, et al. (2012).

Furthermore, applications in ambient assisted living that are based on wearable sensors also fit to transaction analysis as sensing is typically event-based. Lymberopoulos, et al. (2008) proposed a system for automatic extraction of the user's spatio-temporal patterns, encoded as sensor activation from the sensor network deployed inside their home. The proposed method, based on location, time, and duration, was able to extract frequent patterns using the Apriori algorithm and encode the most frequent patterns in the form of a Markov chain. Another area of related work includes the **hidden Markov models** (**HMMs**) that are widely used in traditional activity recognition for modeling a sequence of actions, but these topics are already out of the scope of this book.

Plan recognition

Plan recognition focuses on a mechanism for recognizing the unobservable state of an agent, given observations of its interaction with its environment (Avrahami-Zilberbrand, 2009). Most existing investigations assume discrete observations in the form of activities. To perform anomalous and suspicious behavior detection, plan recognition algorithms may use a hybrid approach. A symbolic plan recognizer is used to filter consistent hypotheses and passes them to an evaluation engine, which focuses on ranking.

These were advanced approaches that were applied to various real-life scenarios, targeted at discovering anomalies. In the following sections, we'll dive into more basic approaches for suspicious and anomalous pattern detection.

Outlier detection using ELKI

ELKI stands for **Environment for Loping KDD applications Index** structures, where **KDD** stands for **Knowledge Discovery in Database**. It is an open source software used mainly for data mining, with an emphasis on unsupervised learning. It supports various algorithms for cluster analysis and outlier detection. The following are some outlier algorithms:

- **Distance-based outlier detection**: This is used to specify two parameters. The object is flagged **outlier** if its fraction, p, for all the data objects that have a distance above d from c. There are many algorithms, such as `DBOutlierDetection`, `DBOutlierScore`, `KNNOutlier`, `KNNWeightOutlier`, `ParallelKNNOutlier`, `ParallelKNNWeightOutlier`, `ReferenceBasedOutlierDetection`, and so on.

- **LOF family methods**: This computes density-based local outlier factors on specific parameters. It includes algorithms such as `LOF`, `ParallelLOF`, `ALOCI`, `COF`, `LDF`, `LDOF`, and so on.

- **Angle-based outlier detection**: This uses the variance analysis of angles, using mostly high-dimensional datasets. Common algorithms include `ABOD`, `FastABOD`, and `LBABOD`.

- **Clustering-based outlier detection**: This uses EM clustering; if the object does not belong to a cluster, it is taken as an outlier. This includes algorithms such as `EMOutlier` and `KMeansOutlierDetection`.

- **Subspace outlier detection**: This uses the outlier detection method for axis-parallel subspaces. It has algorithms such as `SOD`, `OutRankS1`, `OUTRES`, `AggrawalYuNaive`, and `AggrawalYuEvolutionary`.

- **Spatial outlier detection**: This has large datasets based on locations which are collected from different sources and the data point that is an extreme relative to neighbors. It has algorithms such as `CTLuGLSBackwardSearchAlgorithm`, `CTLuMeanMultipleAttributes`, `CTLuMedianAlgorithm`, `CTLuScatterplotOutlier`, and so on.

An example using ELKI

In Chapter 3, *Basic Algorithms – Classification, Regression, and Clustering*, you already saw how to get the required .jar file for ELKI. We will follow a similar process, as follows:

Open Command Prompt or Terminal, and execute the following command:

```
java -jar elki-bundle-0.7.1.jar
```

This will provide the GUI interface, as shown in the following screenshot:

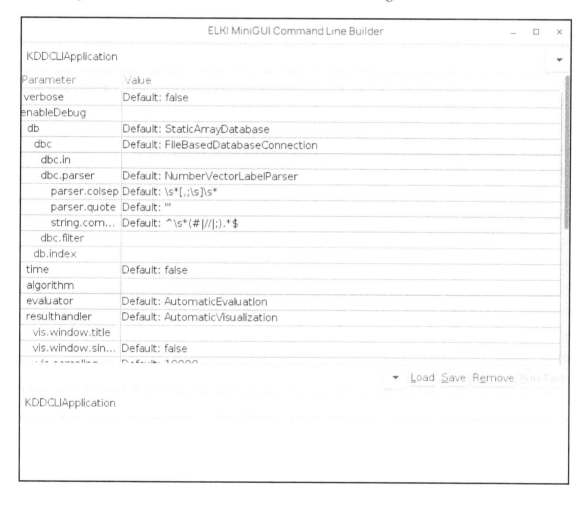

In the GUI, the **dbc.in** and **algorithm** parameters are highlighted and need to be set. We will use `pov.csv` file, as **dbc.in**. This CSV file can be downloaded from `https://github.com/elki-project/elki/blob/master/data/synthetic/ABC-publication/pov.csv`.

For the **algorithm**, select **outlier.clustering.EMOutlier**, and in **em.k**, pass 3 as the value. The following screenshot shows all of the filled-in options:

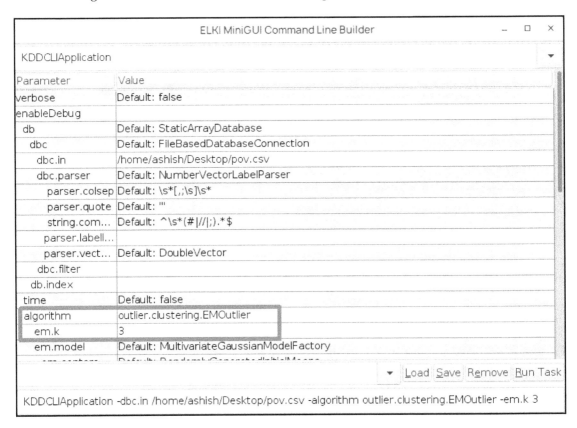

Click on the **Run Task** button, and it will process and generate the following output:

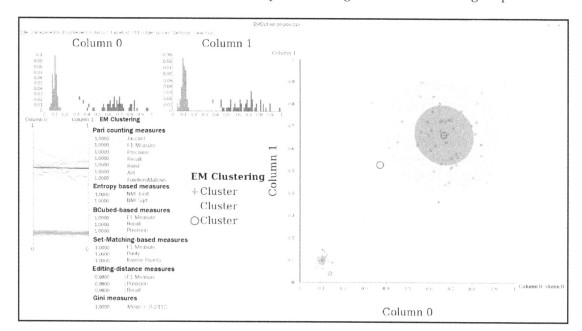

This shows clustering and the possible outliers.

Fraud detection in insurance claims

First, we'll take a look at suspicious behavior detection, where the goal is to learn about patterns of fraud, which corresponds to modeling known knowns.

Dataset

We'll work with a dataset describing insurance transactions, which is publicly available in the Oracle database online documentation at http://docs.oracle.com/cd/B28359_01/ datamine.111/b28129/anomalies.htm.

The dataset describes insurance claims on vehicle incidents for an undisclosed insurance company. It contains 15,430 claims; each claim is comprised of 33 attributes, describing the following components:

- Customer demographic details (**Age**, **Sex**, **MartialStatus**, and so on)
- Purchased policy (**PolicyType**, **VehicleCategory**, number of supplements, agent type, and so on)
- Claim circumstances (day/month/week claimed, policy report filed, witness present, past days between incident-policy report, incident claim, and so on)
- Other customer data (number of cars, previous claims, **DriverRating**, and so on)
- Fraud found (yes or no)

The sample of the database shown in the following screenshot depicts the data that's been loaded into Weka:

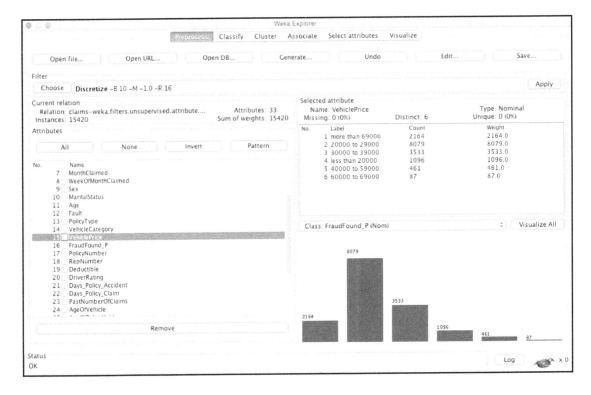

Now, the task is to create a model that will be able to identify suspicious claims in the future. The challenging thing about this task is the fact that only 6% of the claims are suspicious. If we create a dummy classifier saying that no claim is suspicious, it will be accurate in 94% of cases. Therefore, in this task, we will use different accuracy measures: precision and recall.

Let's recall the outcome table from `Chapter 1`, *Applied Machine Learning Quick Start*, where there are four possible outcomes, denoted as true positive, false positive, false negative, and true negative:

		Classified as	
		Fraud	No fraud
Actual	Fraud	TP - true positive	FN - false negative
	No fraud	FP - false positive	TN - true negative

Precision and recall are defined as follows:

- **Precision** is equal to the proportion of correctly raised alarms, as follows:

$$Pr = \frac{TP}{TP + FP}$$

- **Recall** is equal to the proportion of deviant signatures, which are correctly identified as follows:

$$Re = \frac{TP}{TP + FN}$$

- With these measures–our dummy classifier scores–we find that $Pr = 0$ and $Re = 0$, as it never marks any instance as fraud ($TP = 0$). In practice, we want to compare classifiers by both numbers; hence, we use F - *measure*. This is a de facto measure that calculates a harmonic mean between the precision and recall, as follows:

$$F - measure = \frac{2 * Pr * Re}{Pr + Re}$$

Now, let's move on to designing a real classifier.

Modeling suspicious patterns

To design a classifier, we can follow the standard supervised learning steps, as described in `Chapter 1`, *Applied Machine Learning Quick Start*. In this recipe, we will include some additional steps to handle unbalanced datasets and evaluate classifiers based on precision and recall. The plan is as follows:

1. Load the data in the `.csv` format.
2. Assign the class attribute.
3. Convert all of the attributes from a numeric to nominal value to make sure that there are no incorrectly loaded numerical values.
4. **Experiment 1**: Evaluating the models with k-fold cross-validation.
5. **Experiment 2**: Rebalancing the dataset to a more balanced class distribution, and manually perform cross-validation.
6. Compare the classifiers by recall, precision, and f-measure.

First, let's load the data using the `CSVLoader` class, as follows:

```
String filePath = "/Users/bostjan/Dropbox/ML Java
Book/book/datasets/chap07/claims.csv";

CSVLoader loader = new CSVLoader();
loader.setFieldSeparator(",");
loader.setSource(new File(filePath));
Instances data = loader.getDataSet();
```

Next, we need to make sure that all of the attributes are nominal. During the data import, Weka applies some heuristics to guess the most probable attribute type, that is, numeric, nominal, string, or date. As heuristics cannot always guess the correct type, we can set the types manually, as follows:

```
NumericToNominal toNominal = new NumericToNominal();
toNominal.setInputFormat(data);
data = Filter.useFilter(data, toNominal);
```

Before we continue, we need to specify the attribute that we will try to predict. We can achieve this by calling the `setClassIndex(int)` function:

```
int CLASS_INDEX = 15;
data.setClassIndex(CLASS_INDEX);
```

Next, we need to remove an attribute describing the policy number, as it has no predictive value. We simply apply the `Remove` filter, as follows:

```
Remove remove = new Remove();
remove.setInputFormat(data);
remove.setOptions(new String[]{"-R", ""+POLICY_INDEX});
data = Filter.useFilter(data, remove);
```

Now, we are ready to start modeling.

The vanilla approach

The vanilla approach is to directly apply the lesson, just like as it was demonstrated in `Chapter 3`, *Basic Algorithms - Classification, Regression, Clustering*, without any preprocessing, and not taking dataset specifics into account. To demonstrate the drawbacks of the vanilla approach, we will simply build a model with the default parameters and apply k-fold cross-validation.

First, let's define some classifiers that we want to test, as follows:

```
ArrayList<Classifier>models = new ArrayList<Classifier>();
models.add(new J48());
models.add(new RandomForest());
models.add(new NaiveBayes());
models.add(new AdaBoostM1());
models.add(new Logistic());
```

Next, we need to create an `Evaluation` object and perform k-fold cross-validation by calling the `crossValidate(Classifier, Instances, int, Random, String[])` method, providing the `precision`, `recall`, and `fMeasure` as output:

```
int FOLDS = 3;
Evaluation eval = new Evaluation(data);

for(Classifier model : models){
  eval.crossValidateModel(model, data, FOLDS,
  new Random(1), new String[] {});
  System.out.println(model.getClass().getName() + "\n"+
    "\tRecall:    "+eval.recall(FRAUD) + "\n"+
    "\tPrecision: "+eval.precision(FRAUD) + "\n"+
    "\tF-measure: "+eval.fMeasure(FRAUD));
}
```

The evaluation provides the following scores as output:

```
weka.classifiers.trees.J48
   Recall:    0.03358613217768147
   Precision: 0.9117647058823529
   F-measure: 0.06478578892371996
...
weka.classifiers.functions.Logistic
   Recall:    0.037486457204767065
   Precision: 0.2521865889212828
   F-measure: 0.06527070364082249
```

We can see that the results are not very promising. The recall, that is, the share of discovered frauds among all frauds, is only 1-3%, meaning that only 1-3/100 frauds are detected. On the other hand, the precision, that is, the accuracy of alarms, is 91%, meaning that in 9/10 cases, when a claim is marked as fraud, the model is correct.

Dataset rebalancing

As the number of negative examples, that is, instances of fraud, is very small compared to positive examples, the learning algorithms struggle with induction. We can help them by giving them a dataset where the share of positive and negative examples is comparable. This can be achieved with dataset rebalancing.

Weka has a built-in filter, `Resample`, which produces a random subsample of a dataset, using sampling either with replacement or without replacement. The filter can also bias the distribution toward a uniform class distribution.

We will proceed by manually implementing k-fold cross-validation. First, we will split the dataset into *k* equal folds. Fold *k* will be used for testing, while the other folds will be used for learning. To split the dataset into folds, we'll use the `StratifiedRemoveFolds` filter, which maintains the class distribution within the folds, as follows:

```
StratifiedRemoveFolds kFold = new StratifiedRemoveFolds();
kFold.setInputFormat(data);

double measures[][] = new double[models.size()][3];

for(int k = 1; k <= FOLDS; k++){

  // Split data to test and train folds
  kFold.setOptions(new String[]{
    "-N", ""+FOLDS, "-F", ""+k, "-S", "1"});
  Instances test = Filter.useFilter(data, kFold);
  kFold.setOptions(new String[]{
```

```
   "-N", ""+FOLDS, "-F", ""+k, "-S", "1", "-V"});
   // select inverse "-V"
 Instances train = Filter.useFilter(data, kFold);
```

Next, we can rebalance the training dataset, where the -Z parameter specifies the percentage of the dataset to be resampled, and -B biases the class distribution toward uniform distribution:

```
Resample resample = new Resample();
resample.setInputFormat(data);
resample.setOptions(new String[]{"-Z", "100", "-B", "1"}); //with
   replacement
Instances balancedTrain = Filter.useFilter(train, resample);
```

Next, we can build classifiers and perform evaluation:

```
for(ListIterator<Classifier>it = models.listIterator();
   it.hasNext();){
 Classifier model = it.next();
 model.buildClassifier(balancedTrain);
 eval = new Evaluation(balancedTrain);
 eval.evaluateModel(model, test);
// save results for average
 measures[it.previousIndex()][0] += eval.recall(FRAUD);
 measures[it.previousIndex()][1] += eval.precision(FRAUD);
 measures[it.previousIndex()][2] += eval.fMeasure(FRAUD);
}
```

Finally, we calculate the average and provide the best model as output using the following lines of code:

```
// calculate average
for(int i = 0; i < models.size(); i++){
 measures[i][0] /= 1.0 * FOLDS;
 measures[i][1] /= 1.0 * FOLDS;
 measures[i][2] /= 1.0 * FOLDS;
}

// output results and select best model
Classifier bestModel = null; double bestScore = -1;
for(ListIterator<Classifier> it = models.listIterator();
   it.hasNext();){
 Classifier model = it.next();
 double fMeasure = measures[it.previousIndex()][2];
 System.out.println(
   model.getClass().getName() + "\n"+
   "\tRecall:    "+measures[it.previousIndex()][0] + "\n"+
   "\tPrecision: "+measures[it.previousIndex()][1] + "\n"+
```

```
        "\tF-measure: "+fMeasure);
    if(fMeasure > bestScore){
      bestScore = fMeasure;
      bestModel = model;
    }
  }
  System.out.println("Best model:"+bestModel.getClass().getName());
```

Now, the performance of the models has significantly improved, as follows:

```
weka.classifiers.trees.J48
  Recall:    0.44204845100610574
  Precision: 0.14570766048577555
  F-measure: 0.21912423640160392
...
weka.classifiers.functions.Logistic
  Recall:    0.7670657247204478
  Precision: 0.13507459756495374
  F-measure: 0.22969038530557626
Best model: weka.classifiers.functions.Logistic
```

We can see that all of the models have scored significantly better; for instance, the best model, logistic regression, correctly discovers 76% of the fraud, while producing a reasonable amount of false alarms–only 13% of the claims marked as fraud are indeed fraudulent. If an undetected fraud is significantly more expensive than the investigation of false alarms, then it makes sense to deal with an increased number of false alarms.

The overall performance most likely still has some room for improvement; we could perform attribute selection and feature generation and apply more complex model learning, which we discussed in Chapter 3, *Basic Algorithms – Classification, Regression, Clustering*.

Anomaly detection in website traffic

In the second example, we'll focus on modeling the opposite of the previous example. Instead of discussing what typical fraudless cases are, we'll discuss the normal expected behavior of the system. If something cannot be matched against our expected model, it will be considered anomalous.

Dataset

We'll work with a publicly available dataset that was released by Yahoo! Labs, which is useful for discussing how to detect anomalies in time series data. For Yahoo, the main use case is in detecting unusual traffic on Yahoo servers.

Even though Yahoo has announced that their data is publicly available, you have to apply to use it, and it takes about 24 hours before the approval is granted. The dataset is available at `http://webscope.sandbox.yahoo.com/catalog.php?datatype=sdid=70`.

The dataset is comprised of real traffic for Yahoo services, along with some synthetic data. In total, the dataset contains 367 time series, each of which contains between 741 and 1,680 observations, which have been recorded at regular intervals. Each series is written in its own file, one observation per line. A series is accompanied by a second column indicator, with a one being used if the observation was an anomaly, and zero otherwise. The anomalies in real data were determined by human judgment, while those in the synthetic data were generated algorithmically. A snippet of the synthetic times series data is shown in the following table:

timestamp	value	anomaly	change point	trend	noise	12 hour seasonality	daily seasonality	weekly seasonality
1422237600	4333 43	0	0	4599	1.81	-190.95	-128.86	52.44
1422241200	4316 14	0	0	4602	-14.65	-220.5	-105.21	54.51
1422244800	4403 20	0	0	4605	7.04	-190.95	-74.39	56.51
1422248400	4531 20	0	0	4608	13.52	-110.25	-38.51	58.43
1422252000	4967 50	1	0	4911	-3.77	-6.91	-2.33	60.27

Snippet of the synthetic time-series data

In the following section, you'll learn how to transform time series data into an attribute presentation that allows us to apply machine learning algorithms.

Anomaly detection in time series data

Detecting anomalies in raw, streaming time series data requires some data transformation. The most obvious way to do this is to select a time window and sample a time series with a fixed length. In the next step, we want to compare a new time series to our previously collected set to detect whether something is out of the ordinary.

The comparison can be done with various techniques, as follows:

- Forecasting the most probable following value, as well as the confidence intervals (for example, Holt-Winters exponential smoothing). If a new value is out of the forecasted confidence interval, it is considered anomalous.
- Cross-correlation compares a new sample to a library of positive samples, and it looks for an exact match. If the match is not found, it is marked as anomalous.
- Dynamic time wrapping is similar to cross-correlation, but allows for signal distortion in comparison.
- Discretizing signals to bands, where each band corresponds to a letter. For example, A=[min, mean/3], B=[mean/3, mean*2/3], and C=[mean*2/3, max] transforms the signal into a sequence of letters, such as aAABAACAABBA.... This approach reduces the storage and allows us to apply the text mining algorithms that we will discuss in Chapter 10, *Text Mining with Mallet – Topic Modeling and Spam Detection*.
- A distribution-based approach estimates the distribution of values in a specific time window. When we observe a new sample, we can compare whether the distribution matches the previously observed one.

This list is by no means exhaustive. Different approaches are focused on detecting different anomalies (for example, in the value, frequency, and distribution). We will focus on a version of distribution-based approaches in this chapter.

Using Encog for time series

We have to download the time series data from https://solarscience.msfc.nasa.gov/greenwch/spot_num.txt and save the file in the data folder. In the .java file, we will specify the file path, and then we will indicate the format of the file using the following code block:

```
File filename = new File("data/spot_num.txt");
CSVFormat format = new CSVFormat('.', ' ');
VersatileDataSource source = new CSVDataSource(filename, true, format);
VersatileMLDataSet data = new VersatileMLDataSet(source);
```

```
data.getNormHelper().setFormat(format);
ColumnDefinition columnSSN = data.defineSourceColumn("SSN",
ColumnType.continuous);
ColumnDefinition columnDEV = data.defineSourceColumn("DEV",
ColumnType.continuous);
data.analyze();
data.defineInput(columnSSN);
data.defineInput(columnDEV);
data.defineOutput(columnSSN);
```

Now, we will create the feedforward network with the window size 1. When processing a time series, you should keep in mind that it should never be shuffled. We will hold some data back for validation. We will use the following lines of code to do so:

```
EncogModel model = new EncogModel(data);
model.selectMethod(data, MLMethodFactory.TYPE_FEEDFORWARD);

model.setReport(new ConsoleStatusReportable());
data.normalize();

// Set time series.
data.setLeadWindowSize(1);
data.setLagWindowSize(WINDOW_SIZE);
model.holdBackValidation(0.3, false, 1001);
model.selectTrainingType(data);
```

The next step is to run the training with five-fold cross-validation using the following line:

```
MLRegression bestMethod = (MLRegression) model.crossvalidate(5, false);
```

Now, it's time to display the error and the final model. We will do that by using the following lines of code:

```
System.out.println("Training error: " + model.calculateError(bestMethod,
model.getTrainingDataset()));
System.out.println("Validation error: " + model.calculateError(bestMethod,
model.getValidationDataset()));

NormalizationHelper helper = data.getNormHelper();
System.out.println(helper.toString());

// Display the final model.
System.out.println("Final model: " + bestMethod);
```

The output will be similar to the following screenshot:

```
5/5 : Fold #5/5: Iteration #11841, Training Error: 0.00967311, Validation Error: 0.00971101
5/5 : Fold #5/5: Iteration #11842, Training Error: 0.00967347, Validation Error: 0.00971101
5/5 : Fold #5/5: Iteration #11843, Training Error: 0.00967307, Validation Error: 0.00971101
5/5 : Fold #5/5: Iteration #11844, Training Error: 0.00967294, Validation Error: 0.00971101
5/5 : Fold #5/5: Iteration #11845, Training Error: 0.00967279, Validation Error: 0.00971049
5/5 : Cross-validated score:0.014463167741665992
Training error: 0.12863579930769156
Validation error: 0.15095164741019176
[NormalizationHelper:
[ColumnDefinition:SSN(continuous);low=0.000000,high=253.800000,mean=52.093210,sd=44.040046]
[ColumnDefinition:DEV(continuous);low=0.000000,high=90.200000,mean=20.235013,sd=11.781834]
]
Final model: [BasicNetwork: Layers=3]
```

Now, we will test the model using the following code block:

```
while (csv.next() && stopAfter > 0) {
            StringBuilder result = new StringBuilder();

            line[0] = csv.get(2);// ssn
            line[1] = csv.get(3);// dev
            helper.normalizeInputVector(line, slice, false);

            if (window.isReady()) {
                window.copyWindow(input.getData(), 0);
                String correct = csv.get(2); // trying to predict SSN.
                MLData output = bestMethod.compute(input);
                String predicted = helper
                        .denormalizeOutputVectorToString(output)[0];

                result.append(Arrays.toString(line));
                result.append(" -> predicted: ");
                result.append(predicted);
                result.append("(correct: ");
                result.append(correct);
                result.append(")");

                System.out.println(result.toString());
            }

            window.add(slice);

            stopAfter--;
        }
```

The output will be similar to the following screenshot:

```
[85.0, 29.4] -> predicted: 58.32680191027322(correct: 85.0)
[83.5, 29.2] -> predicted: 62.63878508917436(correct: 83.5)
[94.8, 31.1] -> predicted: 69.58458712648326(correct: 94.8)
[66.3, 25.9] -> predicted: 56.15965608742752(correct: 66.3)
[75.9, 27.7] -> predicted: 84.0381501021095(correct: 75.9)
[75.5, 27.7] -> predicted: 82.55787155337393(correct: 75.5)
[158.6, 40.6] -> predicted: 93.87915314626278(correct: 158.6)
[85.2, 29.5] -> predicted: 66.10388017119621(correct: 85.2)
[73.3, 27.3] -> predicted: 75.19251547637754(correct: 73.3)
[75.9, 27.7] -> predicted: 74.80676780610727(correct: 75.9)
[89.2, 30.2] -> predicted: 160.14047862155184(correct: 89.2)
[88.3, 30.0] -> predicted: 84.23268317719584(correct: 88.3)
[90.0, 30.3] -> predicted: 72.70794834119994(correct: 90.0)
[100.0, 32.0] -> predicted: 75.19251547637754(correct: 100.0)
[85.4, 29.5] -> predicted: 88.21265297605454(correct: 85.4)
[103.0, 32.5] -> predicted: 87.31444771405583(correct: 103.0)
[91.2, 30.5] -> predicted: 89.01715854470413(correct: 91.2)
[65.7, 25.7] -> predicted: 99.22600549397221(correct: 65.7)
[63.3, 25.3] -> predicted: 84.43202049932576(correct: 63.3)
[75.4, 27.7] -> predicted: 102.3461160759432(correct: 75.4)
[70.0, 26.6] -> predicted: 90.2255277919527(correct: 70.0)
[43.5, 20.8] -> predicted: 65.54270217716528(correct: 43.5)
[45.3, 21.2] -> predicted: 63.293436645584066(correct: 45.3)
[56.4, 23.8] -> predicted: 74.71041358906953(correct: 56.4)
[60.7, 24.7] -> predicted: 69.58458712648326(correct: 60.7)
[50.7, 22.5] -> predicted: 44.31057240802326(correct: 50.7)
```

Histogram-based anomaly detection

In histogram-based anomaly detection, we split the signals by a selected time window, as shown in the following diagram.

For each window, we calculate the histogram; that is, for a selected number of buckets, we count how many values fall into each bucket. The histogram captures the basic distribution of values in a selected time window, as shown in the center of the diagram.

Histograms can then be directly presented as instances, where each bin corresponds to an attribute. Furthermore, we can reduce the number of attributes by applying a dimensionality-reduction technique, such as **Principal Component Analysis (PCA)**, which allows us to visualize the reduced-dimension histograms in a plot, as shown at the bottom-right of the diagram, where each dot corresponds to a histogram.

In our example, the idea is to observe website traffic for a couple of days, and then create histograms; for example, four-hour time windows, to build a library of positive behavior. If a new time window histogram cannot be matched against a positive library, we can mark it as an anomaly:

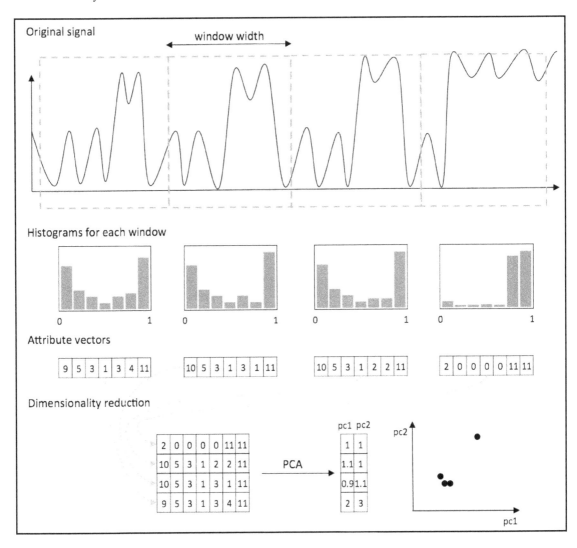

For comparing a new histogram to a set of existing histograms, we will use a density-based k-nearest neighbor algorithm, **Local Outlier Factor** (**LOF**) (Breunig, et al., 2000). The algorithm is able to handle clusters with different densities, as shown in the following diagram. For example, the upper-right cluster is large and widespread, compared to the bottom-left cluster, which is smaller and denser:

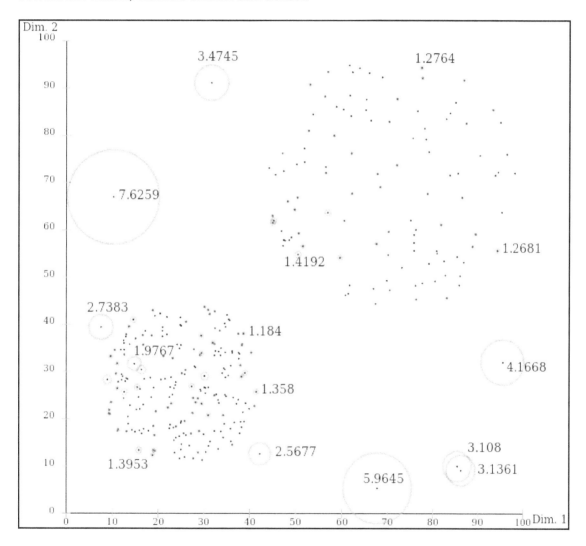

Let's get started!

Loading the data

In the first step, we'll need to load the data from text files to a Java object. The files are stored in a folder, and each file contains one time series, with values per line. We'll load them into a `Double` list, as follows:

```
String filePath = "chap07/ydata/A1Benchmark/real";
List<List<Double>> rawData = new ArrayList<List<Double>>();
```

We will need the `min` and `max` value for histogram normalization; so, let's collect them in this data pass:

```
double max = Double.MIN_VALUE;
double min = Double.MAX_VALUE;

for(int i = 1; i<= 67; i++){
  List<Double> sample = new ArrayList<Double>();
  BufferedReader reader = new BufferedReader(new
     FileReader(filePath+i+".csv"));
  boolean isAnomaly = false;
  reader.readLine();
  while(reader.ready()){
    String line[] = reader.readLine().split(",");
    double value = Double.parseDouble(line[1]);
    sample.add(value);
    max = Math.max(max, value);
    min = Double.min(min, value);
    if(line[2] == "1")
      isAnomaly = true;
  }
  System.out.println(isAnomaly);
  reader.close();
  rawData.add(sample);
}
```

The data has been loaded. Next, let's move on to histograms.

Creating histograms

We will create a histogram for a selected time window with the `WIN_SIZE` width.

The histogram will hold the `HIST_BINS` value buckets. The histograms consisting of lists of doubles will be stored in an array list:

```
int WIN_SIZE = 500;
int HIST_BINS = 20;
```

```
int current = 0;

List<double[]> dataHist = new ArrayList<double[]>();
for(List<Double> sample : rawData){
  double[] histogram = new double[HIST_BINS];
  for(double value : sample){
    int bin = toBin(normalize(value, min, max), HIST_BINS);
    histogram[bin]++;
    current++;
    if(current == WIN_SIZE){
      current = 0;
      dataHist.add(histogram);
      histogram = new double[HIST_BINS];
    }
  }
  dataHist.add(histogram);
}
```

The histograms are now completed. The last step is to transform them into Weka's `Instance` objects. Each histogram value will correspond to one Weka attribute, as follows:

```
ArrayList<Attribute> attributes = new ArrayList<Attribute>();
for(int i = 0; i<HIST_BINS; i++){
  attributes.add(new Attribute("Hist-"+i));
}
Instances dataset = new Instances("My dataset", attributes,
    dataHist.size());
for(double[] histogram: dataHist){
  dataset.add(new Instance(1.0, histogram));
}
```

The dataset has been now loaded, and is ready to be plugged into an anomaly detection algorithm.

Density-based k-nearest neighbors

To demonstrate how LOF calculates scores, we'll first split the dataset into training and testing sets by using the `testCV(int, int)` function. The first parameter specifies the number of folds, while the second parameter specifies which fold to return:

```
// split data to train and test
Instances trainData = dataset.testCV(2, 0);
Instances testData = dataset.testCV(2, 1);
```

The LOF algorithm is not a part of the default Weka distribution, but it can be downloaded through Weka's package manager at `http://weka.sourceforge.net/packageMetaData/localOutlierFactor/index.html`.

The LOF algorithm has two implemented interfaces: as an unsupervised filter that calculates LOF values (known unknowns), and as a supervised k-nearest neighbors classifier (known knowns). In our case, we want to calculate the outlierness factor, and therefore, we'll use the unsupervised filter interface:

```
import weka.filters.unsupervised.attribute.LOF;
```

The filter is initialized in the same way as a usual filter. We can specify k number of neighbors (for example, k=3) with the -min and -max parameters. LOF allows us to specify two different k parameters, which are used internally as the upper and lower bound, to find the minimum or maximum number of lof values:

```
LOF lof = new LOF();
lof.setInputFormat(trainData);
lof.setOptions(new String[]{"-min", "3", "-max", "3"});
```

Next, we load the training instances into the filter that will serve as a positive example library. After we complete the loading, we will call the `batchFinished()` method to initialize the internal calculations:

```
for(Instance inst : trainData){
    lof.input(inst);
}
lof.batchFinished();
```

Finally, we can apply the filter to the test data. The `Filter()` function will process the instances and append an additional attribute at the end, containing the LOF score. We can simply provide the score as output in the console:

```
Instances testDataLofScore = Filter.useFilter(testData, lof);

for(Instance inst : testDataLofScore){
    System.out.println(inst.value(inst.numAttributes()-1));
}
```

The LOF score of the first couple of test instances is as follows:

```
1.306740014927325
1.318239332210458
1.0294812291949587
1.1715039094530768
```

To understand the `LOF` values, we need some background on the LOF algorithm. It compares the density of an instance to the density of its nearest neighbors. The two scores are divided, producing the LOF score. An LOF score of around 1 indicates that the density is approximately equal, while higher LOF values indicate that the density of the instance is substantially lower than the density of its neighbors. In such cases, the instance can be marked as anomalous.

Summary

In this chapter, we looked into detecting anomalous and suspicious patterns. We discussed the two fundamental approaches, focusing on library encoding, either positive or negative patterns. Next, we got our hands on two real-life datasets, and we discussed how to deal with unbalanced class distributions and how to perform anomaly detection on time series data.

In the next chapter, we'll dive deeper into patterns and more advanced approaches to building pattern-based classifiers, and discuss how to assign labels to images using deep learning automatically.

8
Image Recognition with Deeplearning4j

Images have become ubiquitous in web services, social networks, and web stores. In contrast to humans, computers have great difficulty in understanding what is in the image and what it represents. In this chapter, we'll first look at the challenges behind teaching computers how to understand images, and then focus on an approach based on deep learning. We'll look at a high-level theory thats required to configure a deep learning model and discuss how to implement a model that is able to classify images using a Java library, Deeplearning4j.

This chapter will cover the following topics:

- Introducing image recognition
- Discussing deep learning fundamentals
- Building an image recognition model

Introducing image recognition

A typical goal of image recognition is to detect and identify an object in a digital image. Image recognition is applied in factory automation to monitor product quality; surveillance systems to identify potentially risky activities, such as moving persons or vehicles; security applications to provide biometric identification through fingerprints, iris, or facial features; autonomous vehicles to reconstruct conditions on the road and environment; and so on.

Digital images are not presented in a structured way with attribute-based descriptions; instead, they are encoded as the amount of color in different channels, for instance, black-white and red-green-blue channels. The learning goal is to identify patterns that are associated with a particular object. The traditional approach for image recognition consists of transforming an image into different forms, for instance, to identify object corners, edges, same-color blobs, and basic shapes. Such patterns are then used to train a learner to distinguish between objects. Some notable examples of traditional algorithms are listed here:

- Edge detection finds boundaries of objects within an image
- Corner detection identifies intersections of two edges or other interesting points, such as line endings, curvature maxima or minima, and so on
- Blob detection identifies regions that differ in a property, such as brightness or color, compared to its surrounding regions
- Ridge detection identifies additional interesting points in the image using smooth functions
- **Scale invariant feature transform** (**SIFT**) is a robust algorithm that can match objects, even if their scale or orientation differs from the representative samples in the database
- Hough transform identifies particular patterns in the image

A more recent approach is based on deep learning. Deep learning is a form of neural network, which mimics how the brain processes information. The main advantage of deep learning is that it's possible to design neural networks that can automatically extract relevant patterns, which in turn can be used to train a learner. With recent advances in neural networks, image recognition accuracy has significantly boosted. For instance, the **ImageNet** challenge, where competitors are provided more than 1.2 million images from 1,000 different object categories, reports that the error rate of the best algorithm was reduced from 28% in 2010, using **support vector machines** (**SVM**), to only 7% in 2014, using a deep neural network.

In this chapter, we'll take a quick look at neural networks, starting from the basic building block, the perceptron, and gradually introducing more complex structures.

Neural networks

The first neural networks, which were introduced in the sixties, were inspired by biological neural networks. The idea of a neural network is to map the biological nervous system, that is, how the brain processes information. It consists of layers with interconnected neurons working together. In computer terms, they are also known as an **artificial neural network** (**ANN**). With computers, it requires training to make this model learn, the same as a human brain. A neuron in the brain gets activated on receiving a signal from nearby interconnected neurons, and the same applies to an ANN. Recent advances in neural networks has proved that deep neural networks fit very well in pattern recognition tasks, as they are able to automatically extract interesting features and learn the underlying presentation. In this section, we'll refresh ourselves on the fundamental structures and components, from a single perceptron to deep networks.

Perceptron

A perceptron is a basic neural network building block and one of the earliest supervised algorithms. It is defined as a sum of features, which is multiplied by the corresponding weights and a bias. When the input signals is received, it multiplies with the assigned weights. These weights are defined for each incoming signal or input, and the weight gets adjusted continuously during the learning phase. The adjustment of weight depends on the error of the last result. After multiplying with the respective weights, all of the inputs are summed up with some offset value called **bias**. The value of the bias is also adjusted by the weights. So, it starts with random weights and bias, and with each iteration, the weights and bias are adjusted so that the next result moves toward the desired output. At the end, the final result is turned into an output signal. The function that sums all of this together is called the **sum transfer function,** and it is fed into an activation function. If the binary step activation function reaches a threshold, the output is 1, otherwise it is 0, which gives us a binary classifier. A schematic illustration is shown in the following diagram:

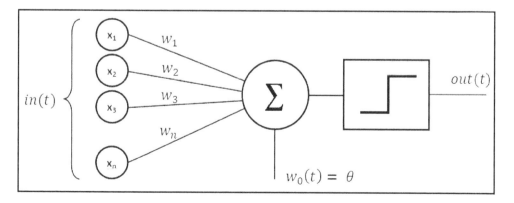

Training perceptrons involves a fairly simple learning algorithm that calculates the errors between the calculated output values and correct training output values, and uses this to create an adjustment to the weights, thus implementing a form of gradient descent. This algorithm is usually called the **delta rule**.

A single-layer perceptron is not very advanced, and nonlinearly separable functions, such as XOR, cannot be modeled using it. To address this issue, a structure with multiple perceptrons was introduced, called the **multilayer perceptron**, also known as the **feedforward neural network**.

Feedforward neural networks

A feedforward neural network is an ANN that consists of several perceptrons, which are organized into layers, as shown in the following diagram: input layer, output layer, and one or more hidden layers. The hidden layers have nothing to do with the outside world, hence the name. Each layer perceptron, also known as a neuron, has direct connections to the perceptrons in the next layer, whereas connections between two neurons carry a weight thats similar to the perceptron weights. So, all the perceptrons in one layer are connected with the perceptrons in the next layer, and the information is fed forward to the next layer. This diagram shows a network with a four-unit **Input layer**, corresponding to the size of the feature vector of length 4, a four-unit **Hidden layer**, and a two-unit **Output layer**, where each unit corresponds to one class value:

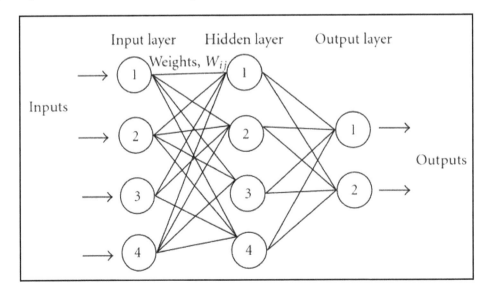

A feedforward neural network learns by finding the relationship between input and output values, which are fed into the network multiple times. The most popular approach to training multilayer networks is backpropagation. In backpropagation, the calculated output values are compared with the correct values in the same way as in the delta rule. The error is then fed back through the network by various techniques, adjusting the weights of each connection in order to reduce the value of the error. The error is calculated using the squared difference between the output value of the network and the original output value. The error indicates how far we are from the original output values. This process is repeated for a sufficiently large number of training cycles, until the error is under a certain threshold.

A feedforward neural network can have more than one hidden layer, where each additional hidden layer builds a new abstraction atop the preceding layers. This often leads to more accurate models; however, increasing the number of hidden layers leads to two known issues:

- **Vanishing gradients problem**: With more hidden layers, the training with backpropagation becomes less and less useful for passing information to the front layers, causing these layers to train very slowly
- **Overfitting**: The model fits the training data too well and performs poorly on real examples

Let's look at some other networks structures that address these issues.

Autoencoder

An autoencoder is a feedforward neural network that aims to learn how to compress the original dataset. Its aim is to copy input to its output. Therefore, instead of mapping features to the input layer and labels to the output layer, we will map the features to both the input and output layers. The number of units in the hidden layers is usually different from the number of units in the input layers, which forces the network to either expand or reduce the number of original features. This way, the network will learn the important features, while effectively applying dimensionality reduction.

An example network is shown in the following diagram. The three-unit input layer is first expanded into a four-unit layer and then compressed into a single-unit layer. The other side of the network restores the single layer unit back in to the four-unit layer, and then to the original three-input layer:

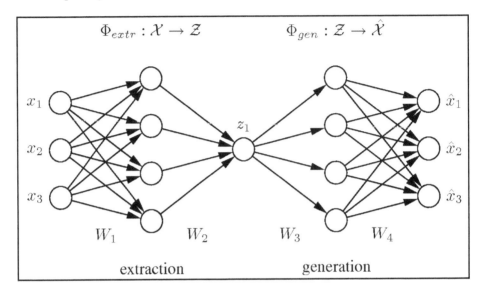

Once the network is trained, we can take the left-hand side to extract the image features like we would with traditional image processing. It consists of encoders and decoders, where the encoder's work is to create or make hidden a layer or layers that captures the essence of the input, and the decoders reconstruct the input from the layers.

The autoencoders can be also combined into **stacked autoencoders**, as shown in the following diagram. First, we will discuss the hidden layer in a basic autoencoder, as described previously. Then, we will take the learned hidden layer (green circles) and repeat the procedure, which in effect learns a more abstract presentation. We can repeat this procedure multiple times, transforming the original features into increasingly reduced dimensions. At the end, we will take all of the hidden layers and stack them into a regular feedforward network, as shown at the top-right part of the diagram:

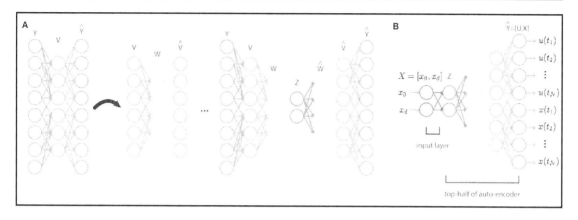

Restricted Boltzmann machine

A restricted Boltzman machine (**RBM**) is an undirected neural network, also denoted as **generative stochastic networks** (**GSNs**), and can learn probability distribution over its set of inputs. As the name suggests, they originate from the Boltzman machine, a recurrent neural network that was introduced in the eighties. In a Boltzmann machine, every node or neuron is connected with all other nodes, which makes it difficult to process when the node count increases. Restricted means that the neurons must form two fully connected layers, an input layer and a hidden layer, as shown in the following diagram:

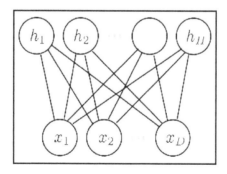

Unlike feedforward networks, the connections between the visible and hidden layers are undirected, hence the values can be propagated in both visible-to-hidden and hidden-to-visible directions.

Training RBMs is based on the contrastive divergence algorithm, which uses a gradient descent procedure, similar to backpropagation, to update weights, and Gibbs sampling is applied on the Markov chain to estimate the gradient, that is the direction on how to change the weights.

RBMs can also be stacked to create a class known as **deep belief networks (DBNs)**. In this case, the hidden layer of an RBM acts as a visible layer for the RBM layer, as shown in the following diagram:

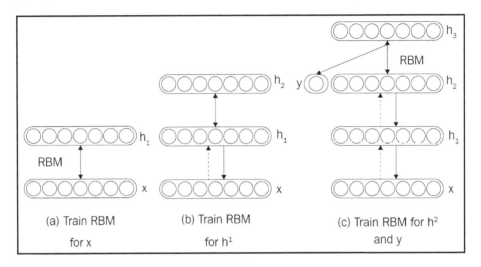

The training, in this case, is incremental: training layer by layer.

Deep convolutional networks

A network structure that recently achieved very good results at image recognition benchmarks is the **convolutional neural network (CNN)** or ConvNet. CNNs are a type of feedforward neural network that are structured in such a way that it emulates the behavior of the visual cortex, exploiting 2D structures of an input image, that is, patterns that exhibit spatially local correlation. It works on the basic principles of how the brain recalls or remembers images. We, as humans, remember images on the basis of features only. Given the features, our brain will start forming the image itself. In computers, consider the following diagram, which shows how a feature is detected:

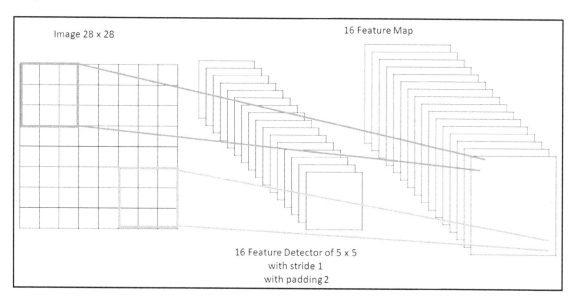

0	0	0
1	1	1
0	0	0

Feature Detector / Kernel / Filter

0	0	0	0	0	0	0	0
0	0	0	0	0	0	0	0
1	1	0	0	1	0	0	0
1	1	1	1	1	1	1	1
1	1	1	1	1	1	1	1
1	1	1	1	1	1	1	1
0	0	0	0	0	0	0	0
0	0	0	0	0	0	0	0

Input Image

Feature Map

In the same way, many features are detected from the image, as shown in the following diagram:

Image 28 x 28

16 Feature Map

16 Feature Detector of 5 x 5
with stride 1
with padding 2

A CNN consists of a number of convolutional and subsampling layers, optionally followed by fully connected layers. An example of this shown in the following diagram. The input layer reads all of the pixels in an image and then we apply multiple filters. In the following diagram, four different filters are applied. Each filter is applied to the original image; for example, one pixel of a 6 x 6 filter is calculated as the weighted sum of a 6 x 6 square of input pixels and corresponding 6 x 6 weights. This effectively introduces filters that are similar to standard image processing, such as smoothing, correlation, edge detection, and so on. The resulting image is called a **feature map**. In the example in the following diagram, we have four feature maps, one for each filter.

The next layer is the subsampling layer, which reduces the size of the input. Each feature map is subsampled typically with mean or max pooling over a contiguous region of 2 x 2 (up to 5 x 5 for large images). For example, if the feature map size is 16 x 16 and the subsampling region is 2 x 2, the reduced feature map size is 8 x 8, where 4 pixels (a 2 x 2 square) are combined into a single pixel by calculating the max, min, mean, or some other functions:

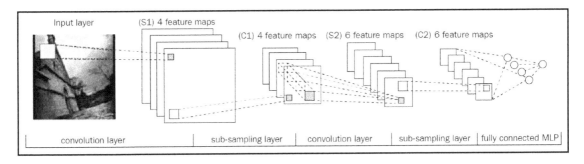

The network may contain several consecutive convolution and subsampling layers, as shown in the preceding diagram. A particular feature map is connected to the next reduced/convoluted feature map, while feature maps at the same layer are not connected to each other.

After the last subsampling or convolutional layer, there is usually a fully connected layer, identical to the layers in a standard multilayer neural network, which represents the target data.

A CNN is trained using a modified backpropagation algorithm that takes the subsampling layers into account and updates the convolutional filter weights based on all the values where this filter is applied.

 Some good CNN designs can be found at the ImageNet competition results page: http://www.image-net.org/. An example is *AlexNet*, which is described in the *ImageNet Classification with Deep Covolutional Neural Networks* paper by *A. Krizhevsky et al.*

This concludes our review of the main neural network structures. In the following section, we'll move on to the actual implementation.

Image classification

In this section, we will discuss how to implement some of the neural network structures with the Deeplearning4j library. Let's get started.

Deeplearning4j

As we discussed in Chapter 2, *Java Libraries and Platforms for Machine Learning*, Deeplearning4j is an open source, distributed deep learning project in Java and Scala. Deeplearning4j relies on Spark and Hadoop for MapReduce, trains models in parallel, and iteratively averages the parameters they produce in a central model. A detailed library summary is presented in Chapter 2, *Java Libraries and Platforms for Machine Learning*.

Getting DL4J

The most convenient way to get Deeplearning4j is through the Maven repository:

1. Start a new Eclipse project and pick **Maven Project**, as shown in the following screenshot:

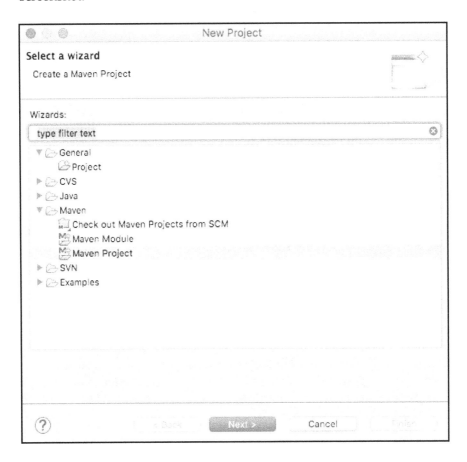

2. Open the `pom.xml` file and add the following dependencies under the `<dependencies>` section:

```
<dependency>
    <groupId>org.deeplearning4j</groupId>
    <artifactId>deeplearning4j-nlp</artifactId>
    <version>${dl4j.version}</version>
</dependency>

<dependency>
    <groupId>org.deeplearning4j</groupId>
    <artifactId>deeplearning4j-core</artifactId>
    <version>${dl4j.version}</version>
</dependency>
```

3. Finally, right-click on **Project**, select **Maven**, and pick **Update project**.

MNIST dataset

One of the most famous datasets is the MNIST dataset, which consists of handwritten digits, as shown in the following image. The dataset consists of 60,000 training and 10,000 test images:

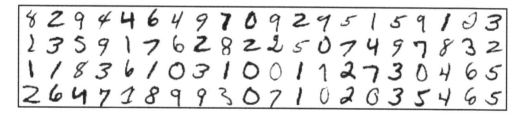

The dataset is commonly used in image recognition problems to benchmark algorithms. The worst recorded error rate is 12%, with no preprocessing and using an SVM in a one-layer neural network. Currently, as of 2016, the lowest error rate is only 0.21%, using the **DropConnect** neural network, followed by a deep convolutional network at 0.23%, and a deep feedforward network at 0.35%.

Now, let's look at how to load the dataset.

Loading the data

Deeplearning4j provides the MNIST dataset loader out of the box. The loader is initialized as DataSetIterator. First let's import the DataSetIterator class and all of the supported datasets that are part of the impl package, for example, iris, MNIST, and others:

```
import org.deeplearning4j.datasets.iterator.DataSetIterator;
import org.deeplearning4j.datasets.iterator.impl.*;
```

Next, we'll define some constants, for instance, the images consist of 28 x 28 pixels and there are 10 target classes and 60,000 samples. We'll initialize a new Mnist.DataSetIterator class that will download the dataset and its labels. The parameters are the iteration batch size, total number of examples, and whether the datasets should be binarized or not:

```
int numRows = 28;
int numColumns = 28;
int outputNum = 10;
int numSamples = 60000;
int batchSize = 100;
int iterations = 10;
int seed = 123;
DataSetIterator iter = new MnistDataSetIterator(batchSize,
numSamples,true);
```

Having an already-implemented data importer is really convenient, but it won't work on your data. Let's take a quick look at how it is implemented and what needs to be modified to support your dataset. If you're eager to start implementing neural networks, you can safely skip the rest of this section and return to it when you need to import your own data.

To load the custom data, you'll need to implement two classes: DataSetIterator, which holds all of the information about the dataset, and BaseDataFetcher, which actually pulls the data either from a file, database, or the web. Sample implementations are available on GitHub at https://github.com/deeplearning4j/deeplearning4j/tree/master/deeplearning4j-core/src/main/java/org/deeplearning4j/datasets/iterator/impl.

Another option is to use the **Canova** library, which was developed by the same authors, at http://deeplearning4j.org/canovadoc/.

Building models

In this section, we'll discuss how to build an actual neural network model. We'll start with a basic single-layer neural network to establish a benchmark and discuss the basic operations. Later, we'll improve this initial result with DBN and a multilayer convolutional network.

Building a single-layer regression model

Let's start by building a single-layer regression model based on the softmax activation function, as shown in the following diagram. As we have a single layer, **Input** to the neural network will be all the figure pixels, that is, 28 x 28 = **748** neurons. The number of **Output** neurons is **10**, one for each digit. The network layers are fully connected, as shown in the following diagram:

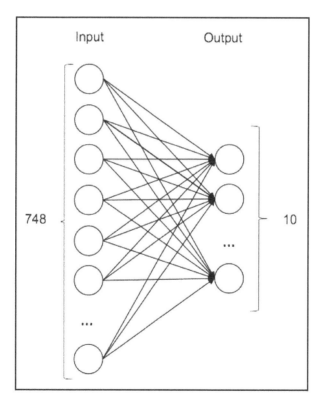

A neural network is defined through a `NeuralNetConfiguration.Builder()` object as follows:

```
MultiLayerConfiguration conf = new NeuralNetConfiguration.Builder()
```

We will define the parameters for gradient search in order to perform iterations with the conjugate gradient optimization algorithm. The `momentum` parameter determines how fast the optimization algorithm converges to an local optimum. The higher the `momentum`, the faster the training; but higher speed can lower the model's accuracy:

```
.seed(seed)
.gradientNormalization(GradientNormalization.ClipElementWiseAbsolu
   teValue)
  .gradientNormalizationThreshold(1.0)
  .iterations(iterations)
  .momentum(0.5)
  .momentumAfter(Collections.singletonMap(3, 0.9))
  .optimizationAlgo(OptimizationAlgorithm.CONJUGATE_GRADIENT)
```

Next, we will specify that the network has one layer and also define the error function, `NEGATIVELOGLIKELIHOOD`, internal perceptron activation function, `softmax`, and the number of input and output layers that correspond to the total image pixels and the number of target variables, as shown in the following code block:

```
.list(1)
.layer(0, new
OutputLayer.Builder(LossFunction.NEGATIVELOGLIKELIHOOD)
.activation("softmax")
.nIn(numRows*numColumns).nOut(outputNum).build())
```

Finally, we will set the network to `pretrain`, disable backpropagation, and actually build the untrained network structure:

```
.pretrain(true).backprop(false)
.build();
```

Once the network structure is defined, we can use it to initialize a new `MultiLayerNetwork`, as follows:

```
MultiLayerNetwork model = new MultiLayerNetwork(conf);
model.init();
```

Next, we will point the model to the training data by calling the `setListeners` method, as follows:

```
model.setListeners(Collections.singletonList((IterationListener)
    new ScoreIterationListener(listenerFreq)));
```

We will also call the `fit(int)` method to trigger end-to-end network training:

```
model.fit(iter);
```

To evaluate the model, we will initialize a new `Evaluation` object that will store batch results:

```
Evaluation eval = new Evaluation(outputNum);
```

We can then iterate over the dataset in batches in order to keep the memory consumption at a reasonable rate and store the results in an `eval` object:

```
DataSetIterator testIter = new MnistDataSetIterator(100,10000);
while(testIter.hasNext()) {
    DataSet testMnist = testIter.next();
    INDArray predict2 =
    model.output(testMnist.getFeatureMatrix());
    eval.eval(testMnist.getLabels(), predict2);
}
```

Finally, we can get the results by calling the `stats()` function:

```
log.info(eval.stats());
```

A basic one-layer model achieves the following accuracy:

```
Accuracy:  0.8945
Precision: 0.8985
Recall:    0.8922
F1 Score:  0.8953
```

Getting 89.22% accuracy, that is, a 10.88% error rate, on the MNIST dataset is quite bad. We'll improve this by going from a simple one-layer network to the moderately sophisticated deep belief network using Restricted Boltzmann machines and a Multilayer Convolutional Network.

Building a deep belief network

In this section, we'll build a deep belief network (DBN) based on the RBM, as shown in the following diagram. The network consists of four layers. The first layer recedes the **748** inputs to **500** neurons, then to **250**, followed by **200**, and finally to the last **10** target values:

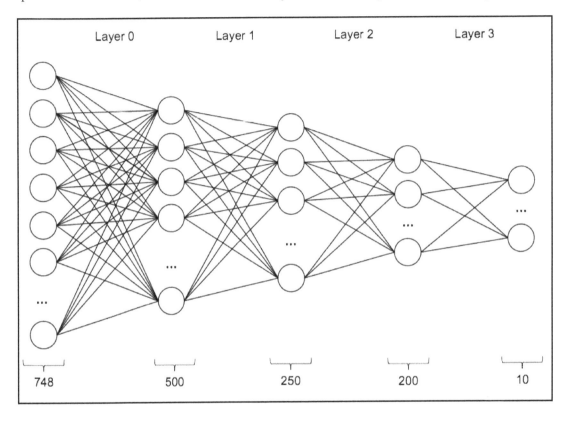

As the code is the same as in the previous example, let's take a look at how to configure such a network:

```
MultiLayerConfiguration conf = new
    NeuralNetConfiguration.Builder()
```

We will define the gradient optimization algorithm, as shown in the following code:

```
.seed(seed)
.gradientNormalization(
GradientNormalization.ClipElementWiseAbsoluteValue)
.gradientNormalizationThreshold(1.0)
.iterations(iterations)
.momentum(0.5)
.momentumAfter(Collections.singletonMap(3, 0.9))
.optimizationAlgo(OptimizationAlgorithm.CONJUGATE_GRADIENT)
```

We will also specify that our network will have four layers:

```
.list(4)
```

The input to the first layer will be 748 neurons and the output will be 500 neurons. We'll use the root mean squared error cross entropy, and the Xavier algorithm to initialize weights by automatically determining the scale of initialization based on the number of input and output neurons, as follows:

```
.layer(0, new RBM.Builder()
.nIn(numRows*numColumns)
.nOut(500)
.weightInit(WeightInit.XAVIER)
.lossFunction(LossFunction.RMSE_XENT)
.visibleUnit(RBM.VisibleUnit.BINARY)
.hiddenUnit(RBM.HiddenUnit.BINARY)
.build())
```

The next two layers will have the same parameters, except for the number of input and output neurons:

```
.layer(1, new RBM.Builder()
.nIn(500)
.nOut(250)
.weightInit(WeightInit.XAVIER)
.lossFunction(LossFunction.RMSE_XENT)
.visibleUnit(RBM.VisibleUnit.BINARY)
.hiddenUnit(RBM.HiddenUnit.BINARY)
.build()
.layer(2, new RBM.Builder()
.nIn(250)
.nOut(200)
.weightInit(WeightInit.XAVIER)
.lossFunction(LossFunction.RMSE_XENT)
.visibleUnit(RBM.VisibleUnit.BINARY)
.hiddenUnit(RBM.HiddenUnit.BINARY)
.build())
```

Now, the last layer will map the neurons to outputs, where we'll use the `softmax` activation function, as follows:

```
.layer(3, new OutputLayer.Builder()
.nIn(200)
.nOut(outputNum)
.lossFunction(LossFunction.NEGATIVELOGLIKELIHOOD)
.activation("softmax")
.build())
.pretrain(true).backprop(false)
.build();
```

The rest of the training and evaluation is the same as in the single-layer network example. Note that training a deep network might take significantly more time compared to a single-layer network. The accuracy should be around 93%.

Now, let's take a look at another deep network.

Building a multilayer convolutional network

In this final example, we'll discuss how to build a convolutional network, as shown in the following diagram. The network will consist of seven layers. First, we'll repeat two pairs of convolutional and subsampling layers with max pooling. The last subsampling layer is then connected to a densely connected feedforward neuronal network, consisting of 120 neurons, 84 neurons, and 10 neurons in the last three layers, respectively. Such a network effectively forms the complete image recognition pipeline, where the first four layers correspond to feature extraction and the last three layers correspond to the learning model:

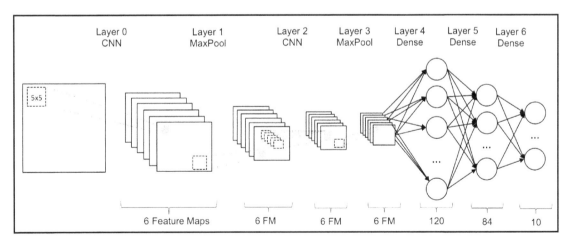

Network configuration is initialized as we did earlier:

```
MultiLayerConfiguration.Builder conf = new
    NeuralNetConfiguration.Builder()
```

We will specify the gradient descent algorithm and its parameters, as follows:

```
.seed(seed)
.iterations(iterations)
.activation("sigmoid")
.weightInit(WeightInit.DISTRIBUTION)
.dist(new NormalDistribution(0.0, 0.01))
.learningRate(1e-3)
.learningRateScoreBasedDecayRate(1e-1)
.optimizationAlgo(
OptimizationAlgorithm.STOCHASTIC_GRADIENT_DESCENT)
```

We will also specify the seven network layers, as follows:

```
.list(7)
```

The input to the first convolutional layer is the complete image, while the output is six feature maps. The convolutional layer will apply a 5 x 5 filter, and the result will be stored in a 1 x 1 cell:

```
.layer(0, new ConvolutionLayer.Builder(
    new int[]{5, 5}, new int[]{1, 1})
    .name("cnn1")
    .nIn(numRows*numColumns)
    .nOut(6)
    .build())
```

The second layer is a subsampling layer that will take a 2 x 2 region and store the max result in a 2 x 2 element:

```
.layer(1, new SubsamplingLayer.Builder(
SubsamplingLayer.PoolingType.MAX,
new int[]{2, 2}, new int[]{2, 2})
.name("maxpool1")
.build())
```

The next two layers will repeat the previous two layers:

```
.layer(2, new ConvolutionLayer.Builder(new int[]{5, 5}, new
    int[]{1, 1})
    .name("cnn2")
    .nOut(16)
    .biasInit(1)
```

```
    .build())
.layer(3, new SubsamplingLayer.Builder
    (SubsamplingLayer.PoolingType.MAX, new
    int[]{2, 2}, new int[]{2, 2})
    .name("maxpool2")
    .build())
```

Now, we will wire the output of the subsampling layer into a dense feedforward network, consisting of 120 neurons, and then through another layer, into 84 neurons, as follows:

```
.layer(4, new DenseLayer.Builder()
    .name("ffn1")
    .nOut(120)
    .build())
.layer(5, new DenseLayer.Builder()
    .name("ffn2")
    .nOut(84)
    .build())
```

The final layer connects 84 neurons with 10 output neurons:

```
.layer(6, new OutputLayer.Builder
    (LossFunctions.LossFunction.NEGATIVELOGLIKELIHOOD)
    .name("output")
    .nOut(outputNum)
    .activation("softmax") // radial basis function required
    .build())
.backprop(true)
.pretrain(false)
.cnnInputSize(numRows,numColumns,1);
```

To train this structure, we can reuse the code that we developed in the previous two examples. Again, the training might take some time. The network accuracy should be around 98%.

 Since model training significantly relies on linear algebra, training can be significantly sped up by using a **graphics processing unit** (GPU) for an order of magnitude. As the GPU backend, at the time of writing this book, is undergoing a rewrite, please check the latest documentation at http://deeplearning4j.org/documentation.

As we saw in different examples, increasingly complex neural networks allow us to extract relevant features automatically, thus completely avoiding traditional image processing. However, the price we pay for this is an increased processing time and a lot of learning examples to make this approach efficient.

Summary

In this chapter, we discussed how to recognize patterns in images in order to distinguish between different classes by covering fundamental principles of deep learning and discussing how to implement them with the Deeplearning4j library. We started by refreshing the basic neural network structure and discussed how to implement them to solve handwritten digit recognition problems.

In the next chapter, we'll look into patterns further; however, instead of patterns in images, we'll tackle patterns with temporal dependencies, which can be found in sensor data.

Activity Recognition with Mobile Phone Sensors

9

While the previous chapter focused on pattern recognition in images, this chapter is all about recognizing patterns in sensor data, which, in contrast to images, has temporal dependencies. We will discuss how to recognize granular daily activities such as walking, sitting, and running using mobile phone inertial sensors. The chapter also provides references to related research and emphasizes best practices in the activity recognition community.

The topics covered in this chapter will include the following:

- Introducing activity recognition, covering mobile phone sensors and the activity recognition pipeline
- Collecting sensor data from mobile devices
- Discussing activity classification and model evaluation
- Deploying an activity recognition model

Introducing activity recognition

Activity recognition is an underpinning step in behavior analysis, addressing healthy lifestyles, fitness tracking, remote assistance, security applications, elderly care, and so on. Activity recognition transforms low-level sensor data from sensors, such as an accelerometer, gyroscope, pressure sensor, and GPS location, to a higher-level description of behavior primitives.

In most cases, these are basic activities, for example, walking, sitting, lying, jumping, and so on, as shown in the following diagram, or they could be more complex behaviors, such as going to work, preparing breakfast, and shopping:

In this chapter, we will discuss how to add the activity recognition functionality into a mobile application. We will first look at what an activity recognition problem looks like, what kind of data we need to collect, what the main challenges are, and how to address them.

Later, we will follow an example to see how to actually implement activity recognition in an Android application, including data collection, data transformation, and building a classifier.

Let's start!

Mobile phone sensors

Let's first review what kind of mobile phone sensors there are and what they report. Most smart devices are now equipped with several built-in sensors that measure the motion, position, orientation, and conditions of the ambient environment. As sensors provide measurements with high precision, frequency, and accuracy, it is possible to reconstruct complex user motions, gestures, and movements. Sensors are often incorporated in various applications; for example, gyroscope readings are used to steer an object in a game, GPS data is used to locate the user, and accelerometer data is used to infer the activity that the user is performing, for example, cycling, running, or walking.

The following diagram shows a couple of examples of what kinds of interactions the sensors are able to detect:

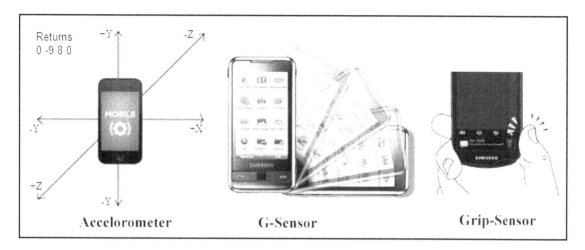

| Accelerometer | G-Sensor | Grip-Sensor |

Mobile phone sensors can be classified into the following three broad categories:

- **Motion sensors:** This sensor measures acceleration and rotational forces along the three perpendicular axes. Examples of sensors in this category include accelerometers, gravity sensors, and gyroscopes.
- **Environmental sensors:** This sensor measures a variety of environmental parameters, such as illumination, air temperature, pressure, and humidity. This category includes barometers, photometers, and thermometers.
- **Position sensors:** This sensor measure the physical position of a device. This category includes orientation sensors and magnetometers.

> More detailed descriptions for different mobile platforms are available at the following links:
>
> - **Android sensors framework**: `http://developer.android.com/guide/topics/sensors/sensors_overview.html`
> - **iOS Core Motion framework**: `https://developer.apple.com/library/ios/documentation/CoreMotion/Reference/CoreMotion_Reference/`
> - **Windows phone**: `https://msdn.microsoft.com/en-us/library/windows/apps/hh202968(v=vs.105).aspx`

In this chapter, we will work only with Android's sensors framework.

Activity recognition pipeline

Classifying multidimensional time series sensor data is inherently more complex than classifying traditional nominal data, as we saw in the previous chapters. First, each observation is temporally connected to the previous and following observations, making it very difficult to apply a straightforward classification of a single set of observations only. Second, the data obtained by sensors at different time points is stochastic, that is, unpredictable due to the influence of sensor noise, environmental disturbances, and many other factors. Moreover, an activity can consist of various sub-activities executed in a different manner and each person performs the activity a bit differently, which results in high intraclass differences. Finally, all these reasons make an activity recognition model imprecise, resulting in new data often being misclassified. One of the highly desirable properties of an activity recognition classifier is to ensure continuity and consistency in the recognized activity sequence.

To deal with these challenges, activity recognition is applied to a pipeline, as shown in the following diagram:

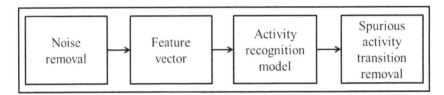

In the first step, we attenuate as much noise as we can, for example, by reducing the sensor sampling rate, removing outliers, applying high-or low-pass filters, and so on. In the next phase, we construct a feature vector. For instance, we convert sensor data from time domain to frequency domain by applying a **discrete Fourier transform** (**DFT**). DFT is a method that takes a list of samples as an input and returns a list of sinusoid coefficients ordered by their frequencies. They represent a combination of frequencies that are present in the original list of samples.

A gentle introduction to the Fourier transform was written by Pete Bevelacqua at `http://www.thefouriertransform.com/`. If you want to get a more technical and theoretical background on the Fourier transform, take a look at the eighth and ninth lectures in the class by Robert Gallager and Lizhong Zheng at this MIT open course: `http://theopenacademy.com/content/principles-digital-communication`.

Next, based on the feature vector and set of training data, we can build an activity recognition model that assigns an atomic action to each observation. Therefore, for each new sensor reading, the model will output the most probable activity label. However, models make mistakes. Hence, the last phase smooths the transitions between activities by removing transitions that cannot occur in reality; for example, it is not physically feasible that the transition between the activities lying-standing-lying occur in less than half a second, hence such a transition between activities is smoothed as lying-lying-lying.

The activity recognition model is constructed with a supervised learning approach, which consists of training and classification steps. In the training step, a set of labeled data is provided to train the model. The second step is used to assign a label to the new unseen data by the trained model. The data in both phases must be preprocessed with the same set of tools, such as filtering and feature vector computation.

The post processing phase, that is, spurious activity removal, can also be a model itself and hence also requires a learning step. In this case, the preprocessing step also includes activity recognition, which makes such arrangement of classifiers into a meta-learning problem. To avoid overfitting, it is important that the dataset used for training the post processing phase is not the same as the one used for training the activity recognition model.

The plan

The plan consists of a training phase and a deployment phase. The training phase boils down to the following steps:

1. Install Android Studio and import `MyRunsDataCollector.zip`.
2. Load the application on your Android phone.
3. Collect your data, for example, standing, walking, and running, and transform the data to a feature vector consisting of FFTs. Don't panic; low-level signal processing functions such as FFTs will not be written from scratch as we will use existing code to do that. The data will be saved on your phone in a file called `features.arff`.
4. Create and evaluate an activity recognition classifier using exported data and implement a filter for spurious activity transition removal.
5. Plug the classifier back into the mobile application.

If you don't have an Android phone, or if you want to skip all the steps related to the mobile application, just grab the collected dataset located in `data/features.arff` and jump directly to the *Building a classifier* section.

Collecting data from a mobile phone

This section describes the first three steps from the plan. If you want to directly work with the data, you can just skip this section and continue to the *Building a classifier* section. The application implements the essentials to collect sensor data for different activity classes, for example, standing, walking, running, and others.

Let's start by preparing the Android development environment. If you have already installed it, jump to the *Loading the data collector* section.

Installing Android Studio

Android Studio is a development environment for the Android platform. We will quickly review the installation steps and basic configurations required to start the app on a mobile phone. For a more detailed introduction to Android development, I would recommend an introductory book, *Android 5 Programming by Example* by Kyle Mew, Packt Publishing.

Grab the latest Android Studio for developers at `https://developer.android.com/studio/` and follow the installation instructions at `http://developer.android.com/sdk/installing/index.html?pkg=studio`. The installation will take around 10 minutes, occupying approximately 0.5 GB of space.

Follow the instructions and select your preferred options for installation, and finally click on **Finish** to start the installation, as shown in the following screenshot:

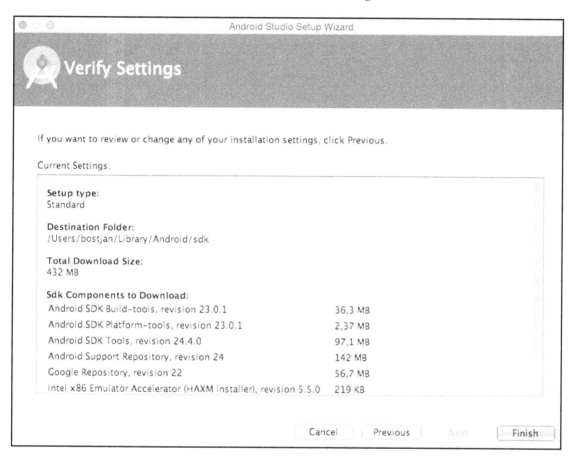

Loading the data collector

First, grab the source code of `MyRunsDataCollector` from GitHub. Once Android Studio is installed, choose the **Open an existing Android Studio project** option, as shown in the following screenshot, and select the `MyRunsDataCollector` folder. This will import the project to Android Studio:

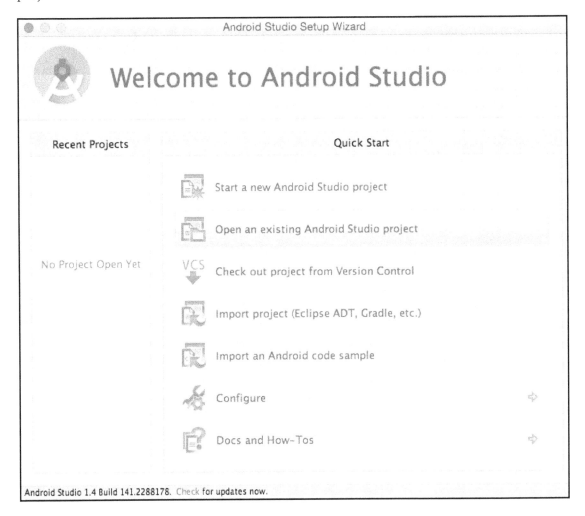

After the project import is completed, you should be able to see the project file structure, as shown in the following screenshot. The collector consists of `CollectorActivity.java`, `Globals.java`, and `SensorsService.java`. The project also shows `FFT.java` implementing low-level signal processing:

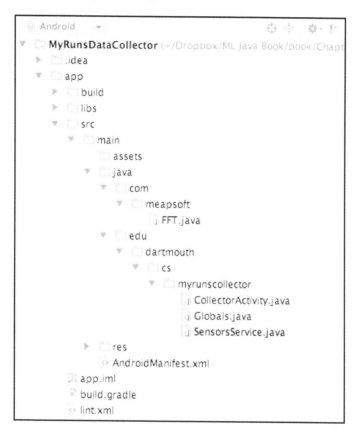

The main `myrunscollector` package contains the following classes:

- `Globals.java`: This defines global constants, such as activity labels and IDs, and data filenames.
- `CollectorActivity.java`: This implements user interface actions, that is, what happens when a specific button is pressed.
- `SensorsService.java`: This implements a service that collects data, calculates the feature vector, as we will discuss in the following sections, and stores the data into a file on the phone.

The next question that we will address is how to design features.

Feature extraction

Finding an appropriate representation of a person's activities is probably the most challenging part of activity recognition. The behavior needs to be represented with simple and general features so that the model using these features will also be general and work well on behaviors different from those in the learning set.

In fact, it is not difficult to design features specific to the captured observations in a training set; such features would work well on them. However, as the training set captures only a part of the whole range of human behavior, overly specific features would likely fail on general behavior:

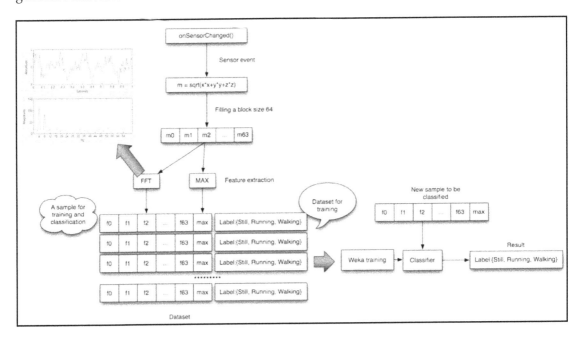

Let's see how this is implemented in `MyRunsDataCollector`. When the application is started, a method called `onSensorChanged()` gets a triple of accelerometer sensor readings (**x**, **y**, and **z**) with a specific timestamp and calculates the magnitude from the sensor readings. The methods buffers up to 64 consecutive magnitudes marked before computing the FFT coefficients.

Now, let's move on to the actual data collection.

Collecting training data

We can now use the collector to collect training data for activity recognition. The collector supports three activities by default, standing, walking, and running, as shown in the following screenshot.

You can select an activity, that is, target class value, and start recording the data by clicking the **START COLLECTING** button. Make sure that each activity is recorded for at least three minutes; for example, if the **Walking** activity is selected, press **START COLLECTING** and walk around for at least three minutes. At the end of the activity, press **Stop collecting**. Repeat this for each of the activities.

You could also collect different scenarios involving these activities, for example, walking in the kitchen, walking outside, walking in a line, and so on. By doing so, you will have more data for each activity class and a better classifier. Makes sense, right? The more data, the less confused the classifier will be. If you only have a little data, overfitting will occur and the classifier will confuse classes—standing with walking, walking with running, and so on. However, the more data, the less they get confused. You might collect less than three minutes per class when you are debugging, but for your final polished product, the more data, the better it is. Multiple recording instances will simply be accumulated in the same file.

Note, the **Delete Data** button removes the data that is stored in a file on the phone. If you want to start over again, hit **Delete Data** before starting; otherwise, the new collected data will be appended at the end of the file:

The collector implements the diagram discussed in the previous sections: it collects accelerometer samples, computes the magnitudes, uses the FFT.java class to compute the coefficients, and produces the feature vectors. The data is then stored in a Weka-formatted features.arff file. The number of feature vectors will vary based on the amount of data you collect. The longer you collect the data, the more feature vectors are accumulated.

Once you stop collecting the training data using the collector tool, we need to grab the data to carry on the workflow. We can use the file explorer in **Android Device Monitor** to upload the `features.arff` file from the phone and to store it on the computer. You can access your Android Device Monitor by clicking on the Android robot icon, as shown in the following screenshot:

By selecting your device on the left, your phone storage content will be shown on the right-hand side. Navigate through `mnt/shell/emulated/Android/data/edu.dartmouth.cs.myrunscollector/files/features.arff`, as shown in the following screenshot:

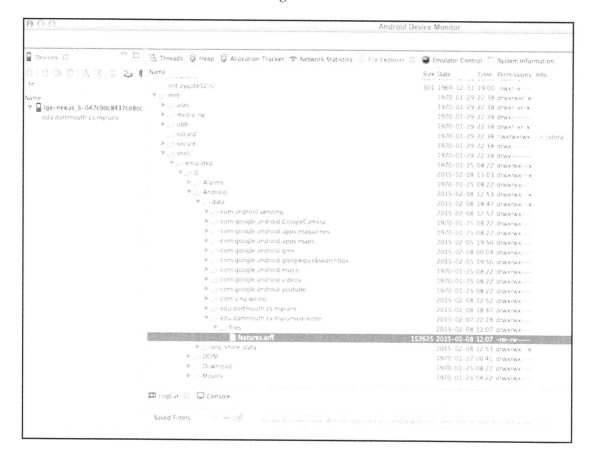

To upload this file to your computer, you need to select the file (it is highlighted) and click on **Upload**.

Now, we are ready to build a classifier.

Building a classifier

Once sensor samples are represented as feature vectors and have the class assigned, it is possible to apply standard techniques for supervised classification, including feature selection, feature discretization, model learning, k-fold cross-validation, and so on. The chapter will not delve into the details of the machine learning algorithms. Any algorithm that supports numerical features can be applied, including SVMs, random forest, AdaBoost, decision trees, neural networks, multilayer perceptrons, and others.

Therefore, let's start with a basic one: decision trees. Here, we will load the dataset, build the set class attribute, build a decision tree model, and output the model:

```
String databasePath = "/Users/bostjan/Dropbox/ML Java
Book/book/datasets/chap9/features.arff";

// Load the data in arff format
Instances data = new Instances(new BufferedReader(new
    FileReader(databasePath)));

// Set class the last attribute as class
data.setClassIndex(data.numAttributes() - 1);

// Build a basic decision tree model
String[] options = new String[]{};
J48 model = new J48();
model.setOptions(options);
model.buildClassifier(data);

// Output decision tree
System.out.println("Decision tree model:\n"+model);
```

The algorithm first outputs the model, as follows:

```
Decision tree model:
J48 pruned tree
------------------
max <= 10.353474
|   fft_coef_0000 <= 38.193106: standing (46.0)
|   fft_coef_0000 > 38.193106
|   |   fft_coef_0012 <= 1.817792: walking (77.0/1.0)
```

```
|  |    fft_coef_0012 > 1.817792
|  |  |    max <= 4.573082: running (4.0/1.0)
|  |  |    max > 4.573082: walking (24.0/2.0)
max > 10.353474: running (93.0)
Number of Leaves   : 5
Size of the tree : 9
```

The tree is quite simplistic and seemingly accurate, as majority class distributions in the terminal nodes are quite high. Let's run a basic classifier evaluation to validate the results, as follows:

```
// Check accuracy of model using 10-fold cross-validation
Evaluation eval = new Evaluation(data);
eval.crossValidateModel(model, data, 10, new Random(1), new
    String[] {});
System.out.println("Model performance:\n"+
    eval.toSummaryString());
```

This outputs the following model performance:

```
Correctly Classified Instances         226               92.623 %
Incorrectly Classified Instances        18                7.377 %
Kappa statistic                          0.8839
Mean absolute error                      0.0421
Root mean squared error                  0.1897
Relative absolute error                 13.1828 %
Root relative squared error             47.519  %
Coverage of cases (0.95 level)          93.0328 %
Mean rel. region size (0.95 level)      27.8689 %
Total Number of Instances              244
```

The classification accuracy scores very high, `92.62%`, which is an amazing result. One important reason why the result is so good lies in our evaluation design. What I mean here is the following: sequential instances are very similar to each other, so if we split them randomly during a 10-fold cross-validation, there is a high chance that we use almost identical instances for both training and testing; hence, straightforward k-fold cross-validation produces an optimistic estimate of model performance.

A better approach is to use folds that correspond to different sets of measurements or even different people. For example, we can use the application to collect learning data from five people. Then, it makes sense to run k-person cross-validation, where the model is trained on four people and tested on the fifth person. The procedure is repeated for each person and the results are averaged. This will give us a much more realistic estimate of the model performance.

Leaving evaluation comments aside, let's look at how to deal with classifier errors.

Reducing spurious transitions

At the end of the activity recognition pipeline, we want to make sure that the classifications are not too volatile, that is, we don't want activities to change every millisecond. A basic approach is to design a filter that ignores quick changes in the activity sequence.

We build a filter that remembers the last window activities and returns the most frequent one. If there are multiple activities with the same score, it returns the most recent one.

First, we create a new `SpuriousActivityRemoval` class, which will hold a list of activities and the `window` parameter:

```
class SpuriousActivityRemoval{
  List<Object> last;
  int window;
  public SpuriousActivityRemoval(int window){
    this.last = new ArrayList<Object>();
    this.window = window;
  }
```

Next, we create the `Object filter(Object)` method, which will take an activity and return a filtered activity. The method first checks whether we have enough observations. If not, it simply stores the observation and returns the same value, as shown in the following code:

```
public Object filter(Object obj){
  if(last.size() < window){
    last.add(obj);
    return obj;
  }
```

If we already collected `window` observations, we simply return the most frequent observation, remove the oldest observation, and insert the new observation:

```
  Object o = getMostFrequentElement(last);
  last.add(obj);
  last.remove(0);
  return o;
}
```

What is missing here is a function that returns the most frequent element from a list of objects. We implement this with a hash map, as follows:

```
private Object getMostFrequentElement(List<Object> list){
    HashMap<String, Integer> objectCounts = new HashMap<String,
        Integer>();
    Integer frequntCount = 0;
    Object frequentObject = null;
```

Now, we iterate over all the elements in the list, insert each unique element into a hash map, or update its counter if it is already in the hash map. At the end of the loop, we store the most frequent element that we found so far, as follows:

```
    for(Object obj : list){
        String key = obj.toString();
        Integer count = objectCounts.get(key);
        if(count == null){
            count = 0;
        }
        objectCounts.put(key, ++count);
        if(count >= frequntCount){
            frequntCount = count;
            frequentObject = obj;
        }
    }
    return frequentObject;
    }
}
```

Let's run a simple example:

```
String[] activities = new String[]{"Walk", "Walk", "Walk", "Run",
    "Walk", "Run", "Run", "Sit", "Sit", "Sit"};
SpuriousActivityRemoval dlpFilter = new
    SpuriousActivityRemoval(3);
for(String str : activities){
    System.out.println(str +" -> "+ dlpFilter.filter(str));
}
```

The example outputs the following activities:

```
Walk -> Walk
Walk -> Walk
Walk -> Walk
Run  -> Walk
Walk -> Walk
Run  -> Walk
Run  -> Run
Sit  -> Run
Sit  -> Run
Sit  -> Sit
```

The result is a continuous sequence of activities, that is, we do not have quick changes. This adds some delay, but unless this is absolutely critical for the application, it is acceptable.

Activity recognition may be enhanced by appending n previous activities, as recognized by the classifier, to the feature vector. The danger of appending previous activities is that the machine learning algorithm may learn that the current activity is always the same as the previous one, as this will often be the case. The problem may be solved by having two classifiers, A and B: classifier B's attribute vector contains n previous activities as recognized by classifier A. Classifier A's attribute vector does not contain any previous activities. This way, even if B gives a lot of weight to the previous activities, the previous activities as recognized by A will change as A is not burdened with B's inertia.

All that remains to do is to embed the classifier and filter it into our mobile application.

Plugging the classifier into a mobile app

There are two ways to incorporate a classifier into a mobile application. The first one involves exporting a model in the Weka format, using the Weka library as a dependency in our mobile application, loading the model, and so on. The procedure is identical to the example we saw in Chapter 3, *Basic Algorithms–Classification, Regression, and Clustering*. The second approach is more lightweight: we export the model as source code, for example, we create a class implementing the decision tree classifier. Then, we can simply copy and paste the source code into our mobile app, without even importing any Weka dependencies.

Fortunately, some Weka models can be easily exported to source code by the toSource(String) function:

```
// Output source code implementing the decision tree
System.out.println("Source code:\n" +
  model.toSource("ActivityRecognitionEngine"));
```

This outputs an `ActivityRecognitionEngine` class that corresponds to our model. Now, let's take a closer look at the output code:

```
class ActivityRecognitionEngine {

  public static double classify(Object[] i)
    throws Exception {

    double p = Double.NaN;
    p = ActivityRecognitionEngine.N17a7cec20(i);
    return p;
  }
  static double N17a7cec20(Object []i) {
    double p = Double.NaN;
    if (i[64] == null) {
      p = 1;
    } else if (((Double) i[64]).doubleValue() <= 10.353474) {
    p = ActivityRecognitionEngine.N65b3120a1(i);
    } else if (((Double) i[64]).doubleValue() > 10.353474) {
      p = 2;
    }
    return p;
  }
...
```

The outputted `ActivityRecognitionEngine` class implements the decision tree that we discussed earlier. The machine-generated function names, such as `N17a7cec20(Object [])`, correspond to decision tree nodes. The classifier can be called by the `classify(Object[])` method, where we should pass a feature vector obtained by the same procedure as we discussed in the previous sections. As usual, it returns a `double`, indicating a class label index.

Summary

In this chapter, we discussed how to implement an activity recognition model for mobile applications. We looked into the completed process, including data collection, feature extraction, model building, evaluation, and model deployment.

In the next chapter, we will move on to another Java library targeted at text analysis: Mallet.

Text Mining with Mallet – Topic Modeling and Spam Detection

10

In this chapter, we'll first discuss what **text mining** is, what kind of analysis it is able to offer, and why you might want to use it in your application. We'll then discuss how to work with **Mallet**, a Java library for natural-language processing, covering data import and text pre-processing. Afterward, we will look into two text-mining applications: **topic modeling**, where we will discuss how text mining can be used to identify topics found in text documents without reading them individually, and **spam detection**, where we will discuss how to automatically classify text documents into categories.

This chapter will cover the following topics:

- Introducing text mining
- Installing and working with Mallet
- Topic modeling
- Spam detection

Introducing text mining

Text mining, or text analytics, refers to the process of automatically extracting high-quality information from text documents, most often written in natural language, where high-quality information is considered to be relevant, novel, and interesting.

While a typical text analytics application is used to scan a set of documents to generate a search index, text mining can be used in many other applications, including text categorization into specific domains; text clustering to automatically organize a set of documents; sentiment analysis to identify and extract subjective information in documents; concept or entity extraction that is capable of identifying people, places, organizations, and other entities from documents; document summarization to automatically provide the most important points in the original document; and learning relations between named entities.

The process based on statistical pattern mining usually involves the following steps:

1. Information retrieval and extraction
2. Transforming unstructured text data into structured data; for example, parsing, removing noisy words, lexical analysis, calculating word frequencies, and deriving linguistic features
3. Discovery of patterns from structured data and tagging or annotation
4. Evaluation and interpretation of the results

Later in this chapter, we will look at two application areas: topic modeling and **text categorization**. Let's examine what they bring to the table.

Topic modeling

Topic modeling is an unsupervised technique and might be useful if you need to analyze a large archive of text documents and wish to understand what the archive contains, without necessarily reading every single document by yourself. A text document can be a blog post, an email, a tweet, a document, a book chapter, a diary entry, and so on. Topic modeling looks for patterns in a corpus of text; more precisely, it identifies topics as lists of words that appear in a statistically meaningful way. The most well-known algorithm is **Latent Dirichlet Allocation** (**LDA**), which assumes that the author composed a piece of text by selecting words from possible baskets of words, where each basket corresponds to a topic. Using this assumption, it becomes possible to mathematically decompose text into the most likely baskets from where the words first came. The algorithm then iterates over this process until it converges to the most likely distribution of words into baskets, which we call *topics*.

For example, if we use topic modeling on a series of news articles, the algorithm would return a list of topics and keywords that most likely comprise of these topics. Using the example of news articles, the list might look similar to the following:

- Winner, goal, football, score, first place
- Company, stocks, bank, credit, business
- Election, opponent, president, debate, upcoming

By looking at the keywords, we can recognize that the news articles were concerned with sports, business, upcoming election, and so on. Later in this chapter, we will learn how to implement topic modeling using the news article example.

Text classification

In text classification, or text categorization, the goal is to assign a text document according to its content to one or more classes or categories, which tend to be a more general subject area, such as vehicles or pets. Such general classes are referred to as topics, and the classification task is then called **text classification**, **text categorization**, **topic classification**, or **topic spotting**. While documents can be categorized according to other attributes such as document type, author, and publication year, the focus in this chapter will be on the document content only. Examples of text classification include the following components:

- Spam detection in email messages, user comments, web pages, and so on
- Detection of sexually explicit content
- Sentiment detection, which automatically classifies a product or service review as positive or negative
- Email sorting according to content
- Topic-specific search, where search engines restrict searches to a particular topic or genre, hence providing more accurate results

These examples show how important text classification is in information retrieval systems; hence, most modern information retrieval systems use some kind of text classifier. The classification task that we will use as an example in this book is text classification for detecting email spam.

We will continue this chapter with an introduction to Mallet, a Java-based package for statistical natural-language processing, document classification, clustering, topic modeling, information extraction, and other machine-learning applications to text. We will then cover two text analytics applications, namely, topics modeling and spam detection as text classification.

Installing Mallet

Mallet is available for download at the UMass Amherst University website at `http://mallet.cs.umass.edu/download.php`. Navigate to the **Download** section as shown in the following screenshot and select the latest stable release (**2.0.8**, at the time of writing this book):

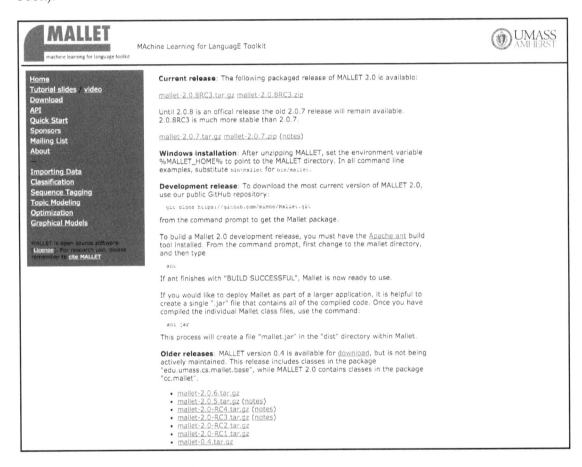

Download the ZIP file and extract the content. In the extracted directory, you should find a folder named `dist` with two JAR files: `mallet.jar` and `mallet-deps.jar`. The first one contains all of the packaged Mallet classes, while the second one packs all of the dependencies. We will include both JARs files in your project as referenced libraries, as shown in the following screenshot:

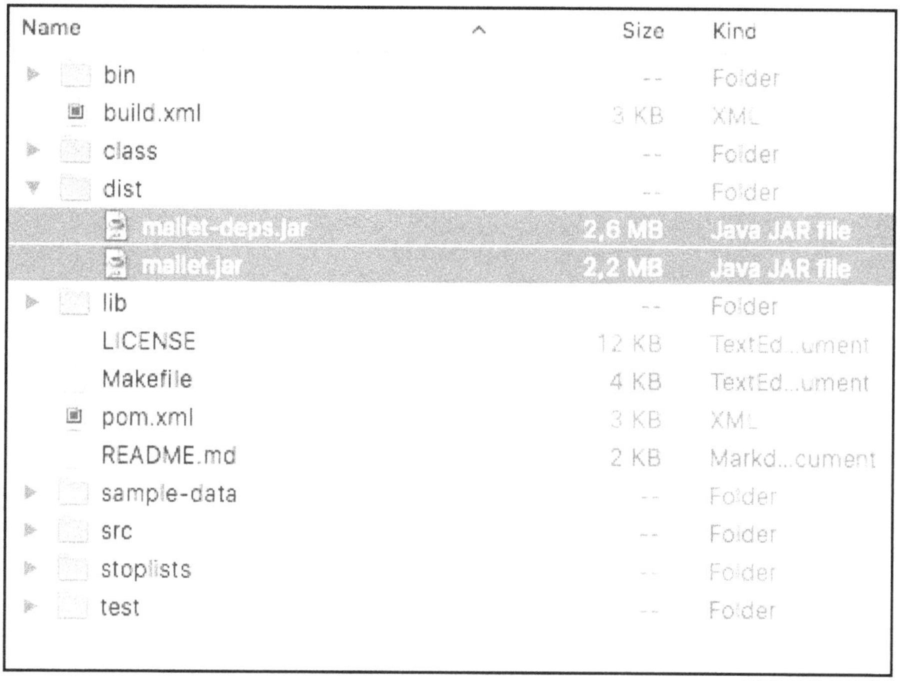

Name	^	Size	Kind
▶ bin		--	Folder
build.xml		3 KB	XML
▶ class		--	Folder
▼ dist		--	Folder
mallet-deps.jar		2,6 MB	Java JAR file
mallet.jar		2,2 MB	Java JAR file
▶ lib		--	Folder
LICENSE		12 KB	TextEd...ument
Makefile		4 KB	TextEd...ument
pom.xml		3 KB	XML
README.md		2 KB	Markd...cument
▶ sample-data		--	Folder
▶ src		--	Folder
▶ stoplists		--	Folder
▶ test		--	Folder

If you are using Eclipse, right-click on **Project**, select **Properties**, and pick **Java Build Path**. Select the **Libraries** tab and click **Add External JARs**. Now, select the two JARs files and confirm, as shown in the following screenshot:

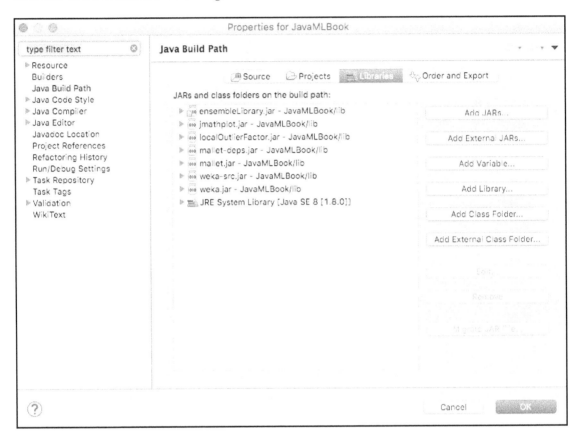

Now we are ready to start using Mallet.

Working with text data

One of the main challenges in text mining is transforming unstructured written natural language into structured attribute-based instances. The process involves many steps, as shown here:

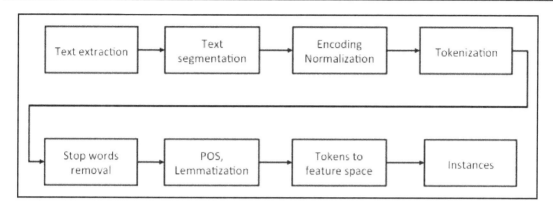

First, we extract some text from the internet, existing documents, or databases. At the end of the first step, the text could still be present in the XML format or some other proprietary format. The next step is to extract the actual text and segment it into parts of the document, for example, title, headline, abstract, and body. The third step is involved with normalizing text encoding to ensure the characters are presented in the same way; for example, documents encoded in formats such as ASCII, ISO 8859-1 and Windows-1250 are transformed into Unicode encoding. Next, tokenization splits the document into particular words, while the next step removes frequent words that usually have low predictive power, for example, the, a, I, and we.

The **Part-Of-Speech** (**POS**) tagging and lemmatization step could be included to transform each token to its basic form, which is known as **lemma**, by removing word endings and modifiers. For example, running becomes run, and better becomes good. A simplified approach is stemming, which operates on a single word without any context of how the particular word is used, and therefore cannot distinguish between words having different meaning, depending on the part of speech, for example, axes as a plural of axe as well as axis.

The last step transforms tokens into a feature space. Most often, feature space is a **Bag-Of-Words** (**BoW**) presentation. In this presentation, a set of all words appearing in the dataset is created. Each document is then presented as a vector that counts how many times a particular word appears in the document.

Consider the following example with two sentences:

- Jacob likes table tennis. Emma likes table tennis too
- Jacob also likes basketball

The BoW in this case consists of {Jacob, likes, table, tennis, Emma, too, also, basketball}, which has eight distinct words. The two sentences could be now presented as vectors using the indexes of the list, indicating how many times a word at a particular index appears in the document, as follows:

- [1, 2, 2, 2, 1, 0, 0, 0]
- [1, 1, 0, 0, 0, 0, 1, 1]

Such vectors finally become instances for further learning.

 Another very powerful presentation based on the BoW model is **word2vec**. Word2vec was introduced in 2013 by a team of researchers led by Tomas Mikolov at Google. Word2vec is a neural network that learns distributed representations for words. An interesting property of this presentation is that words appear in clusters, so that some word relationships, such as analogies, can be reproduced using vector math. A famous example shows that king–man+woman returns queen. Further details and implementation are available at the following link: `https://code.google.com/archive/p/word2vec/`.

Importing data

In this chapter, we will not look into how to scrap a set of documents from a website or extract them from database. Instead, we will assume that we have already collected them as set of documents and stored them in the `.txt` file format. Now let's look at two options for loading them. The first option addresses the situation where each document is stored in its own `.txt` file. The second option addresses the situation where all of the documents are stored in a single file by taking one per line.

Importing from directory

Mallet supports reading from directory with the `cc.mallet.pipe.iterator.FileIterator` class. A file iterator is constructed with the following three parameters:

- A list of `File[]` directories with text files
- A file filter that specifies which files to select within a directory
- A pattern that is applied to a filename to produce a class label

Consider the data structured into folders as shown in the following screenshot. We have documents organized in five topics by folders (tech, entertainment, politics, sport, and business). Each folder contains documents on particular topics, as shown in the following screenshot:

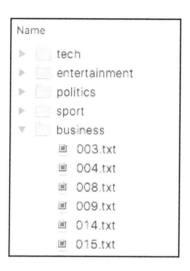

In this case, we initialize iterator as follows:

```
FileIterator iterator =
  new FileIterator(new File[]{new File("path-to-my-dataset")},
  new TxtFilter(),
  FileIterator.LAST_DIRECTORY);
```

The first parameter specifies the path to our root folder, the second parameter limits the iterator to the .txt files only, while the last parameter asks the method to use the last directory name in the path as class label.

Importing from file

Another option to load the documents is through
`cc.mallet.pipe.iterator.CsvIterator.CsvIterator(Reader, Pattern, int, int, int)`, which assumes all of the documents are in a single file and returns one instance per line extracted by a regular expression. The class is initialized by the following components:

- `Reader`: This is the object that specifies how to read from a file
- `Pattern`: This is a regular expression, extracting three groups: data, target label, and document name
- `int, int, int`: These are the indexes of data, target, and name groups as they appear in a regular expression

Consider a text document in the following format, specifying the document name, category, and content:

```
AP881218 local-news A 16-year-old student at a private
    Baptist...
AP880224 business The Bechtel Group Inc. offered in 1985 to...
AP881017 local-news A gunman took a 74-year-old woman hostage...
AP900117 entertainment Cupid has a new message for lovers
    this...
AP880405 politics The Reagan administration is weighing w...
```

To parse a line into three groups, we can use the following regular expression:

```
^(\\S*)[\\s,]*(\\S*)[\\s,]*(.*)$
```

There are three groups that appear in parenthesies `()`, where the third group contains the data, the second group contains the target class, and the first group contains the document ID. `iterator` is initialized as follows:

```
CsvIterator iterator = new CsvIterator (
fileReader,
Pattern.compile("^(\\S*)[\\s,]*(\\S*)[\\s,]*(.*)$"),
    3, 2, 1));
```

Here, the regular expression extracts the three groups separated by an empty space and their order is `3, 2, 1`.

Now let's move to the data-preprocessing pipeline.

Pre-processing text data

Once we initialize an iterator that will go through the data, we need to pass the data through a sequence of transformations as described at the beginning of this section. Mallet supports this process through a pipeline and a wide variety of steps that could be included in a pipeline, which are collected in the `cc.mallet.pipe` package. Some examples are as follows:

- `Input2CharSequence`: This is a pipe that can read from various kinds of text sources (either URL, file, or reader) into `CharSequence`
- `CharSequenceRemoveHTML`: This pipe removes HTML from `CharSequence`
- `MakeAmpersandXMLFriendly`: This converts `&` into `&amp` in tokens of a token sequence
- `TokenSequenceLowercase`: This converts the text in each token in the token sequence in the data field into lowercase
- `TokenSequence2FeatureSequence`: This converts the token sequence in the data field of each instance into a feature sequence
- `TokenSequenceNGrams`: This converts the token sequence in the data field into a token sequence of ngrams, that is, a combination of two or more words

The full list of processing steps is available in the following Mallet documentation: `http://mallet.cs.umass.edu/api/index.html?cc/mallet/pipe/iterator/package-tree.html`.

Now we are ready to build a class that will import our data. We will do that using the following steps:

1. Let's build a pipeline, where each processing step is denoted as a pipeline in Mallet. Pipelines can be wired together in a serial fashion with a list of `ArrayList<Pipe>` objects:

```
ArrayList<Pipe> pipeList = new ArrayList<Pipe>();
```

2. Let's begin by reading data from a file object and converting all of the characters into lowercase:

```
pipeList.add(new Input2CharSequence("UTF-8"));
pipeList.add( new CharSequenceLowercase() );
```

3. We will tokenize raw strings with a regular expression. The following pattern includes unicode letters and numbers and the underscore character:

```
Pattern tokenPattern =
Pattern.compile("[\\p{L}\\p{N}_]+");

pipeList.add(new CharSequence2TokenSequence(tokenPattern));
```

4. We will now remove stop words, that is, frequent words with no predictive power, using a standard English stop list. Two additional parameters indicate whether stop-word removal should be case-sensitive and mark deletions instead of just deleting the words. We'll set both of them to `false`:

```
pipeList.add(new TokenSequenceRemoveStopwords(new
File(stopListFilePath), "utf-8", false, false, false));
```

5. Instead of storing the actual words, we can convert them into integers, indicating a word index in the BoW:

```
pipeList.add(new TokenSequence2FeatureSequence());
```

6. We'll do the same for the class label; instead of the label string, we'll use an integer, indicating a position of the label in our bag of words:

```
pipeList.add(new Target2Label());
```

7. We could also print the features and the labels by invoking the `PrintInputAndTarget` pipe:

```
pipeList.add(new PrintInputAndTarget());
```

8. We store the list of pipelines in a `SerialPipes` class that will covert an instance through a sequence of pipes:

```
SerialPipes pipeline = new SerialPipes(pipeList);
```

Now let's take a look at how apply this in a text-mining application!

Topic modeling for BBC News

As discussed earlier, the goal of topic modeling is to identify patterns in a text corpus that correspond to document topics. In this example, we will use a dataset originating from BBC News. This dataset is one of the standard benchmarks in machine-learning research, and is available for non-commercial and research purposes.

The goal is to build a classifier that is able to assign a topic to an uncategorized document.

BBC dataset

In 2006, Greene and Cunningham collected the BBC dataset to study a particular document—*Clustering challenge using support vector machines*. The dataset consists of 2,225 documents from the BBC News website from 2004 to 2005, corresponding to the stories collected from five topical areas: business, entertainment, politics, sport, and technology. The dataset can be seen at the following website: `http://mlg.ucd.ie/datasets/bbc.html`.

We can download the raw text files under the **Dataset: BBC** section. You will also notice that the website contains an already processed dataset, but, for this example, we want to process the dataset by ourselves. The ZIP contains five folders, one per topic. The actual documents are placed in the corresponding topic folder, as shown in the following screenshot:

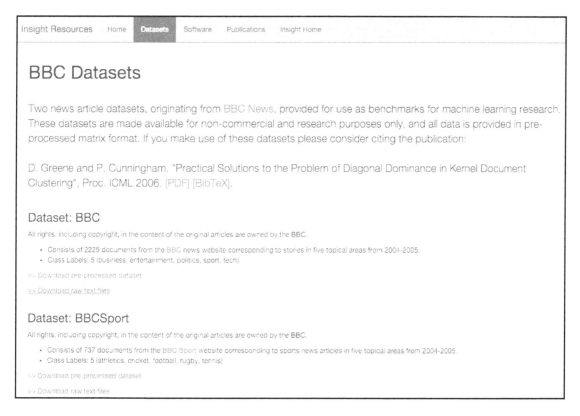

Now, let's build a topic classifier.

Modeling

We will begin the modeling phase using the following steps:

1. We will start by importing the dataset and processing the text using the following lines of code:

```
import cc.mallet.types.*;
import cc.mallet.pipe.*;
import cc.mallet.pipe.iterator.*;
import cc.mallet.topics.*;

import java.util.*;
import java.util.regex.*;
import java.io.*;

public class TopicModeling {

    public static void main(String[] args) throws Exception {

String dataFolderPath = "data/bbc";
String stopListFilePath = "data/stoplists/en.txt";
```

2. We will then create a default `pipeline` object as previously described:

```
ArrayList<Pipe> pipeList = new ArrayList<Pipe>();
pipeList.add(new Input2CharSequence("UTF-8"));
Pattern tokenPattern = Pattern.compile("[\\p{L}\\p{N}_]+");
pipeList.add(new CharSequence2TokenSequence(tokenPattern));
pipeList.add(new TokenSequenceLowercase());
pipeList.add(new TokenSequenceRemoveStopwords(new
File(stopListFilePath), "utf-8", false, false, false));
pipeList.add(new TokenSequence2FeatureSequence());
pipeList.add(new Target2Label());
SerialPipes pipeline = new SerialPipes(pipeList);
```

3. Next, we will initialize the `folderIterator` object:

```
FileIterator folderIterator = new FileIterator(
    new File[] {new File(dataFolderPath)},
    new TxtFilter(),
    FileIterator.LAST_DIRECTORY);
```

4. We will now construct a new instance list with the `pipeline` that we want to use to process the text:

```
InstanceList instances = new InstanceList(pipeline);
```

5. We process each instance provided by `iterator`:

```
instances.addThruPipe(folderIterator);
```

6. Now let's create a model with five topics using the
`cc.mallet.topics.ParallelTopicModel.ParallelTopicModel` class that
implements a simple threaded LDA model. LDA is a common method for topic
modeling that uses Dirichlet distribution to estimate the probability that a
selected topic generates a particular document. We will not dive deep into the
details in this chapter; the reader is referred to the original paper by D. Blei et al.
(2003).

Note: There is another classification algorithm in machine learning with
the same initialism that refers to **Linear Discriminant Analysis** (**LDA**).
Beside the common acronym, it has nothing in common with the LDA
model.

The class is instantiated with parameters alpha and beta, which can be broadly
interpreted as follows:

- High alpha value means that each document is likely to contain a mixture of
  most of the topics, and not any single topic specifically. A low alpha value puts
  less of such constraints on documents, and this means that it is more likely that a
  document may contain mixture of just a few, or even only one, of the topics.
- A high beta value means that each topic is likely to contain a mixture of most of
  the words, and not any word specifically; while a low value means that a topic
  may contain a mixture of just a few of the words.

In our case, we initially keep both parameters low (alpha_t = `0.01`, beta_w =
`0.01`) as we assume topics in our dataset are not mixed much and there are many
words for each of the topics:

```
int numTopics = 5;
ParallelTopicModel model =
new ParallelTopicModel(numTopics, 0.01, 0.01);
```

7. We will add `instances` to the model, and since we are using parallel
implementation, we will specify the number of threads that will run in parallel,
as follows:

```
model.addInstances(instances);
model.setNumThreads(4);
```

8. We will now run the model for a selected number of iterations. Each iteration is used for better estimation of internal LDA parameters. For testing, we can use a small number of iterations, for example, 50; while in real applications, use `1000` or `2000` iterations. Finally, we will call the `void estimate()` method that will actually build an LDA model:

```
model.setNumIterations(1000);
model.estimate();
```

The model outputs the following result:

```
0 0,06654   game england year time win world 6
1 0,0863    year 1 company market growth economy firm
2 0,05981   people technology mobile mr games users music
3 0,05744   film year music show awards award won
4 0,11395   mr government people labour election party blair
[beta: 0,11328]
<1000> LL/token: -8,63377
Total time: 45 seconds
```

`LL/token` indicates the model's log-likelihood, divided by the total number of tokens, indicating how likely the data is given the model. Increasing values mean the model is improving.

The output also shows the top words describing each topic. The words correspond to initial topics really well:

- **Topic 0**: `game, england, year, time, win, world, 6` $\Rightarrow$ sport
- **Topic 1**: `year, 1, company, market, growth, economy, firm` $\Rightarrow$ finance
- **Topic 2**: `people, technology, mobile, mr, games, users, music` $\Rightarrow$ tech
- **Topic 3**: `film, year, music, show, awards, award, won` $\Rightarrow$ entertainment
- **Topic 4**: `mr, government, people, labor, election, party, blair` $\Rightarrow$ politics

There are still some words that don't make much sense, for instance, `mr`, `1`, and `6`. We could include them in the stop word list. Also, some words appear twice, for example, `award` and `awards`. This happened because we didn't apply any stemmer or lemmatization pipe.

In the next section, we'll take a look to check whether the model is any good.

Evaluating a model

As statistical topic modeling has an unsupervised nature, it makes model selection difficult. For some applications, there may be some extrinsic tasks at hand, such as information retrieval or document classification, for which performance can be evaluated. However, in general, we want to estimate the model's ability to generalize topics regardless of the task.

In 2009, Wallach et al. introduced an approach that measures the quality of a model by computing the log probability of held-out documents under the model. The likelihood of unseen documents can be used to compare models—higher likelihood implies a better model.

We will evaluate the model using the following steps:

1. Let's split the documents into training and test sets (that is, held-out documents), where we use 90% for training and 10% for testing:

   ```
   // Split dataset
   InstanceList[] instanceSplit= instances.split(new Randoms(), new
       double[] {0.9, 0.1, 0.0});
   ```

2. Now let's rebuild our model using only 90% of our documents:

   ```
   // Use the first 90% for training
   model.addInstances(instanceSplit[0]);
   model.setNumThreads(4);
   model.setNumIterations(50);
   model.estimate();
   ```

3. We will initialize an `estimator` object that implements Wallach's log probability of held-out documents, `MarginalProbEstimator`:

   ```
   // Get estimator
   MarginalProbEstimator estimator = model.getProbEstimator();
   ```

   An intuitive description of LDA is summarized by Annalyn Ng in her blog: `https://annalyzin.wordpress.com/2015/06/21/laymans-explanation-of-topic-modeling-with-lda-2/`. To get deeper insight into the LDA algorithm, its components, and its working, take a look at the original paper LDA by David Blei et al. (2003) at `http://jmlr.csail.mit.edu/papers/v3/blei03a.html`, or take a look at the summarized presentation by D. Santhanam of Brown University at `http://www.cs.brown.edu/courses/csci2950-p/spring2010/lectures/2010-03-03_santhanam.pdf`.

The class implements many estimators that require quite deep theoretical knowledge of how the LDA method works. We'll pick the left-to-right evaluator, which is appropriate for a wide range of applications, including text mining, and speech recognition. The left-to-right evaluator is implemented as the `double evaluateLeftToRight` method, accepting the following components:

- `Instances heldOutDocuments`: This tests the instances.
- `int numParticles`: This algorithm parameter indicates the number of left-to-right tokens, where the default value is 10.
- `boolean useResampling`: This states whether to resample topics in left-to-right evaluation; resampling is more accurate, but leads to quadratic scaling in the length of documents.
- `PrintStream docProbabilityStream`: This is the file or `stdout` in which we write the inferred log probabilities per document.

4. Let's run `estimator`, as follows:

```
double loglike = estimator.evaluateLeftToRight(
   instanceSplit[1], 10, false, null););
System.out.println("Total log likelihood: "+loglike);
```

In our particular case, the `estimator` outputs the following `log likelihood`, which makes sense when it is compared to other models that are either constructed with different parameters, pipelines, or data—the higher the log likelihood, the better the model is:

```
Total time: 3 seconds
Topic Evaluator: 5 topics, 3 topic bits, 111 topic mask
Total log likelihood: -360849.4240795393
```

Now let's take a look at how to make use of this model.

Reusing a model

As we are usually not building models on the fly, it often makes sense to train a model once and use it repeatedly to classify new data.

Note that, if you'd like to classify new documents, they need go through the same pipeline as other documents—the pipe needs to be the same for both training and classification. During training, the pipe's data alphabet is updated with each training instance. If you create a new pipe with the same steps, you don't produce the same pipeline as its data alphabet is empty. Therefore, to use the model on new data, we have to save or load the pipe along with the model and use this pipe to add new instances.

Saving a model

Mallet supports a standard method for saving and restoring objects based on serialization.

We simply create a new instance of the `ObjectOutputStream` class and write the object into a file, as follows:

```
String modelPath = "myTopicModel";

//Save model
ObjectOutputStream oos = new ObjectOutputStream(
new FileOutputStream (new File(modelPath+".model")));
oos.writeObject(model);
oos.close();
//Save pipeline
oos = new ObjectOutputStream(
new FileOutputStream (new File(modelPath+".pipeline")));
oos.writeObject(pipeline);
oos.close();
```

Restoring a model

Restoring a model saved through serialization is simply an inverse operation using the `ObjectInputStream` class:

```
String modelPath = "myTopicModel";

//Load model
ObjectInputStream ois = new ObjectInputStream(
  new FileInputStream (new File(modelPath+".model")));
ParallelTopicModel model = (ParallelTopicModel) ois.readObject();
ois.close();

// Load pipeline
ois = new ObjectInputStream(
  new FileInputStream (new File(modelPath+".pipeline")));
SerialPipes pipeline = (SerialPipes) ois.readObject();
ois.close();
```

We discussed how to build an LDA model to automatically classify documents into topics. In the next example, we'll look into another text mining problem—text classification.

Detecting email spam

Spam or electronic spam refers to unsolicited messages, typically carrying advertising content, infected attachments, links to phishing or malware sites, and so on. While the most widely recognized form of spam is email spam, spam abuses appear in other media as well: website comments, instant messaging, internet forums, blogs, online ads, and so on.

In this chapter, we will discuss how to build Naive Bayesian spam filtering, using BoW representation to identify spam emails. Naive Bayes spam filtering is one of the basic techniques that was implemented in the first commercial spam filters; for instance, Mozilla Thunderbird mail client uses native implementation of such filtering. While the example in this chapter will use email spam, the underlying methodology can be applied to other type of text-based spam as well.

Email spam dataset

In 2000, Androutsopoulos et al. collected one of the first email spam datasets to benchmark spam-filtering algorithms. They studied how the Naive Bayes classifier can be used to detect spam, if additional pipes such as stop list, stemmer, and lemmatization contribute to better performance. The dataset was reorganized by Andrew Ng in OpenClassroom's machine-learning class, available for download at `http://openclassroom.stanford.edu/MainFolder/DocumentPage.php?course=MachineLearningdoc=exercises/ex6/ex6.html`.

Select and download the second option, `ex6DataEmails.zip`, as shown in the following screenshot:

OpenClassroom

Machine Learning
Andrew Ng

Exercise 6: Naive Bayes

RESOURCES

Syllabus
FAQ
Credits/Acknowledgments

In this exercise, you will use Naive Bayes to classify email messages into spam and nonspam groups. Your dataset is a preprocessed subset of the Ling-Spam Dataset, provided by Ion Androutsopoulos. It is based on 960 real email messages from a linguistics mailing list.

There are two ways to complete this exercise. The first option is to use the Matlab/Octave-formatted features we have generated for you. This requires using Matlab/Octave to read prepared data and then writing an implementation of Naive Bayes. To choose this option, download the data pack ex6DataPrepared.zip.

The second option is to generate the features yourself from the emails and then implement Naive Bayes on top of those features. You may want this option if you want more practice with features and a more open-ended exercise. To choose this option, download the data pack ex6DataEmails.zip.

The ZIP contains the following folders:

- The `nonspam-train` and `spam-train` folders contain the pre-processed emails that you will use for training. They have 350 emails each.
- The `nonspam-test` and `spam-test` folders constitute the test set, containing 130 spam and 130 nonspam emails. These are the documents that you will make predictions on. Notice that, even though separate folders tell you the correct labeling, you should make your predictions on all of the test documents without this knowledge. After you make your predictions, you can use the correct labeling to check whether your classifications were correct.

To leverage Mallet's folder iterator, let's reorganize the folder structure as follows. We will create two folders, `train` and `test`, and put the `spam/nospam` folders under the corresponding folders. The initial folder structure is as shown in the following screenshot:

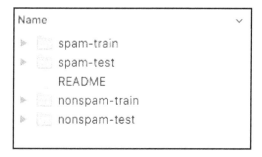

The final folder structure will be as shown in the following screenshot:

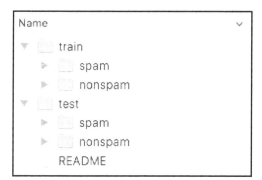

The next step is to transform email messages to feature vectors.

Feature generation

We will perform feature generation using the following steps:

1. We will create a default pipeline, as described previously:

```
ArrayList<Pipe> pipeList = new ArrayList<Pipe>();
pipeList.add(new Input2CharSequence("UTF-8"));
Pattern tokenPattern = Pattern.compile("[\\p{L}\\p{N}_]+");
pipeList.add(new CharSequence2TokenSequence(tokenPattern));
pipeList.add(new TokenSequenceLowercase());
pipeList.add(new TokenSequenceRemoveStopwords(new
    File(stopListFilePath), "utf-8", false, false, false));
pipeList.add(new TokenSequence2FeatureSequence());
pipeList.add(new FeatureSequence2FeatureVector());
pipeList.add(new Target2Label());
SerialPipes pipeline = new SerialPipes(pipeList);
```

Note that we added an additional `FeatureSequence2FeatureVector` pipe that transforms a feature sequence into a feature vector. When we have data in a feature vector, we can use any classification algorithm, as we saw in the previous chapters. We'll continue our example in Mallet to demonstrate how to build a classification model.

2. We initialize a folder iterator to load our examples in the `train` folder comprising email examples in the `spam` and `nonspam` subfolders, which will be used as example labels:

```
FileIterator folderIterator = new FileIterator(
    new File[] {new File(dataFolderPath)},
    new TxtFilter(),
    FileIterator.LAST_DIRECTORY);
```

3. We will construct a new instance list with the `pipeline` object that we want to use to process the text:

```
InstanceList instances = new InstanceList(pipeline);
```

4. We will process each instance provided by the iterator:

```
instances.addThruPipe(folderIterator);
```

We have now loaded the data and transformed it into feature vectors. Let's train our model on the training set and predict the `spam`/`nonspam` classification on the `test` set.

Training and testing

Mallet implements a set of classifiers in the `cc.mallet.classify` package, including decision trees, Naive Bayes, AdaBoost, bagging, boosting, and many others. We'll start with a basic classifier, that is, a Naive Bayes classifier. A classifier is initialized by the `ClassifierTrainer` class, which returns a classifier when we invoke its `train(Instances)` method:

```
ClassifierTrainer classifierTrainer = new NaiveBayesTrainer();
Classifier classifier = classifierTrainer.train(instances);
```

Now let's see how this classier works and evaluate its performance on a separate dataset.

Model performance

To evaluate the classifier on a separate dataset, we will use the following steps:

1. Let's start by importing the emails located in our `test` folder:

```
InstanceList testInstances = new
    InstanceList(classifier.getInstancePipe());
folderIterator = new FileIterator(
    new File[] {new File(testFolderPath)},
    new TxtFilter(),
    FileIterator.LAST_DIRECTORY);
```

2. We will pass the data through the same pipeline that we initialized during training:

```
testInstances.addThruPipe(folderIterator);
```

3. To evaluate classifier performance, we'll use the `cc.mallet.classify.Trial` class, which is initialized with a classifier and set of test instances:

```
Trial trial = new Trial(classifier, testInstances);
```

4. The evaluation is performed immediately at initialization. We can then simply take out the measures that we care about. In our example, we'd like to check the precision and recall on classifying spam email messages, or F-measure, which returns a harmonic mean of both values, as follows:

```
System.out.println(
  "F1 for class 'spam': " + trial.getF1("spam"));
System.out.println(
  "Precision:" + trial.getPrecision(1));
```

```
System.out.println(
    "Recall:" + trial.getRecall(1));
```

The evaluation object outputs the following results:

```
F1 for class 'spam': 0.9731800766283524
Precision: 0.9694656488549618
Recall: 0.9769230769230769
```

The results show that the model correctly discovers 97.69% of spam messages (recall), and when it marks an email as spam, it is correct in 96.94% cases. In other words, it misses approximately 2 per 100 spam messages and marks 3 per 100 valid messages as spam. So, it's not really perfect, but it's more than a good start!

Summary

In this chapter, we discussed how text mining is different than traditional attribute-based learning, requiring a lot of pre-processing steps to transform written natural language into feature vectors. Further, we discussed how to leverage Mallet, a Java-based library for NLP by applying it to two real-life problems. First, we modeled topics in a news corpus using the LDA model to build a model that is able to assign a topic to new document. We also discussed how to build a Naive Bayesian spam-filtering classifier using the BoW representation.

This chapter concludes the technical demonstrations of how to apply various libraries to solve machine-learning tasks. As we weren't able to cover more interesting applications and give further details at many points, the next chapter gives some further pointers on how to continue learning and dive deeper into particular topics.

11
What Is Next?

This chapter brings us to the end of our journey of reviewing machine learning in Java libraries and discussing how to leverage them to solve real-life problems. However, this should not be the end of your journey by all means. This chapter will give you some practical advice on how to start deploying your models in the real world, what are the catches, and where to go to deepen your knowledge. It also gives you further pointers about where to find additional resources, materials, venues, and technologies to dive deeper into machine learning.

This chapter will cover the following topics:

- Important aspects of machine learning in real life
- Standards and markup languages
- Machine learning in the cloud
- Web resources and competitions

Machine learning in real life

Papers, conference presentations, and talks often don't discuss how the models were actually deployed and maintained in a production environment. In this section, we'll look into some aspects that should be taken into consideration.

Noisy data

In practice, data typically contains errors and imperfections due to various reasons such as measurement errors, human mistakes, and errors of expert judgment in classifying training examples. We refer to all of these as **noise**. Noise can also come from the treatment of missing values when an example with unknown attribute value is replaced by a set of weighted examples corresponding to the probability distribution of the missing value. The typical consequences of noise in learning data are low prediction accuracy of a learned model in new data and complex models that are hard to interpret and understand for the user.

Class unbalance

Class unbalance is a problem we come across in `Chapter 7`, *Fraud and Anomaly Detection*, where the goal was to detect fraudulent insurance claims. The challenge is that a very large part of the dataset, usually more than 90%, describes normal activities, and only a small fraction of the dataset contains fraudulent examples. In such a case, if the model always predicts normal, then it is correct 90% of the time. This problem is extremely common in practice and can be observed in various applications, including fraud detection, anomaly detection, medical diagnosis, oil spillage detection, and facial recognition.

Now, knowing what the class unbalance problem is and why it is a problem, let's take a look at how to deal with this problem. The first approach is to focus on measures other than classification accuracy, such as recall, precision, and f-measure. Such measures focus on how accurate a model is at predicting minority class (**recall**) and what is the share of false alarms (**precision**). The other approach is based on resampling, where the main idea is to reduce the number of overrepresented examples in such a way that the new set contains a balanced ratio of both classes.

Feature selection

Feature selection is arguably the most challenging part of modeling that requires domain knowledge and good insights into the problem at hand. Nevertheless, properties of well-behaved features are as follows:

- **Reusability**: Features should be available for reuse in different models, applications, and teams.
- **Transformability**: You should be able to transform a feature with an operation, for example, `log()`, `max()`, or combine multiple features together with a custom calculation.

- **Reliability**: Features should be easy to monitor and appropriate unit tests should exist to minimize bugs or issues.
- **Interpretability**: To perform any of the previous actions, you need to be able to understand the meaning of features and interpret their values.

The better you are able to capture the features, the more accurate your results will be.

Model chaining

Some models might produce output, which is used as the feature in another model. Moreover, we can use multiple models—ensembles—turning any model into a feature. This is a great way to get better results, but this can lead to problems too. Care must be taken that the output of your model is ready to accept dependencies. Also, try to avoid feedback loops, as they can create dependencies and bottlenecks in the pipeline.

The importance of evaluation

Another important aspect is model evaluation. Unless you apply your models to new data and measure a business objective, you're not doing predictive analytics. Evaluation techniques, such as cross-validation and separated train/test sets, simply split your test data, which can give only you an estimate of how your model will perform. Life often doesn't hand you a train dataset with all of the cases defined, so there is a lot of creativity involved in defining these two sets in a real-world dataset.

At the end of the day, we want to improve a business objective, such as improve ad conversion rate, and get more clicks on recommended items. To measure the improvement, execute A/B tests, measuring differences in metrics across statistically identical populations that each experience a different algorithm. Decisions on the product are always data-driven.

 A/B testing is a method for a randomized experiment with two variants: A, which corresponds to the original version, controlling the experiment; and B, which corresponds to a variation. The method can be used to determine whether the variation outperforms the original version. It can be used to test everything from website changes to sales emails to search ads. Udacity offers a free course, covering design and analysis of A/B tests at https://www.udacity.com/course/ab-testing--ud257.

Getting models into production

The path from building an accurate model in a lab to deploying it in a product involves collaboration of data science and engineering, as shown in the following three steps:

1. **Data research and hypothesis building** involves modeling the problem and executing initial evaluation.
2. **Solution building and implementation** is where your model finds its way into the product flow by rewriting it into more efficient, stable, and scalable code.
3. **Online evaluation** is the last stage where the model is evaluated with live data using A/B testing on business objectives.

This is better illustrated in the following diagram:

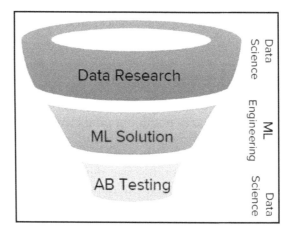

Model maintenance

Another aspect that we need to address is how the model will be maintained. Is this a model that will not change over time? Is it modeling a dynamic phenomenon requiring the model to adjust its prediction over time?

The model is usually built in an offline batch training and then used on live data to serve predictions as shown in the following diagram. If we are able to receive feedback on model predictions, for instance, whether the stock went up as the model predicted, and whether the candidate responded to campaign, the feedback should be used to improve the initial model:

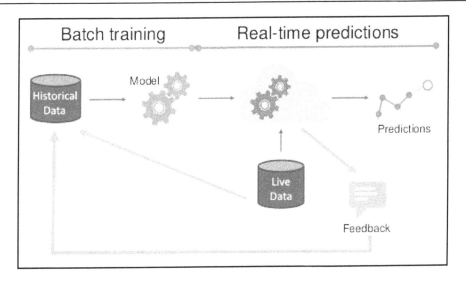

The feedback could be really useful to improve the initial model, but make sure to pay attention to the data you are sampling. For instance, if you have a model that predicts who will respond to a campaign, you will initially use a set of randomly contacted clients with specific responded/not responded distribution and feature properties. The model will focus only on a subset of clients that will most likely respond and your feedback will return you a subset of clients that responded. By including this data, the model is more accurate in a specific subgroup, but might completely miss some other group. We call this problem exploration versus exploitation. Some approaches to address this problem can be found in Osugi et al. (2005) and Bondu et al. (2010).

Standards and markup languages

As predictive models become more pervasive, the need for sharing the models and completing the modeling process leads to formalization of development process and interchangeable formats. In this section, we'll review two de facto standards, one covering data science processes and the other specifying an interchangeable format for sharing models between applications.

CRISP-DM

Cross Industry Standard Process for Data Mining (CRISP-DM) describes a data-mining process commonly used by data scientists in industry. CRISP-DM breaks the data-mining science process into six major phases:

- **Business understanding**
- **Data understanding**
- **Data preparation**
- **Modeling**
- **Evaluation**
- **Deployment**

In the following diagram, the arrows indicate the process flow, which can move back and forth through the phases. Also, the process doesn't stop with model deployment. The outer arrow indicates the cyclic nature of data science. Lessons learned during the process can trigger new questions and repeat the process while improving previous results:

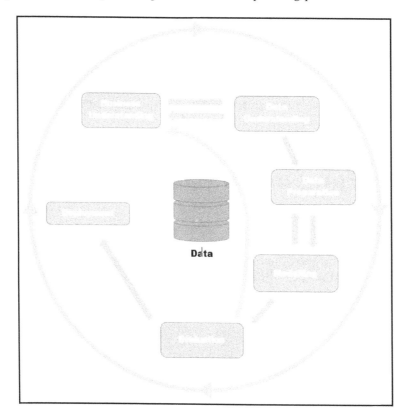

SEMMA methodology

Another methodology is **Sample, Explore, Modify, Model, and Assess** (**SEMMA**). SEMMA describes the main modeling tasks in data science, while leaving aside business aspects such as data understanding and deployment. SEMMA was developed by SAS Institute, which is one of the largest vendors of statistical software, aiming to help the users of their software to carry out core tasks of data mining.

Predictive model markup language

Predictive Model Markup Language (**PMML**) is an XML-based interchange format that allows machine- learning models to be easily shared between applications and systems. Supported models include logistic regression, neural networks, decision trees, naïve Bayes, regression models, and many others. A typical PMML file consists of the following sections:

- Header containing general information
- Data dictionary, describing data types
- Data transformations, specifying steps for normalization, discretization, aggregations, or custom functions
- Model definition, including parameters
- Mining schema listing attributes used by the model
- Targets allowing post-processing of the predicted results
- Output listing fields to be output and other post-processing steps

The generated PMML files can be imported to any PMML-consuming application, such as Zementis **adaptive decision and predictive analytics** (**ADAPA**) and **universal PMML Plug-In** (**UPPI**) scoring engines; Weka, which has built-in support for regression, general regression, neural network, TreeModel, RuleSetModel, and **support vector machine** (**SVM**) model; Spark, which can export k-means clustering, linear regression, ridge regression, lasso model, binary logistic model, and SVM; and cascading, which can transform PMML files into an application on Apache Hadoop.

The next generation of PMML is an emerging format called **portable format for analytics** (**PFA**), providing a common interface to deploy the complete workflows across environments.

Machine learning in the cloud

Setting up a complete machine learning stack that is able to scale with the increasing amount of data could be challenging. A recent wave of the **Software as a Service (SaaS)** and **Infrastructure as a Service** (**IaaS**) paradigm has spilled over to the machine learning domain as well. The trend today is to move the actual data preprocessing, modeling, and prediction to cloud environments and focus on modeling tasks only.

In this section, we'll review some of the promising services offering algorithms, predictive models already train in specific domain, and environments empowering collaborative workflows in data science teams.

Machine learning as a service

The first category is algorithms as a service, where you are provided with an API or even graphical user interface to connect preprogrammed components of data science pipeline together:

- **Google Prediction API**: It was one of the first companies that introduced prediction services through its web API. The service is integrated with Google Cloud Storage serving as data storage. The user can build a model and call an API to get predictions.
- **BigML**: It implements a user-friendly graphical interface, supports many storage providers (for instance, Amazon S3) and offers a wide variety of data processing tools, algorithms, and powerful visualizations.
- **Microsoft Azure Machine Learning**: This provides a large library of machine learning algorithms and data processing functions, as well as graphical user interface, to connect these components to an application. Additionally, it offers a fully-managed service that you can use to deploy your predictive models as ready-to-consume web services.
- **Amazon Machine Learning**: It entered the market quite late. It's main strength is seamless integration with other Amazon services, while the number of algorithms and user interface needs further improvements.

- **IBM Watson Analytics**: It focuses on providing models that are already handcrafted to a particular domain such as speech recognition, machine translations, and anomaly detection. It targets a wide range of industries by solving specific use cases.
- **Prediction.IO**: It is a self-hosted open source platform, providing the full stack from data storage to modeling to serving the predictions. Prediction.IO can talk to Apache Spark to leverage its learning algorithms. In addition, it is shipped with a wide variety of models targeting specific domains, for instance, recommender system, churn prediction, and others.

Predictive API is an emerging new field, so these are just some of the well-known examples; **KDnuggets** compiled a list of 50 machine-learning APIs at `http://www.kdnuggets.com/2015/12/machine-learning-data-science-apis.html`.

 To learn more about it, you can visit PAPI, the International Conference on Predictive APIs and apps at `http://www.papi.io` or take a look at this book: *Bootstrapping Machine Learning*, L Dorard, *Createspace Independent Pub, 2014.*

Web resources and competitions

In this section, we'll review where to find additional resources for learning, discussing, presenting, or sharpening our data science skills.

Datasets

One of the most well-known repositories of machine learning datasets is hosted by the University of California Irvine. The UCI repository contains over 300 datasets covering a wide variety of challenges, including poker, movies, wine quality, activity recognition, stocks, taxi service trajectories, advertisements, and many others. Each dataset is usually equipped with a research paper where the dataset was used, which can give you a hint on how to start and what the prediction baseline is.

The UCI machine-learning repository can be accessed at `https://archive.ics.uci.edu`, as follows:

Another well-maintained collection by Xiaming Chen is hosted on GitHub: `https://github.com/caesar0301/awesome-public-datasets`.

The awesome public dataset repository maintains links to more than 400 data sources from a variety of domains, ranging from agriculture, biology, economics, psychology, museums, and transportation. Datasets, specifically targeting machine learning, are collected under the image processing, machine learning, and data challenges sections.

Online courses

Learning how to become a data scientist has became much more accessible due to the availability of online courses. The following is a list of free resources to learn different skills online:

- **Udemy—Learn Java Programming From Scratch** at `https://www.udemy.com/learn-java-programming-from-scratch`.
- **Udemy—Java Tutorial for Complete Beginners** at `https://www.udemy.com/java-tutorial`.
- **LearnJAvaOnline—Interactive Java tutorial** at `http://www.learnjavaonline.org`.

Some online courses to learn more about machine learning are as follows:

- **Coursera—Machine Learning (Stanford) by Andrew Ng**: This teaches you the math behind many machine-learning algorithms, explains how they work, and explores why they make sense at `https://www.coursera.org/learn/machine-learning`.
- **Statistics 110 (Harvard) by Joe Biltzstein**: This course lets you discover the probability of related terms that you will hear many times in your data science journey. Lectures are available on YouTube at `http://projects.iq.harvard.edu/stat110/youtube`.
- **Data Science CS109 (Harvard) by John A. Paulson**: This is a hands-on course where you'll learn about Python libraries for data science, as well as how to handle machine-learning algorithms at `http://cs109.github.io/2015/`.

Competitions

The best way to sharpen your knowledge is to work on real problems and, if you want to build a proven portfolio of your projects, machine-learning competitions are a viable place to start:

- **Kaggle**: This is the number one competition platform, hosting a wide variety of challenges with large prizes, strong data science community, and lots of helpful resources. You can check it out at `https://www.kaggle.com/`.
- **CrowdANALYTIX**: This is a crowdsourced data analytics service that is focused on the life sciences and financial services industries at `https://www.crowdanalytix.com`.
- **DrivenData**: This hosts data science competitions for social good at `http://www.drivendata.org/`.

Websites and blogs

In addition to online courses and competitions, there are numerous websites and blogs publishing the latest developments in the data science community, their experience in attacking different problems, or just best practices. Some good starting points are as follows:

- **KDnuggets**: This is the de facto portal for data mining, analytics, big data, and data science, covering the latest news, stories, events, and other relevant issues at `http://www.kdnuggets.com/`.
- **Machine Learning Mastery**: This is an introductory-level blog with practical advice and pointers where to start. Check it out at `http://machinelearningmastery.com/`.
- **Data Science Central**: This consists of practical community articles on a variety of topics, algorithms, caches, and business cases at `http://www.datasciencecentral.com/`.
- **Data Mining Research** by Sandro Saitta at `http://www.dataminingblog.com/`.
- **Data Mining: Text Mining, Visualization and Social Media** by Matthew Hurst, which covers interesting text and web mining topics, frequently with applications to Bing and Microsoft at `http://datamining.typepad.com/data_mining/`.
- **Geeking with Greg** by Greg Linden, inventor of the Amazon recommendation engine and internet entrepreneur. You can check it out at `http://glinden.blogspot.si/`.

- **DSGuide**: This is a collection of over 150 data science blogs at `http://dsguide.biz/reader/sources`.

Venues and conferences

The following are a few top-tier academic conferences with the latest algorithms:

- **Knowledge Discovery in Databases (KDD)**
- **Computer Vision and Pattern Recognition (CVPR)**
- **Annual Conference on Neural Information Processing Systems (NIPS)**
- **International Conference on Machine Learning (ICML)**
- **International Conference on Data Mining (ICDM)**
- **International Joint Conference on Pervasive and Ubiquitous Computing (UbiComp)**
- **International Joint Conference on Artificial Intelligence (IJCAI)**

Some business conferences are as follows:

- O'Reilly Strata Conference
- The Strata + Hadoop World Conferences
- Predictive Analytics World
- MLconf

You can also check local meet-up groups.

Summary

In this chapter, we concluded this book by discussing some aspects of model deployment, and we looked into standards for the data science process and the interchangeable predictive model format. We also reviewed online courses, competitions, web resources, and conferences that could help you in your journey towards mastering the art of machine learning.

I hope this book inspired you to dive deeper into data science and has motivated you to get your hands dirty, experiment with various libraries, and get a grasp of how different problems could be attacked. Remember, all of the source code and additional resources are available on the Packt Publishing website: `https://www.packtpub.com/`.

Other Books You May Enjoy

If you enjoyed this book, you may be interested in these other books by Packt:

Mastering Java Machine Learning

Dr. Uday Kamath, Krishna Choppella

ISBN: 9781785880513

- Master key Java machine learning libraries, and what kind of problem each can solve, with theory and practical guidance.
- Explore powerful techniques in each major category of machine learning such as classification, clustering, anomaly detection, graph modeling, and text mining.
- Apply machine learning to real-world data with methodologies, processes, applications, and analysis.
- Techniques and experiments developed around the latest specializations in machine learning, such as deep learning, stream data mining, and active and semi-supervised learning.
- Build high-performing, real-time, adaptive predictive models for batch- and stream-based big data learning using the latest tools and methodologies.
- Get a deeper understanding of technologies leading towards a more powerful AI applicable in various domains such as Security, Financial Crime, Internet of Things, social networking, and so on.

Natural Language Processing with Java - Second Edition
Richard M Reese, AshishSingh Bhatia

ISBN: 9781788993494

- Understand basic NLP tasks and how they relate to one another
- Discover and use the available tokenization engines
- Apply search techniques to find people, as well as things, within a document
- Construct solutions to identify parts of speech within sentences
- Use parsers to extract relationships between elements of a document
- Identify topics in a set of documents
- Explore topic modeling from a document

Leave a review - let other readers know what you think

Please share your thoughts on this book with others by leaving a review on the site that you bought it from. If you purchased the book from Amazon, please leave us an honest review on this book's Amazon page. This is vital so that other potential readers can see and use your unbiased opinion to make purchasing decisions, we can understand what our customers think about our products, and our authors can see your feedback on the title that they have worked with Packt to create. It will only take a few minutes of your time, but is valuable to other potential customers, our authors, and Packt. Thank you!

Index

E

Eclipse
  Apache Mahout, configuring with Maven plugin 144, 145, 146
edit distance 23
ELKI, packages
  de.lmu.ifi.dbs.elki.algorithm 50
  de.lmu.ifi.dbs.elki.data 51
  de.lmu.ifi.dbs.elki.database 51
  de.lmu.ifi.dbs.elki.index 51
  de.lmu.ifi.dbs.elki.outlier 50
  de.lmu.ifi.dbs.elki.statistics 50
email spam dataset
  reference 254
email spam detection
  build 254
  email spam dataset, using 254, 255
  feature generation, performing 256
  model performance, evaluating 257, 258
  testing 257
  training 257
Encog
  about 49
  BasicActiveSummation class 50
  BasicFreeConnection class 50
  BasicFreeformLayer interface 50
  FreeformConnection class 50
  FreeformContextNeuron class 50
  FreeformNeuron class 50
  InputSummation class 50
  MLClassification interface 50
  MLClustering interface 50
  MLData class 50
  MLDataPair class 50
  MLDataSet class 50
  MLRegression interface 50
  reference 50
  used, for classification 68, 69, 70, 71
  used, for clustering 92
  used, for linear regression 82, 83
energy efficiency dataset
  reference 78
ensemble learning 27
ensemble methods

Massive Online Analysis (MOA), using 115, 117, 118, 120, 121, 123
ensembleLibrary package
  reference 108
ensembles
  advanced modeling 107
  attributes, selecting 110
  data preprocessing 109
  ensembleLibrary package, using 108
  model selection 111, 112, 113
  performance, evaluation 114, 115
Environment for Loping KDD applications Index (ELKI)
  about 50, 168
  example 169, 170, 171
  reference 50
  used, for clustering 94, 95, 96
  used, for outlier detection 168
Euclidean distance 21
evaluation 33
evaluation framework
  features 75
expectation maximization (EM) 90
exploitation
  versus exploration 143

F

feature map 200
feature selection
  about 60, 61
  features 260
feedforward neural network 194, 195
file
  text data, importing 244
FilteredAssociator 42
FP-Growth algorithm 42, 131, 132
fraud detection, in insurance claims
  dataset, rebalancing 176, 177, 178
  dataset, using 172, 173
  example 171
  suspicious patterns, modeling 174, 175
  vanilla approach 175, 176

G

generalization error
  estimating 35
  estimating, with cross-validation 36
  estimating, with test sets 36
  estimating, with train sets 36
  leave-one-out validation 37
  stratification 37
generalization
  about 33
  overfitting 34, 35
  underfitting 34, 35
Generalized Sequential Patterns (GSP) 42
generative stochastic networks (GSNs) 197
GNU General Public License (GNU GPL) 41
graphics processing unit (GPU) 212

H

Hadoop Distributed File System (HDFS) 46
Hadoop
  about 54
  reference 54
Hamming distance 23
HBase
  about 54
  reference 54
Hidden layer
  about 194
  issues 195
hidden Markov model (HMM) 45, 167
Hierarchical agglomerative clustering (HAC) 94
hotSpot 42

I

image classification
  about 201
  with Deeplearning4j (DL4J) 201
image recognition
  about 191, 192
  neural networks 193
ImageNet challenge 192
Infrastructure as a Service (IaaS) 266
Input layer 194
intrusion detection (ID) 167

Iris dataset
  reference 68
item-based analysis 141
item-based filtering 156, 157

J

Jaccard distance 22
Java Machine Learning Library (Java-ML),
   packages
  net.sf.javaml.classification 44
  net.sf.javaml.clustering 44
  net.sf.javaml.core 44
  net.sf.javaml.distance 44
  net.sf.javaml.featureselection 44
  net.sf.javaml.filter 44
  net.sf.javaml.matrix 44
  net.sf.javaml.sampling 44
  net.sf.javaml.tools 44
  net.sf.javaml.utils 44
Java Machine Learning Library (Java-ML)
  about 43
  reference 43
Java
  need for 40

K

k-nearest neighbor (KNN) 77
kernel methods 27
Knowledge Discovery in Database (KDD) 168
known knowns 164
known unknowns 165

L

L1-norm 21
L2-norm 21
labelled point 46
Latent Dirichlet Allocation (LDA) 236
lazy learning 77
leave-one-out validation 37
lemma 241
Linear discriminant analysis (LDA) 20
Linear Discriminant Analysis (LDA)
  about 249
  reference 252
linear regression

Massive Online Analysis (MOA), packages
  moa.classifiers 51
  moa.clusters 51
  moa.evaluation 51
  moa.streams 51
Massive Online Analysis (MOA)
  about 51
  active learning 77
  baseline classifiers 76
  decision tree 76
  evaluation 75
  lazy learning 77
  reference 51, 72
  used, for classification 72, 74, 75
  used, for regression 83, 85, 86
  using 115, 117, 118, 120, 121, 123
Maven plugin
  Apache Mahout, configuring in Eclipse 144, 145, 146
mean absolute error (MAS) 32
mean squared error (MSE) 32
measurement scales 11, 12, 13
mobile app
  classifier, plugging 232, 233
mobile phone sensors
  about 216
  environmental sensors 217
  motion sensors 217
  position sensors 217
  reference 217
mobile phone
  Android Studio, installing 220, 221
  data collector, loading 222, 223
  data, collecting 220
  feature extraction 224, 225
  training data, collecting 225, 226, 227, 228
models
  evaluating 105, 106
MongoDB
  about 54
  reference 54
multilayer perceptron 194
myrunscollector package
  CollectorActivity.java class 223
  Globals.java class 223

SensorsService.java class 223

N

Naive Bayes baseline
  implementing 106, 107
Naive Bayes classifier
  about 101
  data, loading 103, 104
  data, obtaining 101, 102
neural networks
  about 193
  autoencoder 195, 196
  deep convolutional networks 198, 199, 200, 201
  feedforward neural network 194, 195
  perceptron 193, 194
  restricted Boltzman machine (RBM) 197, 198
no-change classifier 76
non-Euclidean distance 22

O

online learning engine 159
outlier algorithms
  angle-based outlier detection 168
  clustering-based outlier detection 168
  distance-based outlier detection 168
  LOF family methods 168
  spatial outlier detection 168
  subspace outlier detection 168
outlier detection
  with ELKI 168
Output layer 194
overfitting 34, 35

P

p-norm distance 21
part-of-speech (POS) tagging 241
pattern analysis 167
perceptron 27, 193, 194
plan recognition 167
portable format for analytics (PFA) 265
precision 28
predictive Apriori 42
predictive model markup language (PMML) 265
Principal Component Analysis (PCA) 20, 183
probabilistic classifiers 26

www.ingramcontent.com/pod-product-compliance
Lightning Source LLC
Chambersburg PA
CBHW080628060326
40690CB00021B/4850